Brecht on Art and Politics

Brecht's Plays, Poetry and Prose
Series Editors: John Willett, Ralph Manheim and Tom Kuhn

BRECHT COLLECTED PLAYS: ONE
Baal, Drums in the Night, In the Jungle of Cities, The Life of Edward II of England; A Respectable Wedding; The Beggar or The Dead Dog; Driving Out a Devil; Lux in Tenebris; The Catch

BRECHT COLLECTED PLAYS: TWO
Man Equals Man; The Elephant Calf; The Threepenny Opera; The Rise and Fall of the City of Mahogonny; The Seven Deadly Sins

BRECHT COLLECTED PLAYS: THREE
Lindbergh's Flight; The Baden-Baden Lesson on Consent; He Said Yes/He Said No; The Decision; The Mother; The Exception and the Rule; The Horatians and the Curiatians; St Joan of the Stockyards

BRECHT COLLECTED PLAYS: FOUR
Round Heads and Pointed Heads; Fear and Misery of the Third Reich; Señora Carrar's Rifles; Dansen: How Much is Your Iron?; The Trial of Lucullus

BRECHT COLLECTED PLAYS: FIVE
Life of Galileo; Mother Courage and Her Children

BRECHT COLLECTED PLAYS: SIX
The Good Person of Szechwan; The Resistable Rise of Arturo Ui; Mr Puntila and his Man Matti

BRECHT COLLECTED PLAYS: SEVEN
The Visions of Simone Machard; Schweyk in the Second World War; The Caucasian Chalk Circle; The Duchess of Malfi

BRECHT COLLECTED PLAYS: EIGHT*
The Days of the Commune; Antigone; Turandot

Poetry
POEMS 1913–1956
POEMS AND SONGS FROM THE PLAYS
BAD TIME FOR POETRY: 152 POEMS AND SONGS
FURTHER POEMS*

Prose
BRECHT ON THEATRE, VOL. 1
BRECHT ON THEATRE, VOL. 2
DIARIES 1920–1922
JOURNALS 1934–1955
LETTERS 1913–1956
SHORT STORIES 1921–1946
BRECHT ON ART AND POLITICS
BRECHT ON FILM AND RADIO (*edited by Marc Silberman*)

*in preparation

Brecht on
Art and Politics

BERTOLT BRECHT

Edited by
Tom Kuhn and Steve Giles

Part Five edited by
*Stephen Parker, Matthew Philpotts
and Peter Davies*

Translations by
Laura Bradley, Steve Giles and Tom Kuhn

Methuen

Published by Methuen 2003

1 3 5 7 9 10 8 6 4 2

First published in 2003 by
Methuen Publishing Limited
215 Vauxhall Bridge Road
London SW1V 1EJ

Translations of texts by Brecht copyright © Stefan S. Brecht

Texts by Brecht originally published in
*Bertolt Brecht Grosse Kommentierte Berliner
und Frankfurter Ausgabe* copyright
© Suhrkamp Verlag, Frankfurt am Main 1988-2000

Methuen Publishing Limited Reg. No. 3543167

A CIP catalogue record for this title is available from the British Library

ISBN 0 413 75890 7

Designed by Helen Ewing

Typeset by SX composing DTP, Rayleigh, Essex
Printed and bound in Great Britain by
Creative Print and Design (Wales), Ebbw Vale

Translations: Parts One, Three and Five Laura Bradley and Tom Kuhn;
Parts Two and Four Steve Giles, with the exception of the following
in Part Five: no. 61 'The *Other* Germany' (translation Eric Russell Bentley);
nos. 69-71, the pieces on formalism (translation Steve Giles);
and no. 72 'The Discussion about the Condemnation of Lucullus'
(translation John Willett from *Collected Plays 4*).
The translators have asserted their rights under the Copyright, Designs and
Patents Act, 1988, to be identified as translators of this work.

Selections, introductions, notes and commentaries of this work
copyright © 2003 by Tom Kuhn and Steve Giles.
Tom Kuhn, Steve Giles, Stephen Parker, Matthew Philpotts and Peter Davies
have asserted their rights to be identified as the authors of the various
introductions, notes and commentaries of this work.

Contents

PART THREE:
Nazism and Anti-Fascism 1933–1939

Contents

PART FOUR:
Realism and Formalism 1938–1940

PART FIVE:
Brecht and German Socialism 1942–1956

General Introduction and Acknowledgements

Waste no thought on
That which cannot be changed!
(BFA 14/154)

There is an aspect to Bertolt Brecht which has too long remained inaccessible to an English-speaking readership. Brecht is known, as well as for his poems and plays, above all for his theory of the theatre, outlined in John Willett's ground-breaking selection, *Brecht on Theatre* (first published in 1964) and in *The Messingkauf Dialogues* (1965). The theatre theory is, however, just a fragment. The writings presented here (nearly all of which appear in English for the first time) reveal one of the twentieth century's most innovative, entertaining and thought-provoking writers reflecting on a far wider range of cultural, aesthetic and political concerns. To read the Brecht of these pages is to experience a dynamic intellect, radically engaged with social, political and cultural processes, convinced that the world needs change, and that we can change it.

The most commonplace misapprehension about Brecht's 'theory' is that there is some single body of doctrine about a simple set of concerns. There is not. A very large proportion of his writings is about the theatre, but even here his ideas are continually changing and shifting their ground and their emphases. And elsewhere the texts that have survived (over two thousand pages of 'Schriften' in the new German edition) are a bewildering array of essays, speeches, short sketches and fragments, thoughts without contexts, published and unpublished bits of ideas, to which we can often only cautiously ascribe a chronology, let alone a single philosophy. To a certain extent we might wish to account for the variety and confusion in terms of Brecht's personal intellectual habits: he had a lively, alert, sometimes slippery intellect; he enjoyed a good opinion, relished a nice argument, and was sometimes maddeningly nonchalant about shifting his frame of reference; he turned his mind eclectically to a great many different matters, and to other writers, as they presented themselves to him (in theatre, literature, art, politics, human relations generally); he did not set out to be a 'systematic thinker'. However, there are also essential reasons why Brecht's ideas might seem changeable, fragmentary, even contradictory. For a start, he soon decided that thought was not the 'property' of the individual, and argued that 'it is wrong to take a philosophy as the expression of a particular head, rather than as the play of the intellect itself'.[1] And he increasingly came to think of the divorce of theory from practice as a problem of 'bourgeois philosophy'; for him, theory was to be inseparable from practice, whether in the theatre or in the political resistance to Nazism. For the modern Marxist, philosophy could not be simply a question of cooking up theories about a fixed object and an unchanging world. On the contrary, the ideas had to be able to intervene and participate in the reality (the fragmented, collectivist, late capitalist reality), just as the reality intervenes in the ideas. Both had to be amenable to change. 'Change' and 'contradiction' become key categories in Brecht's thinking.

The German editors of the thirty-volume Berlin/Frankfurt edition of Brecht's works (completed in 2000)[2] have responded to the challenge represented by Brecht's 'non-literary' writings by publishing everything (or almost everything) in a best approximation to chronological order, making no distinction between what Brecht published or left unpublished and unfinished, nor dividing the corpus according to its subject matters. We, in contrast, present only a selection, and on this we have imposed divisions, and occasionally deviated slightly from the chronological order. Our purpose has always been to make better sense of the material, to avoid repetitions and to facilitate access, but we are conscious of the danger of introducing distortions too. It is, for example, vain to try to separate Brecht's writings on theatre entirely from his writings on aesthetics or on politics; these strands of his thinking develop together and are intertwined. So, although we have largely excluded the material already published in *Brecht on Theatre* and *Brecht on*

Film, the theatre is never far away. Brecht himself, in his own publishing practice, did not for the most part make a distinction even between the literary and the non-literary, or between the genres. In his own pamphlet series of his writings, *Versuche* (*Experiments*), he set poems, plays, stories, sketches and essays one alongside the other. (For example, the 1950 volume 9 of the *Versuche* contains both *Mother Courage* and *Five Difficulties in Writing the Truth*, as the 20th and 21st 'experiments' respectively).

The current volume is called *Brecht on Art and Politics*, but it is, to a certain extent, a compendium of 'Brecht on everything else'. It gathers together some of what we consider to be his most significant writings on culture generally, the arts (excluding theatre and film), society and politics. The material is presented in five parts, governed both by chronology and by the desire to give a sense of the central concerns of different periods of Brecht's intellectual development (hence the broadly thematic titles). But the parts are not evenly balanced in scope or focus. Part One includes many short pieces from a period of fourteen years and with a wide range of subjects and approaches; Part Four, in contrast, collects the crucial and substantial writings on the realist aesthetic from just three years. The unevenness is partly determined by the available surviving material from different periods of Brecht's life, and partly also by the changing emphases of Brecht's own energies. He wrote, for example, far more longer essays on aesthetics and politics in the years 1927 to 1940 than he did at any other time of his life. It is, of course, also a product of our editorial decisions about what is most significant and interesting. Each part is prefaced with a short essay by the editors, introducing and summarising Brecht's thought in the relevant years, and setting it in context.

It is, however, worth emphasising that Brecht's ideas are not only of antiquarian or nostalgic interest. He was never merely a Communist dogmatic or propagandist. Rather, his critical engagement with the dialectics of Marx, Lenin and their contemporary interpreters, and his take on the political and cultural developments of his own time, in dialogue with such thinkers as Walter Benjamin, Theodor Adorno and Georg Lukács, gesture insistently forwards.

Brecht's thought has played a significant role: in the intellectual life of the GDR and in Socialist Europe; in the West German and European student movements; and for the Marxist left generally, from Europe to Central and South America, and beyond. His intellectual attitude was taken up above all by Roland Barthes, and so fed into the French tradition of cultural criticism, where it has re-emerged again especially in the work of Pierre Bourdieu; and his 'method' has been rediscovered and expounded, for example, by Fredric Jameson, who compares his contribution to, amongst many others, those of Gramsci or Althusser.[3] The essays of the current volume may help to explain why Brecht has been so useful to later cultural theorists, and how his critiques of the social context and function of culture still resonate for us today, even with a certain urgency.

As far as their style is concerned, Brecht's writings present problems, both for the translator and for the reader. Brecht could be aggressive, laconic, allusive, lapidary or convoluted: indeed, coming to these essays for the first time one might well not think they were all by the same author. In our translations we have tried to maintain some sense of the energy, but also of the fluid nature of Brecht's style. After the early disdainful polemics there is perhaps a progressive lucidity, but the bunched and knotted clauses, especially of some of the pieces which were never finished for publication, remain challenging. And the contradictory and elliptical nature of the writing on philosophy and social theory in the late 1920s and early 1930s may be traced to Brecht's own difficulties in sorting out his theoretical and epistemological position. We have been concerned not to render Brecht's texts with a phoney elegance, but to preserve the hard-edged character of his writing.

The German texts on which we have based our translations are those printed in the *Berliner und Frankfurter Ausgabe*. The titles given to the individual essays are translations of the BFA titles, the German original appearing with the BFA reference after each piece. Most titles are Brecht's own, or the titles under which the essays were published in Brecht's own lifetime; titles adopted by later editors are marked by an asterisk. We are very much indebted to the work of the editors of the BFA and other German editions. Further cross-references are above all to the other volumes of Brecht's writings already published in the Methuen edition, and especially to the indispensable companion volumes *Brecht on Theatre* and *Brecht on Film and Radio*. A short bibliography, including a fuller list of Brecht's non-literary writings in English, is included at the back of the volume.

We should like to record our thanks first of all to John Willett, who died during the preparation of this volume, but without whose inspiration and leadership there might be no English Brecht. Our gratitude goes also to the Suhrkamp Verlag and the Brecht heirs for permission, and also encouragement, to undertake this volume, and to our colleagues at Methuen for supporting the project. We are also especially indebted to the Brecht Archive and its director Erdmut Wizisla, and to Marc Silberman, Elizabeth Chadwick, Laura Bradley and Rebecca Beard for advice and suggestions. Finally, we acknowledge the financial assistance of the Arts and Humanities Research Board and of the Modern Languages Faculty of the University of Oxford, as well as the support of our various institutions (St Hugh's College, Oxford, and Nottingham, Manchester and Edinburgh Universities), without which we would not have been able to complete our work so efficiently.

The Editors

---

[1] BFA 21/563.

[2] The *Grosse kommentierte Berliner und Frankfurter Ausgabe* (Berlin and Frankfurt: Aufbau and Suhrkamp, 1988–2000), to which references are given in the abbreviated form: BFA volume number/page(s).

[3] The key texts are Barthes's *Mythologies* and Bourdieu's *Outline of a Theory of Praxis*. Fredric Jameson discusses these and other connections in his *Brecht and Method* (London, New York: Verso, 1998).

Part One

Early Writings and Polemics
1914–1928

(Augsburg–Munich–Berlin)

Introduction to Part One

The pieces in this first part range from relatively trivial, if energetic, juvenilia to the beginnings of a serious political aesthetic, which Brecht develops further in the later 1920s and early 1930s. Apart from the very early and somewhat anomalous 'Augsburg War Letters', the focus is on just two years: 1920 and 1926. There are only a few fragmentary notes and very occasional published articles from other years. It is not, however, merely an accident of history that such a scant scattering of Brecht's notes on political and philosophical matters has survived from this period. It seems also to be a fact that, at this stage, the focus of his interest lay elsewhere, namely on literature and on his own writing. The early journals (unpublished in English) can contribute a little to the picture, and the *Letters* (and third-person accounts) help to flesh out at least a sketch of Brecht's intellectual concerns in his twenties. And, of course, the literary works themselves. For, if the other writings of these years are sparse, Brecht's output in poetry and drama is enormously rich. These are the years of the poems of *The Domestic Breviary*, of *Baal*, *Drums in the Night*, *Man Equals Man* and so on. In terms of his literary career, these are the years in which he made it: in which he moved from provincial Augsburg to Munich to Berlin (in 1924), in which he attracted the attention of leading theatre critics Alfred Kerr (who reviled him) and Herbert Ihering (who championed him), won the Kleist Prize (in 1922), and became something of an *enfant terrible* of the theatre scene of the Weimar Republic.

This early literature is often described as nihilistic, and certainly it seems to embrace a sort of chaotic iconoclasm, directed at the prevailing standards of taste and morality. In one notebook from

9

1920 Brecht remarked, 'Values are in demand: I have a good sense of values (inheritance from my father). But I am also sensitive to the fact that one can set aside the concept of value altogether (Baal).'[1] A closer look at the writings of the years 1914 to 1926 reveals, however, a more complex picture.

In 1914 Brecht was only sixteen. Like many other young men, he was initially caught up in the tide of military enthusiasm which swept across Germany (and Europe) at the outbreak of the First World War. He wrote patriotic poems and pieces for a local newspaper, in a somewhat breathless, journalistic style. This is a writing that is produced primarily to meet a demand. Relatively unquestioning in its attitudes of patriotism and sympathy for the suffering, it gives little inkling of what was to come later. All the same, there is, quite early on, a shift towards a growing awareness of the pain involved in war and of the social misery (especially in poems from this period), and in 1916 Brecht caused a little scandal at school when he wrote what was, in this climate, a scurrilous essay on the subject of the famous line from Horace, '*Dulce et decorum est pro patria mori*'. A schoolfriend recalls the argument:

The saying, that it is sweet and fitting to die for the fatherland, can only be understood as propaganda. To depart this life must always be hard, whether in bed or in battle, and surely all the more so for young men in the blossom of their years. Only simpletons could be so vain as to speak of an easy step through that dark gate – and even then only so long as they think themselves still far removed from their final hour. When the bogeyman does come to fetch them, then they'll take their shields upon their backs and run for it, just like the bloated imperial jester at Philippi, who thought up this adage.[2]

As the war continued, Brecht became more and more con-scientiously determined not to conform, and not to fulfil the expectations of his upbringing. Like many of his generation, he opposed the war, as a stupid gesture by the old bourgeois order of the doomed Wilhelmine Empire and by the previous generation. In fact, Brecht's own father helped him to avoid being called up, the fate of many teenagers in the last months of the war, and he only served briefly, while still living at home, as a medical orderly in an Augsburg hospital – as he remembers in 'Republication Forbidden!' (no. 15). As he also recalls here, he was not much involved either in the turmoil of post-war political developments. In November 1918 a revolution was proclaimed in both Berlin and Munich, but Brecht seems to have been only marginally involved in all the politicking and excitement; he was more concerned with revising his first play, *Baal*, and then with a literary exploitation of contemporary events in *Drums in the Night*, in which the anti-hero proclaims at the end,

> The bagpipes play, the poor people are dying around the newspaper buildings, the houses fall on top of them, the dawn breaks, they lie like drowned kittens in the roadway, I'm a swine and the swine's going home.
>
> (*Collected Plays*, vol. 1, p. 115)

Not only was he determined to be anti-bourgeois and anti-patriotic, he was pretty determined not to commit himself, at this stage, to anything whatsoever. The sarcastic, contrary attitude to German political developments is still clear to see in the 1920 essay 'On Habitual Patriotism', and even in 'The Fun of Writing', some five years further down the road (nos 3 and 6).

In some way, despite all this, the war and its aftermath left a mark on him. Perhaps it was the very lack of stability and clear authority in these years which helped him (in this he is like many of his generation) towards a more radical questioning of the values of his humanist education, of received standards of order, morality, religious belief and so on. 'On Habitual Patriotism' is interesting as well because it so bitterly condemns 'the teachers' for society's ills. It is also just one amongst many pieces of evidence of Brecht's early interest in Nietzsche, that perpetual familiar of the clever, disillusioned, ambitious young man.[3] The cultural climate of the early decades of the twentieth century provided a fertile ground for the reception of Nietzsche's radical relativism and inversion of values. In fact, the first sign of Brecht's own reception dates from way back in 1915, in a letter in which he talks of discussing *Zarathustra* with friends. Only a year later we find him maintaining that he is already tired of Nietzsche and has turned to Spinoza.[4] Certainly he picked up ideas from these and other thinkers, but we should not for one moment suppose that his engagement amounted to anything like a conscientious reading, or to the development of a clear philosophical position. For a start, Spinoza is one of the most variously interpreted of philosophers, and Nietzsche is notorious for his rhetorical excess and his wild contradictions. Besides, Brecht was reading voraciously, and flitting from one idea to the next. One friend later summed it up like this:

> In the light of Brecht's later development one cannot help wondering what he thought about philosophy and about the theory of art at this early stage. A conclusive answer is probably impossible even for the most assiduous scholar of the young Brecht. Questions like that take no account of the zest and capriciousness of youth, in which it is possible to admire both Cesare Borgia and St Francis at one and the same time.
>
> (*The Young Brecht*, p. 45)

All in all, it is hard to say what came from books and what from his own experience; but it should not be surprising that a lot happened, in terms of Brecht's intellectual development, between the ages of seventeen and twenty-two: between war and revolution, school and university, a string of relationships and the beginnings of a literary career. There are, nevertheless, some constant concerns. The young Brecht's attraction to desolate philosophies and anti-creeds is very apparent; for him, God is dead beyond all resurrection. Much of his early philosophising can be understood as a restless casting around for what, having decided this, the next step should be. We should be wary of calling this nihilism. For all the attitudes of rejection, there are positive gestures too. After all, Nietzsche himself only rejects what he calls the 'Judaeo-Christian' tradition in the name of higher, 'naturalistic' values. Brecht too may have little patience with transcendental values but, beyond the minimalist earthbound materialism, there are signs also, around 1920, of an almost vitalistic investment in the creative process (in which instinct is valued over reason) and in the energy and productivity of a life (even if this should not be conceived in simple individualistic terms). Characteristically profanely, and humorously:

> If all you do is shit, says Baal, I say,
> that's still worth more than doing sweet f.a.
>
> (*The Young Brecht*, p. 61)

There is, moreover, a sort of exuberant enjoyment of ideas for their own sake, of 'opinions', which resonates through the writings of these early years. As Brecht noted in 1920,

> A man with one theory is lost. He must have several, four, many! He must stuff them in his pockets like newspapers, always the most recent, you can live well between them, you can dwell easily between the theories.
>
> (BFA 26/160)

Amongst the writings of the early years which were actually published at the time the most important group consists of the many reviews which Brecht wrote for local newspapers in Augsburg, Munich and, later, Berlin. Most are theatre reviews and so are excluded from the current collection. The first few items in *Brecht on Theatre* give an impression. Brecht wrote on Shaw and Wedekind, and on theatre as a sporting institution. He exercised himself about debates and scandals which may mean very little to us now. He wrote reviews of everything from Schiller to popular musical theatre, from Ibsen to Tagore. His judgements are vigorous and often scathing. Above all, his determination to reject contemporary literary trends (especially nos 4, 5 and 7, below) and his fixation that his own generation must represent a completely new departure are striking. Brecht's is a creativity derived from opposition.

Where he might take all this only very gradually becomes a little clearer. Around 1920 his vision is of a constantly, vitally self-renewing avant-garde ('On Dadaism'), the purpose of which is to vent the intellectual and spiritual contribution of the author (his 'opinions'). By the mid-1920s the vision is a much more social one. Art is still very much a part of life (Brecht will have nothing of Mann's or Rilke's polarities of life and art, or the 'spirit'), but it is no longer a matter of opinions (see no. 9), and the creativity of the individual is irretrievably bound up with his class (as well as his generation). Brecht still plays the immoderate polemicist, exploiting his differences with Alfred Kerr and with Germany's most established novelist, Thomas Mann, as a means to define his own position, and as a perverse source of energy for his creative productivity. But gradually one big idea (and one which has huge consequences for Brecht's whole output) begins to emerge: that literature must not only have and express a social base, but that literary value itself can only be understood in terms of social function. This rejection of a Kantian, Schillerian, Rilkean aesthetic is expressed almost stridently in his writings on poetry from 1927, in which he develops clearly for the first time the all-important notion of the 'use value' of art (no. 13, and compare also no. 8).

Brecht uses these occasions not only to expound his ideas, but also to develop his own provocative posture and voice. Throughout the opinionated diatribes, belligerent exchanges and epigrammatic throwaways of these early writings, a style is emerging. To an extent, the contribution to this of philosophers (and again especially of Nietzsche) is as *material* for literary processing, no different from the contribution of, say, Rimbaud or G. K. Chesterton. The young Brecht is not a philosopher, more a pillager of ideas and gestures. That does not, however, mean that he is unaware of the relationship between style and intellectual content. There is a tendency to view Brecht as the great political rationalist, for whom language, even literary language, is a transparent medium for the expression of ideas. Clear signs of a more radical questioning of language will only appear later (for example, in the essay 'On "the Thing in Itself"' of 1930, no. 25 below), but passing remarks even from 1920 and 1926 (the last sentence of 'On Expressionism', or the first of 'From: On Art and Socialism') give some inkling of a budding linguistic scepticism.

Finally, these early years provide, of course, Brecht's first encounters with a socialist politics. Brecht was not much involved in the brief turmoil of the Bavarian revolution, but he at least attended political meetings and talked with friends. Even if his real interests lay elsewhere, it cannot have escaped his notice that many of his contemporaries in the left-wing cultural scene were close to, or actually joined, the Independent Social Democrats (the splinter group out of which the German Communist Party emerged). According to one friend, Brecht described himself as an 'independent Independent'.[5] In 1920, however, he was still dismissing the Communists as wretched 'minor revolutionaries' (no. 3). Whatever the fluctuations in his attitude, gradually, the social concern (evident in even the earliest pieces), the sympathy for the underdog and the all-important anti-bourgeois resentment became more focused. Brecht's political inclinations and his anti-metaphysical stance led him to question the relationship of the individual to the natural world, to humanity and to the social group. And although he started out from an apparently rampant and self-confident individualism (in *Baal* especially), feelings, attitudes and opinions were increasingly understood, not as individual, but as the expression of a social situation, of 'interests'. This has consequences also for his theories of artistic creation and collective achievement, of intellectual property and the status of the artwork (which were only worked out fully later).

In 1926 Brecht read Lenin and Marx, or at least he began to, and he discovered interests in social conflict which chimed in with his own: even if he was still very far from embracing a Marxist position, he recognised, 'it is here that the fruitful oppositions lie' (no. 9). Around this time the attacks on what he understands as bourgeois ideology become more sustained and more considered. Nonetheless, despite the proclamation that the future will be dominated by revolutionary socialism, there is still a real fear of what that might look like: the almost Heinesque distaste at the thought of surrendering the individual life in the name of equality is very apparent in 'On Socialism'. And at times Brecht's ideas – for example, with his talk of the collective will in 'Terror Against Literature' (no. 9) – are more reminiscent of Rousseau than they are of Marx. It remains quite unclear, at least for another year or two, where his own sympathies and allegiances in all of this will lie. He has certainly not achieved the 'conversion' he would sometimes later laconically describe, nor yet discovered how to make the apparently so simple move of the autobiographical poem, 'Driven out with good reason': 'I left my own class and allied myself / With insignificant people'.

Often this early period has been underestimated by critics of Brecht, or it has been interpreted in relatively narrow ideological terms. Socialist critics during the Cold War were intent on discovering signs of the social critique and engagement considered central to Brecht's later work. Critics in the West were more likely to seek out evidence of the poet whose creativity was held to be independent of his later political commitment; for them the young Brecht was, if a thinker at all, a nihilist Nietzschean. More recently, Brecht's early work has been the ground on which to erect a 'post-modern Brecht'.[6] Many of these accounts, even the most recent, seduced by the conventions of the biography of the developing artist, have inclined to impose an implausible coherence on what was clearly a lively chaos of various, uneven and contradictory impulses. However, even if these early years provide no clear picture of the rationalist proto-Marxist that some critics are seeking, they are nonetheless revealed as a rich seedbed of ideas, intellectual poses and theories. Like his critics, Brecht was himself inclined to make sense, retrospectively, of his early development, in terms of the positions he later reached (or wanted to have reached).[7] It may, however, also be productive to bear these early writings in mind when we look at some of the later work. Even decades later (to name just one example: Azdak in *The Caucasian Chalk Circle*), there are still traces of the anarchic energies and unresolved conflicts, the exuberant contrariness and the profane anti-bourgeois gestures of this young Brecht.

---

[1] BFA 26/116.

[2] Quoted from Hanns Otto Münsterer, *The Young Brecht* (London, 1992),

a book of memoir and biographical material which provides a full account of the years 1917 to 1922. Further references to this are in brackets in the text.

[3] The influence of Nietzsche on Brecht was investigated in a pioneering study by Reinhold Grimm, *Brecht und Nietzsche oder Geständnisse eines Dichters* (Frankfurt a.M., 1979).

[4] BFA 28/28 and 26/108.

[5] *The Young Brecht*, p.149.

[6] In the first category there are the classic studies by Ernst Schumacher and Werner Mittenzwei; in the second, works by Martin Esslin and Reinhold Grimm; in the third, Elizabeth Wright's *Postmodern Brecht: A Re-Presentation*, amongst others.

[7] In no. 56 below, or in 'On looking through my first plays' (BFA 23/239–45).

1

Extracts from the 'Augsburg War Letters'

14 August 1914

Battalion upon battalion is marching off, through Königsplatz and Schrannenstrasse down to the station. The cheering crowds mill and jostle round them; and they march on, with firm and steady stride, off to join the great war. The people have brought flowers to the barracks, and the soldiers' helmets and rifles are all bedecked with blossoms. Beneath the flowery helmets their eyes burn bright in faces glowing with sweat.

Not a single one of those who are marching does so other than gladly. One or other, maybe a farmer's lad with a rough, honest face, may clench his teeth, as he grits them when there's hard work to be done. Some contemplate the coming war with something like relief, and regret for those who stay at home. And thoughts such as these, though they may later fall silent, keep their joy in check and lay a profound and quiet seriousness over all the company.

At the kerbside, those who stay at home. The hurrahs swell and ring out, kerchiefs flutter and wave goodbyes. Those whose sons and brothers are marching off are quiet. Mothers stand with still, despairing faces and sob into their handkerchiefs. Men look on, strong men, chewing on their beards, biting back the tears.

There is sadness in plenty. But I was most moved by the bearing of an old man standing by the side of the road watching his three sons. He stood erect and straight, his wizened body stiff. He did not cry out, nor wave. He watched in silence as his sons marched past, calling their farewells. Not a hand did he lift. Not a tear to be seen in his wide, alert eyes. But that coarse face was like a prayer.

20 August 1914

The first list of the lost and missing. People are not a little relieved. So far, it seems, no Bavarians have fallen.

Nonetheless there is continual talk of officers from Augsburg who they say are dead.

The news of the capture of 3,000 Russians excites great joy. But it is a silent joy. Day and night the newspaper kiosk on Königsplatz is besieged by crowds hungry for news. Most of the telegrams are read out loud. People debate, and doubt.

Half the week passes with little to report.

On Wednesday evening the first rumours of the fall of Belfort. Quiet excitement. Everyone knows that Belfort is the key to the French defences in the Vosges. The rumour is denied by the *München-Augsburger Abendzeitung*.

By noon the next day the news seems to be firming up. On the streets people call out to one another 'Belfort has fallen'. They have already announced it to the soldiers, they say.

Evening. The newspapers still won't confirm the rumour.

I have just come in from the streets. It was quiet.

And as I write this now, I wonder whether, over there in the Vosges, the joy of victory is spreading through the mountains, it must be good to be there now, uplifting, or whether . . .

And I imagine: the last rays of sun wander over a corpse-strewn battlefield . . . Thousands lie dead: dead or with twitching limbs.

And I think of the many heavy sacrifices that such a victory costs.

Sacrifices offered by the fatherland – for the fatherland.

10 September 1914

We have so many worries.

There is still no list of the missing from the local regiments. Individual families have received news of the death of a family member. But the fate of the regiments themselves remains unclear.

Rumours of terrible losses circulate. People have no confidence, but in the end they believe the rumours. Lists of the missing have appeared for every other regiment in the Reich. Just not for ours.

Worry haunts our town.

Contributions to the war effort are plentiful. Every ruse is tried to get more money. Recently they've set up little boxes, with two flags stuck in them, so people can make their contributions as they pass. Paper bags are distributed for collections for the Red Cross.

But still the money is far too little to assuage all the misery the war has unleashed. Thousands storm the War Welfare office. Widows whose sons are at the front. Worker wives who have given their husbands. They all come with justified demands.

What's more, there is fear that the eagerness of the men to sacrifice themselves may diminish in the coming months. And in the coming months winter will be upon us. Much, much more must be done. People are still playing cards, billiards. While thousands stand on the brink of the abyss. –

Worry haunts our town.

27 September 1914

Amidst the thunder of the big guns, the struggles and the worries, summer is coming to an end. We scarcely notice that the days are getting shorter, cooler, that in the natural world around us things are falling ever quieter.

We err through these days, lost in thought. Our eyes are fixed on the distant future. Our sense for our surroundings is weak. What care is it to us that nature has bedecked herself in new treasures and shines once more in all her glory . . .

The days are fine and sunny. It is as if the golden sun, paler all the while, wanted to prove once more her tenderness, as she gleams through the tops of the chestnut trees, paints golden yellow patches on the browning leaves.

An aching tiredness, a mild melancholy in nature announces that the great dying has begun. The sun still shines, day after day,

over the autumnal landscape. But the great storms are approaching, drawing ever nearer, anticipated – it almost seems – by a tired
nature.

And recently when I passed the graveyard in Haunstetter Street,
in contemplative mood, I thought that this year nature is decked
up for a greater celebration than in other years.

And I thought, a grand and weighty memorial is to be celebrated
when the great storms ring in All Hallows.

['*Augsburger Kriegsbriefe*'. BFA 21/10, 14–15, 22 and 31.]

These pieces are extracts from a number of articles Brecht published while
he was still at school, under the pseudonym 'Berthold Eugen', his given
forenames in reverse order. They appeared on the front page of a local
newspaper, the *München-Augsburger Abendzeitung*. In the last piece he
looks forward to 2 November, All Souls' Day, when, according to Catholic
doctrine, the souls of the dead are purified in purgatory before their
reception into heaven.

2

From the 1920 Notebooks

Salvation of an Individual

When an individual has got so far that it can only be preserved
through the transformation of another, then it should be allowed to
fail.

It is like the case of a man who wants to sell another man a knife and,
in order to show him what a good knife he's getting, stabs him to
death. –

Patriotism

Only in states where the subjects are such swine that they would otherwise piss in their trousers is it really necessary to consecrate the urinals as temples.

Putting up with the state is as necessary as putting up with having to shit. However, loving the state is not *so* necessary.

No Help

I always thought, when I saw people in pain or grief wringing their hands or crying laments, that such people had not grasped their situation in its full seriousness. For they had completely forgotten that there is no help, they had not yet realised that they had not just been abandoned or abused by God, but that there simply is no God, and that a man who, alone on his island, makes such a fuss must be mad.

['*Rettung eines Individuums*'*, '*Patriotismus*', '*Keine Hilfe*'*, BFA 21/45 and 52.]

These epigrammatic fragments are examples of the notes on more or less political and philosophical matters which have survived from early notebooks of 1920. Others are on the monarchy, death, God, and so on. One sheet contains the sentence, 'Free will – that is a capitalist invention!' (BFA 26/114). Most, however, are more autobiographical, or else literary sketches. They were not intended for publication.

3

On Habitual Patriotism

Now that I have warned you against habitual drinking, habitual philosophising, habitual being in love, I am going to warn you against habitual love of the fatherland. I have told you that the worst thing for a habitual drinker is not forgetting how to walk, how to do business or how to be good, but instead forgetting how to drink. In the same way, someone who is ready, every hour of the day, to sacrifice his life for the fatherland will gradually lose his love of his fatherland, just as someone who always chops wood will exchange the love of chopping wood for the habit of chopping wood, and that is something completely different, even though it is still quite useful. In the end the habitual patriot loves only one thing, one hero: namely himself. Yet those are still the better sort; most of them just spend the whole time *talking*. Talkers and heroes are quite useful people, but they have nothing whatsoever in common. Usually people's love of the fatherland is nothing more than their love of holding forth. It is agreeable to rave about the irreproachable, commendable nature of one's own convictions. And it is almost equally agreeable and easy to curse about the convictions of others. This, however, is not commendable, my dear friend, and it is certainly not irreproachable. Cursing is a habit which disappointed people succumb to; cursing is the revenge of the lackey. Now we have, once again, arrived at the origins of this evil: the lackeys, the teachers, etc. Habitual patriots are always talking about 'our *Volk*'. The phrase itself demonstrates how inclined they are to stand to one side and watch the people, their people, file past. It is *their* people, they are the owners. They know what they are like, they know what is good for them. They are prepared to make various sacrifices for them, they demand something from them in return. When they are just about satisfied with their people, then they join them and say 'we'. By this, they mean themselves and their people. And now, in this mood, they have the feeling that there are many of them, a great many, an entire herd, and because they believe that strength lies in unity (this is still their most excusable mistake!) they feel now, more than ever before, that they are the masters. There you have it: rulers and lackeys, they are two of a kind. If you lick his arse, then he is a master, and if you spit in his face, then he must be a slave. Whatever he is, he is always a teacher. A teacher is someone who makes a living from chatter. The teacher is the obstacle in the way of progress, the sanctuary of stragglers, the pillar of old age, for nations and for ideas, the fortress of everything old – which he calls 'hard-won'. The teacher is someone who presumes to know something just because he enjoys the promise of being a know-*all*, who teaches and is therefore unteachable, who never loves anything as it is, but always thinks that he could do everything better. The serpent in Paradise was the first teacher; it wanted to 'teach' mankind what is good. Amongst the ranks of teachers we also find the revolutionaries, that is to say the minor revolutionaries, those who are currently getting rid of the Kaiser and introducing Communism, and their conservative opponents are teachers too. On right and left the barricades are manned by teachers. But let me tell you this: the man who bows on principle and the man who refuses to bow on principle are brothers, they belong to the same wretched breed. Teachers have bestowed an honourable name on their sort: they are men of character. But free men need no principles in matters of such indifference. The out-and-out pacifist and the out-and-out militarist are the same kind of fool.

['*Über den Gewohnheitspatriotismus*', BFA 21/92–4.]

A further sketch from the 1920 notebooks. Brecht several times returned to the subject of patriotism.

4

On Expressionism and Dadaism

On Expressionism

Expressionism means: crude oversimplification.

Where it is not a question of allegory (as it is in *Alcibiades Saved*, *Gas*, or *The Son*), it is all about exorcising or exaggerating the spirit and the ideal. Since developments in literature were (coincidentally) just like those in politics, where there was a new parliament but no new parliamentarians, here there was a great love of the idea, but no ideas. As a result, it became a movement instead of a phenomenon, and its proponents clung to external appearances; i.e., instead of filling human bodies with spirit, they bought skins (the more brightly coloured, the better) for the spirits to dwell in, and instead of drawing out the (supposedly misunderstood) souls in the bodies, they turned the souls themselves into bodies, oversimplifying them and making the intangible spirit material. In the days when the spirit still lived in caves, it was unheeded but free. Although, in those days, it was not yet maintained by Wolff Publishing, it also did not have to bow coquettishly to dealers and whores. If a young man becomes a philosopher (and nothing else) because he has great ideas, then that is nice. However, if he becomes nothing (and a philosopher) because it's nice to have great ideas, then that is definitely not nice. That is, if Wolff goes bust.

To write in such a way that as few people as possible dare to claim they understand you is no great art, if you have studied Sternheim and Kaiser closely.

['*Über den Expressionismus*', BFA 21/48–9.]

On Dadaism

One of the Dadaists' worst mistakes lies in having their works published, even though they seem to have been produced unmediatedly and for the most immediate present. The effect of this is embarrassing.

Whatever its mode or genre, art always concerns itself with the spiritual equilibrium of the recipient. Its ambition is to confirm it or to destroy it. Against its pursuit of this goal, the recipient, subject to the famous law of inertia, seeks to stabilise himself at all costs, consciously or unconsciously. The formal aspects of the artwork help him to do so. However, the most extreme effect of a work of art (hinted at above) only ever occurs once.

The same tricks never work twice. The recipient is generally immune to a second invasion of new ideas which employ familiar techniques, even the successful ones.

Perhaps this explains why the first works of a (currently) new genre leave behind a deeper impression than the more perfect works which follow on, which last longer. (Because their formal qualities are stronger.)

If forces are recognised by their effects, then Dadaism counts as art. In Dadaism, intellectual exertions [*the text breaks off here*]

['*Über den Dadaismus*', BFA 21/51–2.]

These two texts are taken, like nos 2 and 3, from Brecht's notebooks of 1920. 'On Expressionism' may be a response to the efforts of the Munich Professor for Theatre Studies, Artur Kutscher, in whose seminars Brecht participated, to win over his students and the wider public to the theatre of Expressionism. The references are to Georg Kaiser's plays, *Alcibiades Saved* and *Gas* (a production in Augsburg of the first part of which Brecht reviewed for *Der Volkswille* in March 1920) and Walter Hasenclever's *The Son*. Brecht's interest in Kaiser is well documented (see also below, no. 18). The Kurt Wolff Verlag was the leading publisher of Expressionist literature.

5

On German Literature

We Germans are very conceited about our seriousness, we feel that the opposite of seriousness is frivolity and that frivolity must be condemned. Other nations feel differently.

We think that humour is a bad and lazy method of dealing with things. We presuppose that things always give cause for concern, that our opinion about them is correct, and we hope that we will be taken more seriously if we are serious ourselves. We harbour a deep mistrust of everything that is easy, we suspect immediately that if someone is slapdash the emphasis is on the slap above all, and not the dash, and that it's not the man who is better, but that his work is worse.

Now some nations agree with us that things can demand serious treatment; indeed, some even think they have to take some of the things seriously which we find comical (for we have pretty crude ideas about comedy; in our country clowns represent humour), and

I would like to believe that it is their sense of humour that enables them to do so.

Humour is a feeling of distance.

I have read that an Englishman would not think of insisting on his views on principle unless it were a matter of commercial interest. We are used to annexing certain points of view straight away and then to throwing ourselves cheerfully – or rather, seriously – into the subject matter. We consume the sausage skin with the meat, we turn off our sense of smell where matters of the stomach are concerned. If food poisoning should result then God is to blame, since he created both the sausages and our stomachs.

Our literature is astonishingly free of opinions. When you read Kipling and Hamsun the subject matter is completely different, just like the point of view, but behind the subject matter you can clearly see a standpoint and the man to whom it belongs, and it is the man that counts. He states his opinion, whether right or wrong – that is, whether it suits our taste or not – and the man allows us to place ourselves above him and observe him writing.

It seems, the man takes himself less seriously than he takes his subject matter.

God knows: there is nothing so comical as the deadly seriousness which, for example, raving Kasimir arrogates for himself. Even the comedy of those readers who, in their turn, take him so seriously, him and his printed paper, does not quite live up to his own comedy. There's this philistine sitting there and with no doubt in the divinity of his in- and perspiration, using his left hand to strike down anyone who risks the slightest grin at what his right hand is writing, or at the awe with which mad old Schmidt regards his paper. That is why, when you read such a genuinely German book, you always feel you can smell sweat, instead of glue, sheep's sweat.

And it is all because we have decided that humour belongs in hell, whereas we should not doubt that, in fact, it reigns in heaven.

['*Über die deutsche Literatur*', BFA 21/53–4.]

Again from 1920. The reference is to the Expressionist writer Kasimir Edschmid (a pseudonym for Eduard Schmid).

6

Mood and Opinion

The Fun of Writing

The most important thing for a writer is mercilessly to get rid of a certain sort of mood. If he is writing a Sardanapalus it is no use if he has the feeling that he is sitting amongst Assyrian tapestries; on the contrary, it is much better if he has the feeling he is sitting in front of a piece of paper. For he needs to derive his fun from writing. A powerful thought can achieve sufficient effect with the very minimum of mood. As for a feeling, it is enough that he should once have had it, the memory of it is the most important part of a writer's technique. The desire to have things easy, without losing anything of value overboard, has contributed more to the emergence of periods of blossoming than any wish to be original and to delve deep, amongst people who consider writing itself to be the unpleasant part of the process of production.

The one thing that can depress me in my work is the occasional thought that our own age might not be one of the most wonderful of all ages. Of course it would not depress me if it was one of the worst. Merely the fear that there might be something mediocre behind it all robs me of all the pleasure of work. That is why I am so upset by German history, such as it is taught in schools. I am ashamed of the war of 1870, just like I would be ashamed of a mark for good conduct in school. The Wars of Liberation make me feel sick. Amongst these dispiriting memories, only the achievement of the Treaty of Versailles, by which we compelled half the globe to endure considerable financial sacrifices – in which we ourselves participated only marginally – in order to guarantee every German freedom from war and military service . . . now that is one of the more cheering moments.

['*Spass am Schreiben*'*, BFA 21/116–17.]

Unpublished typescript of 1925. Sardanapalus was an Assyrian king notorious in legend for his love of luxury; he is the eponymous hero of a tragedy by Byron. The further historical references are to the Franco-Prussian war (of 1870–1) which led to the founding of the German Reich; the 1813–14 Prussian Wars of Liberation against Napoleon; and the Versailles Treaty at the end of the First World War – with its constraints on German rearmament and the reparations bill, which ultimately necessitated an international financial plan, the Dawes Plan, to ensure Germany's further solvency.

In this and the following piece, Brecht turns his attention to questions of literary technique and, moving on from the by turns disdainful and scathing attacks of nos 4 and 5, begins conscientiously to define his own voice against those he hears around him.

Letter in the Third Winter of our Discontent

The worst thing is that, whatever topic we want to develop an opinion on, we have to take a big run-up first. And you have to take care not to get tired on the way!

Matters where we understand the old folk are as scarce as hen's teeth. Their whole generation, let's get straight to the point, is categorically, irrevocably and conscientiously misunderstood by our own. It is because this time the third generation has followed straight on the first. The one in between was swallowed up by the earth when it tried to filch the ore mines of Briey. So now the grandsons stare straight into the faces of their grandfathers.

['*Brief im dritten Winter unseres Missvergnügens*', BFA 21/119.]

Unpublished typescript of *c.* 1926. The iron-ore fields of Briey were a target of the German invasion in the First World War.

7

Let's Get Back to Detective Novels!

Two kinds of lady

In my mind it is an advantage of nordic literature that, simply by reading, one can establish whether a book is written by a man or a woman. But isn't it good, when you've read both *Jerusalem* and *Buddenbrooks* and decided they are both by women, that in the first case you are right and in the latter not? With German books in recent decades, even when you know the narrators are men, it sometimes happens that you mistake absolutely similarly written books and think they are written by men, for example, *The Head* and *God's Conic Sections*. The correct identification of the sex of an author in Germany is only possible with the help of a photograph. Let us turn to detective novels.

An ill-willed suggestion

I fear it is an unfriendly impulse of mine to recommend to readers that they study the posture in which a book is written. Consider an example which by no means betrays the full ramifications of this thought: there is not a single detail or turn in Thomas Mann's *Magic Mountain*, for example, by which he could persuade me that he is entirely at home (with his material). That is why all this cheap irony is so suspicious. By the sweat of our brows, there he goes, inventing stuff about which he can only smile ironically. Before anything else is down on paper, this gent must already be, whatever the weather, ironic. I have a good sense of method. I could watch with pleasure while one of our people, in order to recreate a death scene, for example, sets up apparatus about a deathbed, phonetic, optic machines, etc., in order then to create an ironic juxtaposition of the recordings. But I watch with increasing dismay if someone needs something ironic for his machines, and believes that his audacity in using a deathbed scene is itself sufficient to guarantee him a place in literary history (where, by the way, his machines undoubtedly belong). Let us, by all means, get back to detective novels!

An ovation for all the rest
Almost without exception, when a group of men sits down together the outcome will be literature, much abetted, of course, by alcohol and tobacco. So too when Elvestad and Heller sit down together. I don't mean anything unkind by this. Above all, because the resulting literature is very good. It is literature for adults. As an author I was rocked to the core when I watched the extraordinary tributes and the still more extraordinary security measures which the capital city of a nation of 60 million thought appropriate when they summoned a very old man to the highest office of the Reich, an old man whose claim that he hadn't read a single book since his schooldays could be universally believed. Let me join the tributes to this ancient-of-days: there should be fewer books that one cannot read before the end of one's school education. From twenty to eighty years of age a man in these latitudes is dependent on that literature which is the outcome, much abetted, of course, by alcohol and tobacco, when two men sit down together. So let us turn, at last, to detective novels!

What is a writer?
Is it perverse when the thing you love about books is the smell of glue and printer's ink? Whoever can create this smell is a writer. And as for the posture required of the writer: isn't it admirable, if a man can take so much alcohol, that something so sober and testable can come out of him when he is drunk? Let us, simply, get back to detective novels!

You need luck
Literature in some other sense can only come into being if you get lucky. Stendhal, for example. He found a linguistic frame which was more durable than many. It was the language of Napoleon. It only lasted ten years. The stones with which he paved his streets, and

which are indestructible, were only around for ten years. The great ages in which the literati ruled (of the calibre of Napoleon) are few. Let us get back to detective novels!

Gynaecology

It is proof of poor-quality linguistic material if, the more polish an edifice has, the worse it gets. It is proof of good material if an edifice gets all the more lively the more polish it has. Every thought that is written down in this German language, ruined as it is by a hundred years of wets and lackeys, is spoilt by careful stylisation. Linguistically things are just as bad as they are in gynaecology (rural practice). If you can't get hold of the child at the first attempt with the forceps, then you may as well spike him straight through the head. And it is simply better to shape a thought, than to invest all your thoughts in shaping. Let us get back to detective novels!

The only read

Detective novels are the only occasion for me to get abusive about literature. Let us get back to them!

['*Kehren wir zu den Kriminalromanen zurück!*', BFA 21/128–30.]

First published in *Die Literarische Welt*, Berlin, 2 April 1926. The references in the first paragraph are to the following novels: Selma Lagerlöf's *Jerusalem*, Thomas Mann's *Buddenbrooks*, Heinrich Mann's *Der Kopf* (*The Head*), and *Die Kegelschnitte Gottes* (*God's Conic Sections*) by 'Sir Galahad' (i.e., Berta Eckstein-Diener). Sven Elvestad and Frank Heller (§3) were authors of detective stories; and the 'very old man' is Hindenburg, who was seventy-seven when he was elected Reichspräsident and head of state of the German Republic in 1925.

Brecht had a genuine enthusiasm for detective stories. He read Chesterton and others as a young man, and in the late 1930s he wrote knowledgeably on the subject: see below, no. 59. His personal library contained many well-thumbed detective paperbacks.

8

On Being a Suitable Spectator

1 One of the fundamentals of the way we view art is the opinion that great art speaks directly, unmediatedly, from feeling to feeling; that it transcends human differences; rather, having no interests of its own, it brings people together in the act of appreciation by disengaging their interests. Now since neither old nor new art continues to achieve this effect in the present, people either conclude that there is no great art today (and this is indeed the general view), or else they are forced, let us say empowered, to stop making this demand of great art. Let us assume this last step now accomplished.

2 Great art serves great interests. If you want to establish the greatness of a work of art, then ask: what great interests does it serve? Epochs without great interests do not have great art.

3 What interests? Intellectual interests (insofar as they can be traced back to material interests).

4 In our epoch there are several classes of human beings who have quite different interests and correspondingly different intellectual responses. So if great art were to be produced today, it could only ever be produced for *one* of these classes; it would then promote the interests of this class, and this class alone would respond to it. But would this class react to it under all circumstances?

5 No.

['*Über die Eignung zum Zuschauer*', BFA 21/127.]

Written around 1926. The idea that art has no interests of its own (i.e., is an autonomous realm of human activity, with an aesthetics entirely independent of material or moral concerns) goes back to Immanuel Kant's *Critique of Judgement* of 1790.

9

On Art and Socialism

On Socialism

It is an obvious fact that the capitalist class in Europe is a spent force, it has nothing left to offer, least of all desires. The mass on the left wing is a good thing, as long as it is fighting; as soon as it has won it must be replaced. Even the sight of the railways, for instance, is frustrating: they belong to nobody, no one can work with them, they do not serve to bring men fame or destruction, they are simply withdrawn from the frame, useful as civilising aids, no longer as an end in themselves! The only question is whether one wants to chop up happiness into such tiny pieces. One shouldn't. And in any case, it won't work. It would vanish, like snow when you touch it. Don't let them tell you any different: 100,000 marks is a lot of money, but 5 lots of 20,000 are not. Are they supposed to crouch in their freshly painted identical huts between gramophones and tins of mince-meat, with their fixed-price women and their identical pipes? That isn't happiness, all opportunity and risk are missing. Opportunity and risk, the greatest and most moral things of all. What is contentment? Not having a reason to complain, that is just another reason too few, nothing more! And as for a life free of harshness, that is complete nonsense! Goodness and generosity and boldness all count for nothing without the certainty that the normal run is primitive, stupid and tasteless! It is purely due to ignorance when those who are repulsed by the spent bourgeoisie – who themselves are indeed nothing but a socialised, i.e. heavily insured, claque, lacking taste, opportunity and risk – fail to see where the true enemies of the bourgeoisie (and of social democracy) stand.

['*Über den Sozialismus*', BFA 21/140.]

Written in 1926, in a notebook which also contains, amongst other sketches, the next three pieces and the essay on Shaw in *Brecht on Theatre*, pp. 10–13.

From: On Art and Socialism
(Fragment of a Prologue to the Comedy *Man Equals Man*)

Messianic belief in literature
In order to make myself better understood, I had better express myself unclearly: amongst my opponents I am not the least interested in the bourgeoisie, despite all their efforts. On the other hand, I am interested in the proletariat, despite their indifference.

Whatever happens, we are not the filling with which to stuff up the gaping hole in the 'intellectual' history of the bourgeoisie. That can no longer be filled; if we are to identify a role which we are at least still able to perform, it is to make sure the hole gets even bigger.

The desperate, empty-headed plebs will realise, just as their dusk is falling, that if there is one essential criterion for the modernity of ideas it is this: that the corrupt bourgeoisie cannot understand them.

On Baal
When I put Baal, as a type, in full view on the stage, I was seeking, in vain, to provoke the enmity of the bourgeoisie of 'that' time. But they were so irredeemably corrupt that they either criticised just the form, which as form alone was irrelevant – just available that's all – or else they surrendered to the '*je ne sais quoi*' of the formulation. I can only hope for a real opponent in the proletariat. Without *this* enmity, which I could sense, I could never have created this type.

I must admit, it was only when I read Lenin's *State and Revolution* (!) and then Marx's *Kapital* that I understood, philosophically, where I stood. I don't mean to say that I reacted *against* these works, that would seem quite incorrect. I just think that it was here, amidst *these* oppositions, that I felt at home. It is not permitted to the *art* of this (so costly) period of transition to do more than adopt the 'point of view' that it is *here* that the fruitful oppositions lie.

The worries of the bourgeoisie
For example, I was given to understand, without precisely knowing it myself, that they would be happy to permit me, say once a year, to

let one or other of my plays fall flat. I wouldn't have to worry about anything except producing the plays. And it wasn't because they were frightened of the plays, they didn't understand them well enough for that, but rather because they didn't want to have to relinquish their sort of theatre. And it's true, the theatres would have had to be shut down in order to be able to put on my play. The situation, which they were determined to preserve, was very odd: the crowd of people in the stalls were not to be deprived of the opportunity to gawp open-mouthed (and open-eared), and the other crowd – up on the stage – were to keep the opportunity not to become unemployed simpy because of their lack of artistry. It was hard to think of an objection; it seemed appropriate to want to share their worries.

What about the people on the left?
People on the left had real worries, they knew the score and weren't interested in theatricals. The stuff that came from the left was, with the exception of a couple of useful revues, artistically pretty old hat, of a decidedly slavish mentality. A few literati, anxiously orientated to left or right, put together texts which were based on the calculation that a simple lack of intelligence is enough to make plays comprehensible. Typically, they presented themselves to the proletariat as 'the new', as themselves, or else they believed that 'literary feeling' is the feeling which foments revolutions. A harmless mistake. Altogether, the defining characteristic of all these efforts, from left to right, is a harmlessness which is bound to irritate any normal human being. (Even the loutishnesses of ageing literary-supplement hacks, which don't really belong here, share this: they originated in a harmless fear – often expressed in long-winded five- or ten-volume reflections upon the author's own well-being – of being upset by some production or other.) The brusque attitude of the proletariat, and above all of its intellectual leaders, towards art is, in the face of what purports to be art on both left and right, more than understandable. The proletariat adopts the hair-raising view that art is harmful, since it distracts the masses from the struggle. But it has never distracted the bourgeoisie from its struggle, not for

one minute. That is perhaps the reproach one should make as a proletarian. Art has even occasionally pointed the bourgeoisie in the very direction of the struggle. It is understandable, if not such a good thing, if the proletariat now wants to command art to point the masses towards their own struggle. The reproach that Barbusse, for example, levelled against artists of all periods, in the name of the proletariat ... is based on sound evidence, but is nonetheless unjustified. It is no reproach against God that he is always on the winning side. Of course he is. A proletarian art is just as much art as any other: more art than proletarian. It may be unhelpful, and during a struggle it most certainly is unhelpful, but that is of no concern to the art itself. One might even say, with only a little exaggeration, that art is indifferent to the opinions of the artists. Art is not a matter of opinions. Just as corn is likewise not a matter of opinions; it simply grows. If art were something that had to deal with opinions it would be something entirely individual, just as many bourgeois and proletarians have from time to time maintained. But that is not the case. Art is not something individual. Art, both in terms of its origin and its effect, is something collective. The worst thing that could happen as a result of such a view would be that some pile of rubbish that has hitherto been called art should from now on not be called art. A shining advantage! So I would maintain that a view of art, commonly held by us on the left, is false. And I should like to take the opportunity and aver that a great deal of the views on the left are false, it just doesn't matter there so much as on the right. The desperate attempts of the literati to capture the opinions of the proletariat are unbelievably comical. In nine out of ten cases they turn out to be entirely bourgeois opinions. So it is hard to understand why these gentlemen put themselves out so: they are merely expressing their own opinions.

Résumé

In my opinion there can be no doubt that socialism, and by that I mean revolutionary socialism, will transform the face of our land in our own lifetime. Our lives will be dominated by struggles of this kind. As far as the artists are concerned, I reckon they would be best advised to take no heed and do whatever turns them on: otherwise they will be unable to produce good work. For people in whose heads these tensions are absent, it will of course be hard to create art at all. Only they have something to hope for from our age who can profit from a better public and to whom better instincts are an advantage: and there are precious few of them.

['*Aus: Über Kunst und Sozialismus*', BFA 21/142–4.]

For the premiere of *Man Equals Man* in September 1926 Brecht devised texts for a Prologue, but all that has survived are these general remarks, which were never published. As well as the mentions of Brecht's reading of Marx and Lenin at about this time, the text also makes reference to two of his parallel literary projects: *Life Story of the Man Baal* (1926), which he had developed out of the original *Baal* material, and *Joe Fleischhacker*, an unfinished play about the wheat market (hence the remark about corn having no opinions). The parenthetical remark about hacks is a dig in particular at the theatre critic Alfred Kerr, with whom Brecht had a long-running feud (see also below, no. 12) and who had published his collected reviews in seven volumes.

In 1926 and 1927 the French novelist Henri Barbusse, whose First World War novel *Le Feu* (1916, German 1918) had been enormously popular in Germany as well as France, launched a series of attacks, in numerous articles, against the decadence of bourgeois art, and sought to proclaim a new proletarian art which might unite the radical form of the avant-garde with a radical political content. Compare 'Primacy of the Apparatus' (below, no. 17) for more on the relationship between the institutions of the theatre and the new drama.

Terror Against Literature

The great writers of all periods have rightly insisted on the label 'revolutionary'; for their works were collective products. The lesser literati are, according to the prevailing social conditions, some reactionary, some revolutionary. But since their ideas are always concerned only with the immediate conditions – they emerge on the basis and have value only in respect of these conditions – when the conditions need to be changed (which is a matter of collective instinct and not immediately apparent to the writers themselves) these lesser literati need to be socialised by terror – which will be simple enough, given their lack of internal substance and their dependence on external forces. The practical methods of revolution are not always revolutionary; they are dictated by the class struggle. The great revolutionary writers are therefore ill suited for the class struggle, since they incline to treat it as already over, and they concern themselves with the new, collectively willed conditions which are the purpose of the revolution. The revolution of the great writers is a perpetual.

Opinions are Misleading

Insofar as Bolshevism is a matter of opinion it is of little concern to me. Opinions to left and right may well be false. The opinions of the bourgeoisie, for example, vouchsafe no insights concerning the bourgeoisie itself. A large part of the bourgeoisie, for example, considers the making of money to be a dirty business, and yet that is its sole occupation. In fact, their actions are much more sensible than their opinions. And so they demonstrate a truly impressive cynicism, simply letting their newspapers construct the opinions which will justify their actions.

['*Terror gegen Literatur*' and '*Die Ansichten trügen*', both BFA 21/146.]

Both from the 1926 notebook.

10

Literary Judgements

Fitting Comment on Franz Kafka

If it is permissible to speak at all about a truly serious figure like Franz Kafka in a literary environment which simply does not deserve any kind of serious treatment, in a language which might only defend its habitual sloppiness by some polite insight, and when whatever one says will inevitably be insignificant when measured against the subject, then to do so at least requires an apology. To the credit of the present, it has to be said it admits quite frankly that it is not for phenomena like Kafka. Every attempt by the vermin on either side of their shared journalistic red-light district to declare him one of their own would have to be dashed, possibly even by methods whose expediency was widely appreciated only in earlier barbaric times. If necessary, I would not hesitate one moment to destroy someone completely.

Rilke

In several of his poems there is mention of God. I draw your attention to the fact that whenever Rilke is dealing with God, he expresses himself in an utterly camp fashion. Nobody who has ever noticed this can ever again read a line of these verses without a disfiguring smirk.

['*Geziemendes über Franz Kafka*' and '*Rilke*'*, both BFA 21/158.]

Typescripts from *c.* 1926. For more on Brecht's reaction against Rilke's aesthetic, see below, no. 13.

11

An Argument with Thomas Mann

The Difference between the Generations

In the *Berliner Tageblatt* Thomas Mann has taken up some casual comments which I made in the *Tage-Buch* and has established that he did not say, but only opined what he allegedly said in the *Uhu*. As a follow-up, this well-loved representative has set out his position regarding the younger generation. His opinion is that the difference between his generation and mine is rather trivial. To this I can only say that, in my opinion, in the event of a dispute between a horse-drawn carriage and a car, it will certainly be the carriage which considers the difference trivial.

At least the readers of the *Berliner Tageblatt* will have been able to establish that there are certain currents which are against us. Since this is all to do with basically progressive newspapers, one may believe them when they claim that no one finds these currents against us more unpleasant than they do themselves. They find it unpleasant that, in our particular case, they are unable to give free rein to their natural inclination to encourage the young selflessly, for certain reasons which are exclusively our fault. For a while we might have assumed that these newspapers simply did not like our work. But the thorny path of experience soon taught us that instead we ourselves were the ones that they did not like, and that least of all they liked our dislike of them. Our plays were performed in an old-fashioned style suited to quite other things, so you might learn as little about us from the productions as you might learn about the characteristics of a motor car by harnessing it to carriage horses. As for how they did it, I have no idea. But at least they learned that we did not like them. In the hullabaloo which arose against and around us, it always looked chiefly as if *they* had something against *us*, and we were simply unable to explain properly that the main reason for the hullabaloo was that *we* had something against *them*. Indeed, the applause which we received itself prevented us from making the matter clear. We place the greatest emphasis on *not* belonging to particular groups of people (though they be strong in numbers).

Without adopting any other standpoint than that of pure utility, I would like to suggest how the history of the previous generation and of this one ought to be understood . . . [*the text breaks off here*]

['*Unterschied der Generationen*'*, BFA 21/160–1.]

Who Means Whom?

[. . .]

Permit me to inform you that the struggle between your and my generation (of which we have witnessed so far 20 or 30 miniature skirmishes amongst the advance guard) will not be a struggle for opinions but a struggle for the means of production.

For example: in polemics we will fight for the position you hold, not in German cultural history, but in a newspaper with a circulation of 200,000.

Another example: in the theatre it is not Ibsen's opinions and Hebbel's plaster casts we must battle against, but rather those people who want to refuse us access to the theatre spaces and the actors.

Your opinions are harmless, your aesthetic forms have no force, your political stance (towards the *Bürgertum*: deferentially ironic) is insignificant (and redundant even with regard to the *Bürgertum*).

The only thing that is dangerous about you and your dear departed intellectual giants is that they are messing up the all-important means of production for us.

After sitting musing for two whole decades, isn't it despicable just to write a poem, rather than supplying the south seas with automobiles?

[. . .]

['*Wer meint wen?*', BFA 21/166–7.]

This is an extract from a longer, unfinished sketch.

In 1926 the literary monthly *Uhu* (*The Owl*) published an article by Klaus Mann ('The New Parents') and an interview with his father, Thomas Mann

42

('The New Children'). Brecht used the occasion to take a pot-shot at the father, who for him represented all that he deplored in pompous, post-Naturalist, bourgeois literature (see also above, no. 7), and to define what were for him the important differences between the literary generations and their political stances. The argument started with a deeply sarcastic essay entitled 'When the Father with the Son with the *Uhu* . . .' (BFA 21/158–60) in *Das Neue Tage-Buch*, Berlin, 14 August 1926. Unwisely, Mann responded. Brecht (who had already written a not entirely sympathetic review of a public reading by Thomas Mann back in 1920) exploited the dispute to define his own aesthetic and political position, both in public and in a number of unpublished notes. Most of his contributions are so laden with oblique references to more or less obscure literary figures and events that it is hard today to unravel them. The two texts above are just a sample.

Later still, in anti-Nazi exile, the disagreement between Brecht and Mann became even more vitriolic.

12

Challenging Bourgeois Culture

The Opinion of Some Old People

The last new ideas thought by anybody were thought by people who couldn't convey themselves any faster than 60 kilometres per hour, and whose houses required huge quantities of stone and timber – 20 years ago. Maybe the opinion of some old people – that we have no opinions – is really nothing more than the last opinion which these old people had, namely, that young people simply have no opinions. At best, they reckon they've discovered that we create disorder. Chaos. But we have created no more disorder than science itself has, which they always thought was busy creating order. *We know* that, from the moment when science relinquished idealism and grew strong, it set to work to create chaos. It invented microscopes in order to *make* chaos out of an orderly, touchingly harmonious drop of water. I am perfectly aware that people would prefer not to read the word chaos quite so often. Some of our friends – naturally they were the influential ones – had their work cut out proving to the public that we were just beginning to emerge from chaotic conditions. Actually, this was a well-intentioned concession to the forces of reaction, and there was no real reason for calm. On the contrary, *we can only just glimpse the faint beginnings of that large-scale disorder which awaits us.* All those today who seem to have achieved some form of harmony have nothing in common with us, and only harm us by trying to be associated with us; since it is exclusively in order to dissolve order that we ourselves have resorted to simpler, more comprehensible forms. That whole rabble, of the likes of Werfel, Unruh, Zuckmayer, corrupt to the point of commercial viability, has nothing to do with us. We do not see their democratic shallowness, feeble-mindedness and harmlessness as the consequences of lack of talent (unlike some of our friends), but rather as the products of an innate corruptibility, inertia and lack of will-power. They owe their success to the incomprehensible optimism of a class which, in its unstoppable decline, can no longer afford to think about its own flaws.

['*Ansicht einiger alter Leute*'*, BFA 21/168.]

Franz Werfel, Fritz von Unruh and Carl Zuckmayer were popular and successful writers of the time, Werfel and Unruh both of the older, 'Expressionist' generation. Zuckmayer perhaps attracts Brecht's scorn at this time because of the success of his folk comedy, *Der fröhliche Weinberg* (*The Merry Vineyard*), which comes close to the stereotype Brecht criticised in his much later 'Notes on the Folk Play' (1940, see *Brecht on Theatre*, pp. 153–7). This text offers a rare early insight into the young Brecht's attitude to science, both in itself and as a metaphor for social conditions and developments. It would later become much more central to his thought.

On Plagiarism

Certain discrepancies in my work – about which, incidentally, an (unfavourable) overall verdict had long since been reached – were first discovered by people who had already published a general outline of their plans to liberate mankind, at a time when the precise execution and ultimate goal of all such efforts, namely to liberate mankind from me, were becoming increasingly clear. Broader circles were made privy to this discovery at the celebration of my *Edward* premiere by the journalist A. Kerr, in one of those poetical reviews brilliantly divided into Roman numbered sections, which rubbished me all in all roughly nine times in succession. Even though Herr Kerr's diatribes against me belong to my daily reading, along with crime fiction, I did not answer straight away, not only in order to give the newspaper hack his due, namely the last word of the day (at 12 midnight), but mainly because I did not want to abandon my old plan to honour literary plagiarism and to reinvest it with its old accustomed rights, at an inopportune moment, namely when I myself had achieved nothing worthy of note in the field of plagiarism. I wanted to make a big splash. I believe that this small selfish desire is not a crime.

For the plagiarism attributed to me then was nothing of the sort, and even the honest efforts of Herr Kerr could not make it one. Even in this minor field of endeavour, the time when I might be named alongside Shakespeare, Goethe and all the rest had not yet come. At most, I could boast of having created a character for the stage who was able to read out or recite some of Rimbaud's lines. Several other quotations, from Verlaine, Kipling and others – which escaped Kerr's attention, although they might have been apparent to some-one of a literary education – I considered too unrepresentative and too anonymous. Arguments might even have arisen about whether I hadn't written them myself after all. My real, important under-takings in this neglected field still lay locked up in my desk.

['*Über Plagiate*', BFA 21/174–5.]

Written 1926. Brecht is referring to a series of accusations of plagiarism levied against him, beginning with a review of his adaptation of Marlowe's *Life of Edward II* in the *Berliner Tageblatt* in December 1924. For another swipe in the feud with Alfred Kerr, see above, no. 9.

Ban on Truth

1 Up until now everything that the ruling class did not like has been banned, and banned illegally. But now it is *law* that free thought, genuinely natural, untrammelled art, honest, fearless conviction is to be banned.

2 They claim this law should serve to protect the young. We are all in favour of protecting the young. But they can give our young folk neither bread nor truth, they can protect them neither from hunger nor error. How do they protect the young from the trash which drives them into war and oppression? Do they really expect to maintain that the youth of today are in misery because of 'Buffalo Bill' magazines?

3 This law is directed against us. They say Buffalo Bill, and they mean the truth.

['*Verbot der Wahrheit*'*, BFA 21/175.]

Typescript. In December 1926 a law was passed 'For the Protection of the Young from Written Filth and Trash', by which offices for the registration and banning of such literature were instituted. It was a more or less free hand for censorship. Brecht joined many other writers and intellectuals in protesting against the legislation, even in the early stages of its preparation. 'Buffalo Bill' was a popular series of penny dreadfuls.

The Socialisation of Art

Of course, a proletarian-led state will just have to pulp an entire – and incidentally very large – pile of literature which owes its existence to bourgeois prejudices (the marching tread of the workers' battalions will suffice to trample the literature being written at the moment). This branch of literature only consists of mediocre stuff anyway. It was only ever the babble of empty people, devoid of content, that is, with no internal dichotomy. They will be followed immediately by similar (or the selfsame) people, who are on the other side and may now be useful there. It is like the usefulness of soap, which can be very important indeed in times of need. The dichotomy between the individual and the dividual is what makes the artist in every age. Bolshevism's great justification is that in this field it has established primitive and eternal contradictions which, from Greek tragedy onwards, have created all great works of art. Art is nothing particularly individual. A pure individualist would remain silent.

['*Sozialisierung der Kunst*', BFA 21/179–80.]

Another typescript from 1926.

13

On Poetry

Short Report on 400 (Four Hundred) Young Poets

> Mother Goddam's House in Mandalay
> Dirty little hut beside the bay
> Goddam, the finest knocking-shop you ever saw
> With 15 randy men in a queue outside the door
> Watches in their hands, hip hip hooray!
> Are they short of tarts in Mandalay?
> ('The Song of Mandalay')

I must admit, when I agreed to pick over a pile of recent lyric poetry I was being a bit careless. Setting aside my own products (which isn't difficult) I have never been particularly interested in poetry. My own needs, like those of other people, were easily met by the readers we had in primary school, that is to say by works like 'Who would be a soldier' through to 'The wealthy prince' or even 'The steeds of Gravelotte'. So the only justification I can claim for myself is that it seems to me that every human being who is prepared to listen to his reason, without being, in every particular, completely consistent, must be capable of judging what other human beings have made or done. And lyric poetry in particular must surely be something that one can investigate for its use value.

Now I know that a whole load of famous poetry pays no regard at all to whether it can be used. The last epoch of Im- and Expressionism (that 'pressionist art' whose days are numbered) produced poems, the content of which consisted of pretty pictures and aromatic words. There are a few lucky hits too, things which you can neither sing nor give someone as a tonic, but which nonetheless are something. But apart from a few such exceptions, 'pure' lyric products like these are overvalued. They are simply too far distant from the original gesture of the communication of a thought or a feeling which might be of advantage even to a stranger. All great poems have the value of documents. They contain the voice of the author, who was an important man. I should confess at this point that I don't think much of the poetry of Rilke (an otherwise really good man), Stefan George or Werfel, since this is perhaps the best and most radical way of informing my readers about my inability to somehow pass judgement on that sort of product.

Over half a thousand poems were sent in, and I should say right away that I thought none of them was really good. Of course, I always knew that any halfway normal German can write a poem – which itself doesn't tell us a thing about the half of them. But, and this is far worse, in the course of this exercise I got to know a sort of youth whose acquaintance I could have done so much better without. It is in my interest, so to speak, to make a secret of this. What is the point, in terms of propaganda for our cause, of publishing photographs of big cities, if all around us we see a rising generation of bourgeois opinion which can be entirely refuted simply by such photographs? What is the point of striking dead several generations of noxious old people, or better, wishing them dead, if the younger generation is simply innocuous? Given the indescribable personal worthlessness of these people, the same age as me, you could not hope for any effect even if you were to confront one of their number with some random reality: even a salutary derisive laugh couldn't cure them of their sentimentality, insincerity and lack of worldly wisdom (or that of their above-mentioned literary models). Here they are again, those quiet, fine, dreamy souls, the sensitive part of a worn-out bourgeoisie, and I want nothing to do with them!

Perhaps no one will understand why I needed this bitter introduction, in order now to make my suggestion to print a song which I found in a cycle-sport magazine. I don't know if it will please every reader, but in any case, in order to demonstrate my conscientiousness, I have procured the manuscript and a photograph of the author. This song, 'He! He! The Iron Man!' by Hannes Küpper, has an interesting subject, namely the six-day race champion Reggie Mac Namara. It is pretty simple, might even be sung, and it is the best an author could hope to produce. It has, for me at least, a certain documentary value. I recommend to Küpper that he produce more songs like this, and I recommend to the general public that, by their disapproval, they encourage him.

['*Kurzer Bericht über 400 (vierhundert) junge Lyriker*', BFA 21/191–3.]

First published in *Die literarische Welt*, Berlin, 4 February 1927. Brecht had been asked to judge a poetry prize for the young generation for this literary journal. The editors prefaced Brecht's contribution with a disclaimer of all responsibility and the explanation that their judge had found none of the entries worthy of the prize, but had chosen instead to award it to an unknown poet who had not entered. 'He, He! The Iron Man!' (its title and refrain are in English) celebrated the legendary achievements of an Australian cyclist.

Brecht's motto is one of his own songs from *Happy End*. His opening paragraph makes reference to some now relatively obscure nineteenth-century poems and children's songs. His judgement, unsurprisingly, provoked protests, and even the compilation of a new anthology of recent poetry, for which Klaus Mann wrote an afterword attacking Brecht. Brecht, of course, defended himself. In one unpublished contribution ('Neither Useful Nor Beautiful') he wrote, 'I don't know if people will believe me, but I know just as well as most that in art – especially if you employ certain terms – there are values which, so to speak, have no use', and, passing judgement again on Rilke, George (especially) and Werfel: 'In brief, all these people, about whom we should speak calmly and without pious modesty, have no beauty value, and should be made to work.' Their poetry, he went on, could only be understood as a manifestation of the class struggle. 'The reflection of a flock of sheep in the pure gaze of a man of great natural feeling might have immense value, equally the song of a singer immersed in the enjoyment of his own voice. But these people have neither pure gazes nor beautiful voices. And no natural feelings whatsoever. They are the owners of the herds, or they are people who have relinquished their herds as a consequence of their souls' hyperactivity.' (BFA 21/193–4.)

Lyric Poetry as Expression

If we define the lyric as expression we have to be aware that such a description is one-sided. It may be individuals who are expressing themselves, or classes, whole epochs may express themselves, and passions, we soon end up with 'humankind' expressing itself. When bankers express themselves to each other, or politicians, then we know they are doing deals; even when a sick man expresses his pain he also gives the doctor or the onlookers pointers, so there are actions too; but poets, it is said, are concerned only with pure expression, so their actions consist only of expression, and their intention can only be to express themselves. If there are documents showing that such and such a poet struggled like other people, albeit in his own particular way, then they say, well, in this poetry it is the struggle that expresses itself. People also say, such and such a poet experienced terrible things, but his sufferings found beautiful expression – in this respect we'd better thank his sufferings, they achieved something, they expressed him well. When he formulated his sufferings he made use of them, maybe alleviated them a bit. The sufferings have passed, the poems remain, we might exclaim knowingly and rub our hands. But how about if the sufferings have not passed? What if they also remain, if not for the man who sang of them, but for those who cannot sing? Then again, there are other poems which depict a rainy day, or a field of tulips; reading or hearing such poems we lapse into the mood which rainy days or tulip fields evoke, that is to say, even if we observe rainy days and tulip fields with no particular mood, through means of the poems we discover those moods. And so we become better human beings, more capable of enjoyment, more discriminating in our feelings, and that will manifest itself . . . somehow, some day, somewhere.

['*Die Lyrik als Ausdruck*', BFA 21/201–2.]

Typescript *c.* 1927.

14

On Politics and Art

About 1920 the whole of German bourgeois literature – and that was the only sort there was – had sunk so far below any conceivable aesthetic standard that it was, in the name of aesthetics, close to digging its own grave: it had, throughout its development, always maintained a purely aesthetic perspective and, irretrievably sinking, it had dragged aesthetics down with it. Aesthetics had become just as much 'aesthetics', as literature had become 'literature'.

Outwardly this was expressed by the fact that aesthetics (art criticism) became 'poetic' and arrogantly demanded ... aesthetic approval. It claimed, not so unreasonably given the state of the current 'literature', to be able to express a human personality, significant to the generality, with just as much validity (or in the case of A. Kerr with *at least* as much validity) as literature itself. It fixed its gaze obstinately on its own navel at just the same time as the opinion gained general acceptance: that every corner of filth, seen through a 'temperament', had artistic value.

The unhappy man who, trusting to his instinct, might have cast around for a weapon of some sort with which to despatch this unholy heap of irresponsible vanity, called literature, to its grave, could 'only' accuse it of a lack of wider perspectives.

['*Über Politik und Kunst*', BFA 21/212–13.]

Typescript *c.* 1927. This piece bears the subtitle 'Introduction to Borchardt's *Bloody Deed of Germersheim*', but no work by Hans Borchardt with this title has been discovered. For Kerr, see above, nos 9 and 12. The use of the word 'temperament' is an allusion to a saying by the French Naturalist Emile Zola, that a work of art is '*un coin de la nature, vu à travers un tempérament*' (*Le roman expérimental*, 1880). See also below, no. 58.

On 2 June 1927 Brecht published an open letter in the *Berliner Börsen-Courier* addressed to 'Herr X.', in fact the sociologist Fritz Sternberg. The piece was entitled 'Shouldn't We Abolish Aesthetics?' (see *Brecht on Theatre*, pp. 21–2, and below, no. 18). In it Brecht tried to see drama from a sociological rather than an aesthetic point of view, and outlined a new vision of 'epic theatre'. Sociology, he suggested, 'is the only branch of knowledge that enjoys sufficient freedom of thought; all the rest are too closely involved in perpetuating our period's general level of civilisation'. He dismissed the idea of 'eternal' human urges, values and means of expression. It was not a question, he concluded, of 'improving' drama according to the old criteria, but of doing away with those criteria themselves. The essay, and the challenge of its title, are of a piece with the reflections on lyric poetry above, and with the first group of essays in Part Two. This brief unpublished sketch, 'On Politics and Art', also of 1927, perhaps provides a suitable bridge between the earlier 1920s fragments of an anti-bourgeois aesthetics and the more developed essays in culture and society of the later 1920s and early 1930s.

15

Republication Forbidden!

At that time I was a soldiers' representative in a field hospital in Augsburg, and in fact I had only taken up this office after several friends had persuaded me insistently to do so, claiming that it would be in their interest. (As it turned out, however, I was unable to change the state in a way which would have helped them.) We all suffered from a lack of political convictions, and I myself suffered all the more because of my old inability to be enthusiastic about anything. I was saddled with a great deal of work. The Army High Command's plan to send me to the front had already failed six months earlier. Favoured by fortune, I had known how to prevent the military from training me; after six months I had not even learned how to salute and, even though military standards had already been relaxed by then, I was still too slack. Very soon I secured my discharge. In short, I was hardly any different from the overwhelming majority of other soldiers; of course, they had all had enough of the war, but they were not in a position to think in political terms. I do not particularly like to dwell on it.

['*Nachdruck verboten!*', BFA 21/250–1.]

This brief autobiographical self-justification for his inactivity in the revolutionary movement in the dying months and after the war was first published in the *Filmkurier*, Berlin, 9 November 1928, in response to a questionnaire on the occasion of the tenth anniversary of the November Revolution. After the revolution in Bavaria the short-lived soviet republic (*Räterepublik*) had ordered the election of soldiers' delegates from the hospitals and barracks. Having hitherto eluded the call-up, Brecht spent three months, from October 1918, as an orderly in the military hospital in his home town of Augsburg and briefly served on the hospital 'soviet'. From his relatively newly won Marxist standpoint, he understands his earlier career, retrospectively, in social and generational terms.

Part Two

Culture and Society 1927–1933

(Berlin)

Introduction to Part Two

The years from 1927 to 1933 constitute one of the most productive and problematic phases in Brecht's career. He wrote several major plays, a series of fragments and *Lehrstücke*, some four hundred theoretical essays, and also made significant progress in developing the practice of epic theatre. His first major collection of poetry, *Bertolt Brechts Hauspostille* (or *Domestic Breviary*), was published in 1927, while the period in general is dominated by his work on the *Threepenny* project: the *Threepenny Opera* was first performed in 1928, his major theoretical monograph the *Threepenny Lawsuit* appeared in 1932,[1] and the *Threepenny Novel* was published in 1934. Brecht's work at this time tends to be interpreted and evaluated in terms of more general reflections on his intellectual development. This period has often been seen as embodying a fundamental shift in Brecht's writing, as he first abandons the anarchistic nihilism of his early plays in favour of behaviourist materialism in the mid-1920s, and then goes on to adopt a fully-fledged Marxist position as the Weimar Republic reaches its end. As we shall see, however, there are fundamental disagreements about the nature of Brecht's Marxism, not only in relation to the defining characteristics of epic theatre, but also in general theoretical terms.

These controversies have been further complicated by disputes over the precise dating of Brecht's shift to Marxism. While his collaborator Elisabeth Hauptmann argues that his interest in Marxism developed in 1926, it has also been suggested that Brecht did not adopt Marxism until 1929, or even 1932. The first clear indications of Brecht's interest in Marxist theory may be found in his September 1926 notes 'On Art and Socialism' (no. 9), and in a letter to Helene Weigel in 1927, where he asks her to send him Marxist writings dealing with the history of revolutions. The subsequent development of Brecht's Marxism in the Weimar Republic was strongly influenced by his encounters with the sociologist Fritz Sternberg, and the philosophers Otto Neurath and Karl Korsch. However, whereas Neurath's Marxism is relatively orthodox and is grounded in a behaviourist approach to social theory, Korsch was one of the leading critics of orthodox Marxism. Crucially, Korsch rejected the positivist notion that science should be value-free and transcend the interests of scientific investigators; took ideas and ideology to be socially real; advocated the need for intellectual struggle; and stressed the centrality of dialectic and revolutionary praxis in Marxist theory. The inconsistencies between the theoretical views of Korsch and Neurath are reflected in tensions and contradictions in Brecht's own position, which have posed major problems for critics seeking to establish an authentic, coherent and consistent Brechtian perspective on aesthetic and sociological issues at this time.

Werner Hecht, for example, argues that epic theatre is only fully realised when Brecht abandons the social and economic determinism he espoused from the mid-1920s onwards, and moves from an anti-bourgeois conception of theatre based on the modernist principle of the 'shock of recognition', to a revolutionary mode of theatre aiming at active intervention in societal processes. Gerd Irrlitz, on the other hand, stresses the importance for Brecht of Marx's notion that the human essence is intrinsically social, and he concludes that Brecht rejected the view that the individual was a coherent entity with natural qualities, seeing the individual instead as a product of social functions and relationships within which it is located.[2]

The essays in Part Two cover two main areas: the theory and practice of epic theatre from 1927 to 1930, linked to reflections on the cultural heritage and a sociological critique of post-Romantic aesthetic theory; and the development of Brecht's views on philosophy, politics and society between 1929 and 1933, which articulate the epistemological presuppositions guiding his general approach to the critical analysis of contemporary culture.

Brecht's writings on theatre from the mid-1920s display four main areas of concern, reflecting his theatrical work with Erwin Piscator and his intellectual collaboration with Fritz Sternberg. First, Brecht constantly attacks the dominant institution of the theatre, which he wishes to see replaced by a more experimental and politicised form of theatre. In the mid-1920s this type of theatre was best exemplified by the radical and influential productions of Piscator, which attempted to bring together an explicitly Marxist critique of politics and society with a revolution in theatrical representation that incorporated modern technology and film. Second, he advocates a radical shift in the role and response of the audience. Although Piscator's productions had begun to move in this direction by discouraging the audience from identifying with the perspective of the characters on stage, Brecht wanted to encourage the audience to be much more critical and questioning, by adopting the cool, investigative attitude appropriate to the scientific age. Third, he advocates the need for a new kind of writing for the theatre, which will have epic and documentary characteristics. Brecht's argument is based on the assumption, also shared by Piscator, that the collectivising impact of industrial capitalism, together with the mechanised carnage of World War I, had rendered meaningless traditional notions of individualist psychology and human integrity which had been embodied in dramatic form since Shakespeare. Fourth, he tends increasingly to present Marxist accounts of cultural and social phenomena, citing Sternberg in order to insist that a strictly sociological approach to art in general and theatre in particular must abandon aesthetic and moral categories such as eternal value and the notion of an unchanging human nature. By the same token, Brecht rejects the predominant attitude of conservative and deferential reverence to the classical heritage, suggesting that the cultural heritage should be assessed and appropriated instead in terms of its material value: literally, in the case of the Vandals who burnt wood carvings for fuel, and politically and morally for those who might perform classical plays in order to develop their social skills.

In the early 1930s Brecht elaborates on these issues and moves in a more explicitly Marxist direction. He pays increasing attention to the economic structures of capitalist society when specifying the thematic areas appropriate to epic theatre, and presents a more pedagogically orientated conception of theatre, which emphasises the importance of learning how to synthesise action and contemplation, and politics and philosophy. At the same time, Brecht attributes a more judgemental role to the spectator, who must be encouraged to take sides in response to the issues presented in a play, but on the basis of rational consideration. This aim is to be achieved through a process of theatrical estrangement which anticipates his later theory of *Verfremdung*: the actors must attract the spectator's attention by making events striking, in accordance with Brecht's epistemological precept that knowledge is generated thanks to the observer's astonishment. Finally, in 'On New Criticism' (no. 24) he presents a classic Marxist critique of bourgeois literary history, rejecting attempts to define literature in terms of *belles lettres* and insisting on a sociological approach to cultural enquiry. He also argues, with a degree of contemporary resonance, that retrospective accounts of the literary canon based on 'great works' are unhistorical, because they pay insufficient attention to those works that were culturally dominant in their own time, readers' perceptions of them, and their interconnections with other modes of writing such as legal and scientific texts.

Brecht's approach to philosophy, politics and society between 1929 and 1933 rests on the assumption that all thought is rooted in interests, and in particular in socio-economic interests. This means not only that philosophy cannot be construed as an essentially mental or spiritual activity, but also that even intellectuals who support the cause of the proletariat must ultimately remain members of the class faction constituted by the bourgeois intelligentsia. Similarly, Brecht argues that ideologies are a product of specific social relationships, where particular classes adopt sets of ideas on a pragmatic basis according to the principle of utility (see no. 25). In the latter case, Brecht implies that the term ideology can be applied to any set of ideas which is intrinsically connected to opportunism and usefulness, but in 'Who Needs a World-View?' (no. 26) he addresses the specific role of bourgeois ideology. Brecht contends that bourgeois ideology mystifies the nature of social relationships in general, together with the particular ways in which social relationships structure the individual person. Bourgeois ideology must therefore be countered, Brecht maintains, by what he calls a realism of the human functions. The latter concept is clarified in Brecht's critique of literary Naturalism in 'Key Points in Korsch' (no. 32). Taking his cue from the final pages of the introduction to the *Grundrisse*, where Marx demonstrates that modern industrial technology has shattered the world-view underpinning traditional art forms, Brecht asserts that the audience can no longer experience the fate of Naturalist protagonists as tragic in a world where catastrophes can be explained without reference to religion or mythology. Indeed, Brecht takes the very notion of tragedy to be an ideology that must be resisted, because dilemmas which had once been perceived as inevitable and inescapable can, in fact, be resolved by adopting practical social and technical measures.

Brecht's opposition of the realism of human functions to the mystificatory processes of bourgeois ideology implicitly draws on Marx's theory of commodity fetishism. In 'On "the Thing in Itself"' (no. 25), Brecht notes that the emergence of the commodity form and commodified labour caused the observer to perceive relationships between human beings as if they were things or objects, even though such relationships are not visible to the naked eye. Brecht therefore rejects theories of knowledge which hold statements to be true simply because they accurately reflect visible realities, and he proposes instead that the theory of knowledge must involve critique of language. At the same time Brecht's concern with the nature of representation indicates another, non-Marxist, dimension to his repudiation of traditional theories of knowledge.

At several points in his philosophical essays of 1930–1 Brecht assents to the coherence theory of truth, according to which a statement is true not because it corresponds to reality but because it is consistent with all the other statements or propositions which make up a particular theory. In 'On the Process of Knowledge' (no. 25), he stresses the interconnectedness of all statements and their presuppositions, so that the Cartesian principle of doubt, for example, must be applied not to individual objects, but on a holistic basis. Truth, in other words, is a relational concept, which means that philosophical critique must engage with *systems* of ideas. In view of this emphasis on the relational structure of philosophical systems, it is perhaps not surprising that he should construe culture in analogous terms. In 'Theses on the Theory of Superstructure' (no. 31), another essay directly inspired by Korsch, Brecht invests culture with a degree of autonomy in relation to the determining factors of economics and politics, referring to culture (and super-structure) as a process which has its own developmental dynamics. Like Korsch, Brecht emphasises the importance of intellectual struggle, instead of dismissing ideas as passive reflections of socio-economic structures. In 'Who Needs a World-View?' Brecht rejects as defeatist attempts to deprive thought of any deeper influence, and he advocates instead the need for intellectual liberation and transformative thinking.

Taken together with his assertion of the relative autonomy of culture, Brecht's emphasis on power of thought might appear to be bringing him dangerously close to idealism, a suspicion confirmed by his definition of interventionist thinking in 'Who Needs a World-View?', which primarily involves intervention in the realm of thought. On the other hand, assertions made by Brecht elsewhere seem to be designed to dispel such suspicions. He emphasises the interconnectedness of knowledge, power and property in 'On "the Thing in Itself"', and a year or so later suggests in 'Use of Truth' (no. 33) that the notion of intellectual or ideological critique must be pragmatically based, defining the utility of new ideas in terms of their socially transformative power.

The missing link between the apparent idealism of Brecht's view of intellectual struggle and his revolutionary pragmatism is dialectic, or, to be more precise, the application of dialectic in the destruction of ideologies ('On Dialectic: 6', no. 29). Brecht explicitly associates dialectic with open-ended processes and with the power of contradiction to transform reality, and at first sight his con-ception of dialectic seems to be relatively straightforward. However, a fundamental inconsistency at the core of Brecht's understanding of dialectic gradually emerges. On the one hand, he implies that the contradictory processes uncovered by dialectical thinking are themselves objective features of reality ('On Dialectic: 6'). On the other hand, he construes dialectic as a mode of cognition, a way of perceiving and understanding reality, and argues that dialectical concepts do not reflect a dialectic which exists in nature. Moreover, he even suggests that the Marxist dialectic is not so much an objective social fact as a methodological tool which enables us to dissolve fixed ideas and criticise society ('Dialectic'). He moves closer to a more recognisable Marxist position when, in 'On Dialectic: 6', he repudiates explanations of human affairs which are based on metaphysical conceptions of necessity, and asserts instead that historical and social change involves contradictory trends and conflicts grounded in class interests, which are resolved through war and violence. This argument also underpins his critique of Einstein's account of war in the final essay in this section, where he implies that Einstein has adopted a Freudian position by attempting to explain war as an emanation of the dark depths of the human psyche. Brecht, on the other hand, construes war not as a product of the id but as an expression of material interests, class struggle and economic oppression.

---

[1] See *Brecht on Film and Radio*, pp. 147–99. The *Threepenny Lawsuit* was Brecht's most important contribution to the sociology of art and film at this point in his career.

[2] For a more detailed discussion of these issues, see Steve Giles, *Bertolt Brecht and Critical Theory. Marxism, Modernity, and the 'Threepenny Lawsuit'* (Bern, 1998).

16

The Piscator Experiment

The Piscator Experiment

Apart from Engel's crucially important production of *Coriolanus*, experiments in epic theatre were undertaken in dramatic writing only. (The first drama to construct this epic theatre was Brecht's dramatic biography *Baal*, the simplest was Emil Burri's *American Youth*, and the most accomplished so far – because it comes from an author with a quite different perspective – was Bronnen's *East Pole Train*.) Now theatre, too, is bringing grist to the mill: the Piscator experiment.

The essential features of this experiment are as follows:

Film is incorporated to pre-empt those parts of the dramatic action that contain no conflict, so as to take the strain off the spoken word and make it absolutely decisive. The spectator has the opportunity to see and judge for himself certain processes that constitute the preconditions for the decisions of the protagonists, without having to view these processes from the perspective of those who are motivated by them. As the characters no longer have to provide objective information for the spectator, they can express themselves freely: their expression becomes striking. Moreover, the contrast between flat photographed reality and the word placed vividly in front of the film, jumping back and forth thanks to special effects, can also be used to intensify linguistic expression beyond all control. The word, which is full of pathos and simultaneously ambiguous, achieves enhanced status through the calm, photographic display of a real background. Film makes drama's bed for it.

Because the milieu is photographed in its entire breadth, the speaking characters become disproportionately large. Although the milieu has to be compressed or enlarged to fit the unchanging size of the same surface, namely the screen, as, for example, when

Mount Everest constantly changes size, the characters always remain the same size. This is where Engel has collected points for epic theatre. He presented the story of Coriolanus in such a way that each scene was self-contained, and only its outcome was used for the whole. In contrast to dramatic theatre, where everything rushes towards a catastrophe and so almost everything functions as an introduction, here the totality was present, immobile, in each scene. The Piscator experiment will be completed once a series of crucial deficiencies have been removed (for example, thanks to the unexploited transition from word to image, which still takes place quite abruptly, the number of spectators in the theatre is simply increased by the number of actors still busy on stage who are standing in front of the projection screen; for example, the over-emotional operatic style which is still usual today is unmasked dreadfully, ostensibly through carelessness, by the beautiful *naïveté* of photographed machines, technical errors that imbue the Piscator experiment with some of that aroma without which a naive theatre is inconceivable).

Epic theatre still has to put to the test the deployment of film as a pure document of photographed reality, as conscience.

['*Der Piscatorsche Versuch*', BFA 21/196–7.]

Written 1927. Brecht was one of Piscator's collaborators at the Piscator-Bühne in 1927–8, and made numerous allusions to Piscator's work in his writings on theatre from the mid-1920s through to the 1940s (see *Brecht on Theatre*). Erich Engel's production of *Coriolanus* was premiered at the Deutsches Theater, Berlin, on 27 February 1925. Brecht also refers to the 1926 production of his radically revised version of his first major play *Baal, Life Story of the Man Baal*, which is a classic instance of the cooler, more matter-of-fact mode of presentation that characterises his experiments in epic theatre in the mid-1920s.

Piscator Theatre

Not the attempt of politics to seize the theatre, but of the theatre to seize politics . . .

Nowadays, people tend to see Piscator's attempt to renew theatre as revolutionary. But it is revolutionary neither in terms of production nor in terms of politics, but only in terms of theatre. This becomes clear if one considers the history of the theatre in the last hundred years. In this period bourgeois theatre has not fundamentally changed. To take one example: thirty years ago, Naturalism was taken to be a revolutionary transformation. And yet, it was simply a superficial, and at root inconsequential, therefore non-committal, process of drama being influenced by the international bourgeois novel. I saw nothing of this (except its consequences) and today I cannot distinguish this style of stage production from that of the Burgtheater in bygone days. And that's without mentioning Expressionism at all, which was a merely inflationary phenomenon and changed absolutely nothing.

['*Piscatortheater*', BFA 21/197–8.]

Written *c.* 1927. The Burgtheater was the major theatre in Vienna, and a bastion of tradition in terms of repertoire and theatrical style.

17

Primacy of the Apparatus

In a special supplement of the *Frankfurter Zeitung*, the theatre critic Diebold has written about 'Piscator drama'. In this essay, which displays a striking interest in new theatre rare these days, he alludes to a new opportunity for dramatic writing. He asserts, namely, that the Piscator Stage makes a new type of drama possible. This viewpoint is further proof of the extraordinary confusion that bourgeois aesthetics is in. We can assume that Piscator's experiments in directing aim to electrify the theatre and bring it up to the technological standards that most institutions have reached today. Film makes it possible to make the backdrop more realistic and let the scenery play a role. The conveyor belt makes the stage floor mobile, etc. This puts the theatre in the best position to perform modern plays or put on modern performances of older plays. But does this stage, *and this stage alone*, make it possible for new plays to emerge? Do new plays have to be written for this stage?

We can assume that new plays must be written. It was a revolutionary decision of the new dramatic writing to write new plays, come what may. These plays were not stageable. It was not possible to make it clear to anybody that they were not stageable. Why this could not be made clear to anybody was beyond the capacity of aesthetics. Who amongst our critics, schooled only in aesthetics, would be capable of understanding that the self-evident practice of bourgeois criticism, whereby in every single case in aesthetic questions it agrees with theatres rather than producers, has a *political* cause? Here, as everywhere else, the employer gains the upper hand over the worker, the owner of the means of production is assumed to be productive, *eo ipso*. For years, dramatic production has insisted that it is being wrongly staged, that the dominant theatrical style is incapable of coming to terms with it, that, however, it requires and makes possible a completely new theatrical style. Silence in the forest. As ever, because, of course, nothing of note has happened, because no means of production are behind it, because there is no influence to be gained here and no power to fear, the critic judges the new dramas in terms of their suitability for the contemporary theatre, he shakes his magnificent head at everything that is incompatible with an obsolete, worn-out, unimaginative style of staging, and he assumes at best that dramatic writing lacks any really intellectual commitment and has no sense of its own duties. Who is supposed to make him realise that his duty, probably unbeknown to him, is to supply the existing institutions and means of production with material? If a more up-to-date institution emerges, which has just started to replace paraffin lamps with electric light, then dramatic writing does have a duty, namely to supply this institution. Then electricity would at last appear in plays! Nevertheless, not much has been achieved with this modest technological advance; Piscator has his hands full if he is to get any further, and the new dramatic writing that has already appeared is still not stageable.

Piscator has made it possible for us to grasp new materials. It is his duty to make the new materials old. Until they are old, they cannot be grasped by drama.

['*Primat des Apparates*', BFA 21/225–7.]

Written 1928. Ernst Diebold was a leading theatre critic in Germany in the 1920s and is best known for his books on *Georg Kaiser* (1925) and contemporary German Expressionist theatre, *Anarchie im Drama* (1925).

18

New Dramatic Writing

HARDT   . . . why sociology?

BRECHT   My dear Mr Hardt. If you sit in a theatre today, and it started at eight o'clock, then at about eight thirty – whether they are playing *Oedipus* or *Othello* or *Carter Henschel* or *Drums in the Night* – you will feel a certain spiritual depression, and by nine o'clock at the latest you will feel that you have got to leave immediately. You will feel this way not because what's being done is not very nice, but despite its being very nice. It's just not right. Despite that, you hardly ever leave – you don't, I don't, nobody does, and it's very difficult even in theory to somehow object to this type of theatre, because the whole of aesthetics, in other words our theory of beauty, is no help to us in this. With the help of aesthetics alone we cannot do anything about the existing theatre. In order to liquidate this theatre, i.e., dismantle it, get rid of it, sell it off at a loss, we must call on science, just as we have called on science to liquidate a whole lot of other superstitions. In our case, this means sociology, i.e., the theory of human beings' relationships to one another, in other words the theory of the unsightly. Sociology is to help you and us, Mr Ihering, to bury as completely as possible as much as possible of today's dramatic writing and theatre.

IHERING   What you mean by that, if I understand you correctly, is that so-called modern drama is basically no different from the old drama, and therefore also needs to be got rid of. For what reason? Do you want to dismantle all dramas that deal with individual fates, that are thus private tragedies? Incidentally, that would mean that you no longer think Shakespeare is valid, on whom all our contemporary drama is based. Because Shakespeare also wrote dramas of the individual: individual tragedies such as *King Lear*, plays that virtually drive human beings into loneliness, showing them in the end in tragic isolation. So you would deny that drama has any *eternal value*?

BRECHT   Eternal value! To bury eternal value as well we similarly need only to call on science for assistance. Sternberg, what's all this about eternal value?

STERNBERG   There are no eternal values in art. Drama, which was born in a particular cultural milieu, hardly embodies eternal values, just as the epoch in which it was created does not endure for all eternity. The content of drama is made up of conflicts between human beings, conflicts of human beings in their relationships to institutions. Conflicts between human beings are, e.g., all those that are produced by the love of a man for a woman. But these conflicts are not eternal, certainly not, just as certainly as relationships of men and women are fundamentally different in every cultural epoch. Other conflicts are those of human beings in their relation-ships to institutions, e.g., to the state. But these conflicts are not eternal either; they depend on the radius of each human being as an individual, and the radius of state power. And so the relationships of the state to human beings, and thus of human beings to one another, are also absolutely different in different cultural epochs; they are different in antiquity, whose economy was based on slavery – that's why in this respect even classical drama is not eternal for us – they are different in a modern, in a capitalist economy, different again, of course, in an epoch to come which will recognise no classes and no class differences. So we should not speak of eternal values, especially nowadays, as we stand at the turning point of two epochs.

IHERING   Could you apply these general statements of yours to Shakespeare in particular?

STERNBERG   European drama hasn't gone a step further than

Shakespeare. He stood at the turning point of two epochs. What we encapsulate with the term Middle Ages had its effect on him, but Medieval Man had been released from his bonds by the dynamics of the epoch; the individual had been born as an individual, as an indivisible entity that wasn't interchangeable. And that's how Shakespearean drama became the drama of Medieval Man, as well as the drama of human beings who began to discover themselves more and more as individuals and, as such, were involved in dramatic situations with their own kind as well as with superior powers. In this context Shakespeare's choice of materials for his great Roman dramas is significant. He didn't present us with a single drama about Rome's great Republican era, when an individual name didn't yet mean anything and the collective will essentially decided things, *senator populusque romanus*, but chose the period before and after that. The great mythological age, when the individual still opposed the masses in *Coriolanus*, and the age of the empire in dissolution, whose expansion contained the seeds of its downfall (and thereby produced great individuals), in *Julius Caesar* and in *Antony and Cleopatra*.

BRECHT   Yes, the great individuals! The great individuals were the material, and this material produced the form of these dramas. It was the so-called dramatic form, where drama means: furiously turbulent, passionate, contradictory, dynamic. What was this dramatic form like? What was its purpose? In Shakespeare, you can see this exactly. In the course of four acts, Shakespeare drives the great individual, Lear, Othello, Macbeth, out of all his human bonds with family and state on to the heath, into complete isolation, where he has to show his greatness in his downfall. This produces the form, let us say, of an oat field in the wind. The first movement of the tragedy is only there for the second, and all the movements are only there for the final movement. Passion is what keeps this machinery going, and the purpose of the machinery is the great individual experience. Later times will call this drama a drama for cannibals, and will say that Man was devoured at the beginning with contentment as Richard III, and at the end with pity as Carter Henschel, but either way Man was devoured.

STERNBERG   But Shakespeare still embodied the heroic age of drama, and hence the era of heroic experience. The heroic passed away, and the quest for experience remained. The more we approach the nineteenth century, particularly its second half, the more monotonous bourgeois drama became; the entire circle of experience of the bourgeois – in drama! – essentially revolved around the relationship between men/women and women/men. All the variations that can be produced by this problem have been turned into bourgeois drama at one time or another: whether the woman goes to her husband, to a third party, to both or to nobody, whether the men should shoot themselves, and who should kill whom: most of nineteenth-century drama can be reduced to this parody. But what is to happen now, as once again in reality the individual as individual, as individuality, as an indivisible entity that's not interchangeable, is disappearing from view more and more, because with the onset of the capitalist era the collective is the determining force again?

IHERING   In that case one must give up the entire technique of drama. Those theatre people and critics are wrong who maintain that all you need to do is learn your trade with Parisian dramatists, polish up the dialogue, improve scenic structure, refine your technique, and then we'd have drama in Germany again. As if this type of drama hadn't been taken to its conclusion by Ibsen and the French long ago, as if it could somehow still be developed. No, it's not a question of refining an existing serviceable technique, of improvement, of following the Parisian school. That's the big mistake, and the small mistake made, say, by Hasenclever and his comedy *Marriages Are Made in Heaven*. No, it's a question of needing a fundamentally different type of drama.

BRECHT   Yes, epic drama, in other words.

IHERING   Yes, Brecht, you have developed a very specific theory in this area, your theory of epic drama.

BRECHT   Yes, this theory of epic drama is indeed our initiative. We've also tried to put together a few epic dramas. My *Man Equals Man*, Bronnen's *East Pole Train*, Fleisser's Ingolstadt dramas, were all composed using epic techniques. But attempts to put together epic drama have been around for a long time. When did they begin? They began at the time when science really took off in a big way, in the last century. The beginnings of Naturalism were the beginnings of epic drama in Europe. Other cultural areas, China and India, had this more advanced form a good two thousand years ago. Naturalist drama grew out of the bourgeois novel of Zola and Dostoevsky, which, for its part, indicated the incursion of science into the precincts of art. The Naturalists, Ibsen, Hauptmann, tried to put on stage the new material of the new novels, and could find no other form for this than that of these novels: an epic form. When they were at once accused of being undramatic, they abandoned the form at once, together with the material, and their advance faltered; it appeared to be an advance into new areas of material, but in reality it was the advance into epic form.

IHERING   So you are saying that epic drama has a tradition that people generally know nothing about. You maintain that the entire evolution of literature for fifty years has been leading up to epic drama. In your opinion, who's the last representative of this evolutionary trend?

BRECHT   Georg Kaiser.

IHERING   But I don't quite understand that. Georg Kaiser of all people seems to me to signify the final stage of individualist drama, in other words, of a type of drama that is diametrically opposed to epic drama. Kaiser, in particular, is the most short-term of dramatists. He has exhausted his themes through style, and overtaken reality through style. What is the utility of this style? Kaiser's style is a personal signature, is a private style.

BRECHT   Yes, Kaiser is also an individualist. But there is something in his technique that doesn't fit his individualism, and so does suit us. The fact that one can observe technical progress where one otherwise observes no progress at all doesn't happen only in drama. From a technical point of view, a Fordist factory is a Bolshevik organisation; it doesn't fit the bourgeois individual and suits Bolshevik society better. Similarly, Kaiser develops his technique by abandoning the great Shakespearean expedient of suggestibility, which comes about as in epilepsy, where the epileptic carries along with him everyone disposed to epilepsy. Kaiser does appeal to rationality, but with individualistic contents and, moreover, in an exaggeratedly dramatic form, as in *From Morn to Midnight*.

IHERING   Yes, to rationality. But how do you want to complete the long journey to epic drama starting from here?

STERNBERG   The distance from Kaiser to Brecht is short. It's not a continuation, but a dialectical shift. The rationality that in Kaiser was still used to give dramatic form to the spheres of experience of opposing individual fates, this rationality is used in Brecht intentionally to dethrone the individual.

BRECHT   Of course, the pure epic drama, with its collectivist contents, is better at provoking an attitude of discussion.

IHERING   Why? At the moment an active, and hence a dramatic, drama is being performed in Berlin, the *Revolt in the Approved School* by P. M. Lampel. But this dramatic drama has a similar effect, the audience discuss it, not its aesthetic values but its content.

BRECHT   Oh! In that play, public conditions are put up for discussion, namely the intolerable medieval conditions in various approved schools. Such conditions, no matter what form they are reported in, must of course provoke outrage. But Kaiser went a lot further: he made it possible to develop in theatres that quite new attitude of the audience, that cool, investigative, interested attitude, namely the attitude of the audience of the scientific age. In the case of Lampel, we are not, of course, talking about some major transportable dramatic principle.

IHERING   Now you are suddenly claiming that epic drama is an eternal principle, yet we'd agreed after Mr Sternberg's comments that there was no such eternal principle. What is his position on this question, now?

STERNBERG   The epic drama can only be independent of its relationships to contemporary events and thus endure for a while, if the central attitude it adopts anticipates the experiences of future history. Just as it was possible for the journey from Kaiser to Brecht to be short because a dialectical shift had occurred here, so, too, epic drama can endure as soon as a shift in economic relationships creates the situation, the relationships that correspond to it. Epic drama, like any drama, depends in that way on the evolution of history.

IHERING   [*the text breaks off here*]

['*Neue Dramatik*'*, BFA 21/270–5.]

Written 1929. This essay is incomplete, and based on a radio broadcast on 11 January 1929, which involved a discussion between Brecht, Sternberg, Herbert Ihering and Ernst Hardt. Hardt was the artistic director at Radio Cologne, and the broadcast introduced a radio production of Brecht's *Man Equals Man*, directed by Hardt with music by Edmund Meisel. No recording of the programme exists, and Brecht's essay is a retrospective reconstruction which incorporates material from other sources. The words attributed to Sternberg, for example, are drawn primarily from newspaper correspondence published in the *Berliner Börsen-Courier* in May 1927. Brecht's initial response to Sternberg is published in *Brecht on Theatre* ('Shouldn't We Abolish Aesthetics?', pp. 20–2). Herbert Ihering was a leading critic, who edited the theatre section of the *Berliner Börsen-Courier* and was one of Brecht's staunchest advocates from the early 1920s onwards.

In the course of the discussion, Brecht refers to *Carter Henschel*, written by the German Naturalist dramatist Gerhart Hauptmann, the post-Expressionist dramatist Arnolt Bronnen, and Marieluise Fleisser, the author of *Fegefeuer in Ingolstadt* (*Purgatory in Ingolstadt*, 1924) and *Pioniere in Ingolstadt* (*Pioneers in Ingolstadt*, 1926). Georg Kaiser was the most important Expressionist dramatist in the Weimar Republic; Brecht discusses his work in 'On Expressionism' (no. 4).

19

The Individual's Experience of the Apparatus in the Foreground

Fine literature puts the individual's experience of the apparatus in the foreground. The strongly developed belief in the personality was revealed in its funniest light when the problem of war was presented as a psychological problem (in considerations about the adequacy of Czernin's intelligence, or what was going on in Kaiser Bill's mind on the evening of the 14th), according to which personalities had 'succumbed' to a psychosis, war psychosis, in fact. Without psychosis, nothing could be explained, as of course certain commercial differences could have been 'settled' in a 'different' way (by which was meant: more cheaply). The 'philosopher of history', Ludwig, was able to imagine an intelligence of such power that it could have avoided war, e.g., his own intelligence.

Fine literature put the personality utterly and completely in the foreground, and depicted the experience of the apparatus. (Those with the most powerful experiences experienced print runs of up to a million. They demonstrated how awful it was not to have been a personality for four years.) Each one of them felt that the war wasn't his own war, was not the consequence of his deeds, nor the logical outcome of his thoughts (since when had his thoughts had any logic to them?): *nobody had ever asked them*! They had said 'two times two' aloud, and nobody had ever asked them if they also meant 'equals four'! They were primarily psyches and they excused themselves with a psychosis. Did they know where the grain grew that they ate? Did they know the name of the bullock they dined on as fillet steak? They didn't know, yet their heavenly father still fed them. They hadn't realised that they were capitalists (even if they personally had no capital) and that capitalism's time had come, its biggest and most stupendous collectivisation so far, its most consistent and almost impersonal achievement! They didn't realise that this was a societal phenomenon and not an intra-personal one. They saw the individual person being negated by the war, and so they rejected war. But the war was a reality, and the individual person had disappeared. But they hadn't wanted that. So the war was a chance event, and the individual person was there. Couldn't war be avoided, say, through the League of Nations? So war had come about because there hadn't been a League of Nations! The truth was that they couldn't see law-like regularities because they couldn't see the causes of events, and they couldn't see these because they couldn't eliminate them. They couldn't eliminate their actions, and hoped that the consequences of those actions could be avoided! The dualism between their opinions and their actions meant that their literature had no consequences and was absolutely undialectical, thus turning it into the unreal, and hence irrational, side effect which it is. Not only the war, but all the other major capitalist events had to appear to them as being natural in the metaphysical sense, events which human beings confronted as objects by 'experiencing' them. But the war hadn't come about, it had been made, it hadn't only befallen human beings, it had also been waged by human beings, and if the individual was powerless, the sum of all human beings did not constitute humanity, and hence was also powerless. But amongst these, the people who took action did not think, and the people who thought took no action; instead, thinking and acting were diametrical opposites.

['*Apparaterlebnis des einzelnen im Vordergrund*'*, BFA 21/306–7.]

Written 1929. Count Czernin was Austrian Foreign Minister from 1916 to 1918, forced to resign after it was revealed that he had been conducting secret peace negotiations with France. Emil Ludwig was the author of a war novel entitled *Juli vierzehn* (*July '14*), published in Berlin and Vienna in 1929.

20

Conversation about Classics

BRECHT My dear Mr Ihering, when I recently got hold of your pamphlet about the classics – *Reinhardt, Jessner, Piscator or the 'Death of the Classics'* – I thought at first that it would probably be an attack on the classics, and that's probably what our listeners are expecting from us now, an attack, a sort of murder of the classics. However, when I read your pamphlet, I saw that you weren't committing murder, but were simply observing that the classics are already dead. But if they are dead, *when* did they die? The truth is, they died in the war. They are amongst our war victims. If it is true that soldiers going off to war had *Faust* in their kitbag, then the ones who returned from war no longer did. You didn't write your book against the classics any more. The classics are not being killed, or rather they were not killed by books. You wrote your book, and we are talking about the classics, not because the classics are in crisis, but because our theatre is in crisis.

IHERING   This is not an arrogant, superficial craving for modernity, but a conclusion based on the facts. Theatre directors in Berlin and in the Empire are having enormous difficulties in putting together their programmes. There are so many theatres that new plays are quickly worn out. So it's self-evident that theatre directors would fall back on the classics again and again, and more and more frequently, if the audience still needed them or related to them.

BRECHT   So you think that the classics have turned from being an intellectual problem into an economic one. Our theatres are interested in this problem in economic terms. But what has become of *intellectual* interests? The friends of classicism will say that these have just disappeared, that our age utterly lacks intellectual interests. And that, we must admit, is difficult to refute entirely. The middle class had to more or less liquidate its purely intellectual efforts in an age when pleasure in thinking could mean that its economic interests were directly endangered. Where thinking wasn't completely suspended, it became more and more culinary. People did use the classics, but only in a culinary way.

IHERING   Yes, it was abuse. In the age of learning, in the nineteenth century, the classics were considered to be the intellectual furniture of the well-to-do middle class. They ornamented its parlour, they were as much part of the middle class as its plush furnishings, they were applicable and available in all situations. Classical drama served to confirm a world *against* which it had emerged. People used classical verses when they got engaged, brought up their children, watered the garden and went bowling. 'That is the fate of beauty on earth,' declaimed the bearded man and pinched the waitress.

BRECHT   Fine, that was abuse. People shouldn't have overtaxed the classics and called on them at every wedding and christening!

IHERING   They managed to pervert revolutionary works such as *The Robbers* and *Intrigue and Love* into an innocuous ideology. The petty bourgeoisie decontaminated all rebellious thoughts by identifying with them. The philistines appropriated the revolution, and therefore were able to disclaim it in real life all the more smugly. They plundered the contents of the classics and wore them out. There was no tradition, just consumption. But all this consumption was simply the expression of a false, intellectually sterile, conservative reverence.

BRECHT   This deferential attitude has avenged itself on the classics a lot, they were tarnished by deference and blackened by incense. It would have been better for them if people had adopted a more liberated attitude towards them, such as the attitude science has adopted to discoveries, even great ones, which it continually corrected or even rejected, not out of a desire for opposition, but in accord with necessity.

IHERING   Yes, the ownership complex prevented that. Almost the entire nineteenth century was geared towards a feeling of intellectual ownership. Schiller and Goethe belonged to the individual. Everybody spoke of barbarism if the classics weren't performed as they imagined they should be. Everybody was outraged if lines were cut which they did not even know. Everybody thought the nation had been offended if their favourite author was slighted. Nobody identified with the people; everybody identified the people with themselves.

BRECHT   The craze for ownership blocked the advance towards grasping the material value of the classics, which after all could have served to make the classics useful once again, but this was always prevented because people were afraid that it would destroy the classics.

IHERING   This arrogance was fed by schools and universities. German teaching in grammar schools emphasised the orgiastic nature of ownership. The classics were cultivated as a literary nature reserve. Touching them was forbidden; any modification of borders was disapproved of; any transplantation was punished. People hardly knew any more what Goethe and Schiller *meant*, or what went on in Shakespeare's plays, because they knew it all too well, because they uncritically parroted what had been taught for decades; because the words went into their ears and out of their mouths, taken in and returned according to how they sounded, worn-out sequences of notes, hackneyed groups of sentences, like the tunes of bad pop songs: 'The lovely days of Aranjuez . . .', 'I kiss your hand, Madame . . .'

BRECHT   People shouldn't have been so afraid of being accused of vandalism. Fear of vandalism turned people into philistines. People ought to be much more careful when they pass judgement on the Vandals. They probably burnt those wood carvings not simply because they disagreed with their style artistically, perhaps not even because they were against wood carvings as such, but because they needed wood for the fire. People should have approached material value in a relaxed way. For a while, our vandalistic efforts promised quite a lot, even though they were fought against every step of the way. There was already the prospect of saving the classics for our repertoire, not for the sake of the classics, but for the sake of our repertoire.

IHERING   Erwin Piscator tried that with his production of *The Robbers* at the Berlin State Theatre. This experiment exposed the present's relationship to Schiller in a problematic way. In the first two acts of *The Robbers*, Piscator weakened the revolutionary from private sentiment, Karl Moor, in favour of the systematic revolutionary, the revolutionary from conviction, which is what he turned Spiegelberg into. To do that he needed to change the text in the most brutal fashion. That was certainly dangerous and un-Schillerean; nevertheless, this interpretation didn't particularly bring out the high-handedness of the director so much as signify the defeat of the director experimenting with form. This performance, whose second part was simply a bad rendering of Schiller, supplied the theatre not with aesthetic trimmings, but with content, substance, in other words, with material.

BRECHT   Yes, it was a promising experiment. Suddenly another opportunity had come into view. Schiller really flourished again; true, Piscator said, '150 years, that's no small matter', but in the footlights things looked pretty good.

IHERING   Its effect was strange. Instead of being glad that Schiller's play had been plunged back into the river of time, the friends of the classics erupted into howls of rage. Again and again, people wanted human greatness. Human greatness, which had once been an intellectually valid idea, had long since come to refer to everything that was bloated, vague, ideological. Whenever people no longer knew a term for kitsch and histrionics, they said 'that is sublime'. Every charlatan and every reactionary rejected the re-engineering of the classics with the words that the greatness of the characters had been diminished and the greatness of the form had been destroyed. In reality, this greatness was undermined in every conservative performance, and in every pathos-ridden rendering, because they discredited the human content with a colossal form. This dilemma could not be escaped, either by way of a subtly nuanced realism that spelled everything out, or by way of an ecstatic panegyrical style that solemnised everything. In an age when the greatness of the individual had itself become doubtful, pedestals were of no help. A different concept had to be put in place of greatness. You, my dear Brecht, were in the vanguard. In place of greatness, you put: distance. That is your contribution to theatre history. The pivot and turning point in all this was your production of *Edward II* in Munich. You created an example here of how this old work by Marlowe could be rewritten as drama by cooling it down, and brought closer by distancing it. You did not diminish human beings. You did not atomise the characters. You distanced them. You took away from the actor that vivaciously ingratiating cosiness. You called the events to account. You demanded simple gestures. You imposed a clear, cool delivery. No emotional fraud was tolerated. This produced the objective, epic style.

BRECHT   I abandoned those efforts. We tried once again with one of Shakespeare's most magnificent works, when Erich Engel directed *Coriolanus*.

IHERING   That was an attempt at a methodical solution. Now we come to Goethe. There is a difference between form and mellow-ness, between clarity and calm. The rift between the stage and the masses, the false assessment of drama as a cultural affair – how are these to be explained, if not in terms of the overemphasis on Goethe? Goethe, who was the most private of all German creative writers, became the yardstick for art and humanity. His personal experiences were investigated, his personal actions were followed, tributes were paid to his lovers' trysts. But even when it was not only a question of Goethe's private experiences, it was still a question of the private experiences of the rising social stratum to which he belonged, the middle class. The Goethe cult of the Scherer school had a fateful impact on the development of German literature, German theatre and German criticism. This was the source for the spread of an uncontrollable art based on personal experience. Goethe was rich enough to derive knowledge from his experiences, and to give them literary shape. But theatre and criticism were put back by a century because this unique art was held to be exemplary, because an aesthetic was derived from it, and critical standards extracted from it. It turns out to be the case, you see, that, particularly in a critical age which is finding new bearings, it is still possible to stage or interpret material originating from a century with firm views and forms, even if the latter have no longer been valid for a considerable time. This does not apply, however, to material which, lacking binding and generally valid laws, signifies the beginning of a dangerous private art, and hence the beginning of the isolation and alienation between theatre and audience, even if it is much closer to us in time. Investigations were still being conducted into Goethe's most discreet secrets at a time when an industrial age had long since generated a different perspective, and a different world-view. Germanists prattled on about Goethe's love affairs and Goethe's lifestyle, they preened themselves with insignificant details, whilst, in the outside world, events were germinating in relation to which any personal fate would become meaningless, and any emphasis on private life, ridiculous. Hence, German drama, German theatre, German criticism were unprepared when the great upheaval came to pass. Gerhart Hauptmann had veered off into the affectations of Goethe's old age. No criticism and no aesthetic had built a reception point. The collapse came about like a catastrophe.

BRECHT   The purpose makes the style . . . And the worst thing you can do is hold on to something that no longer has a purpose, just because it used to be beautiful.

IHERING   Fine, you don't think ornaments are useful. But in your opinion, what would the classics have to be in order to be useful? What ought to constitute their value?

BRECHT   In order to establish this value, we must do an intellectual experiment. Let's simply imagine that some classical work, say *Faust* or *William Tell*, is being performed by boys, by a class of schoolkids. Do you think this would have a value for these boys? Would the thoughts they have to express represent education to them? Would they, or other human beings, gain any benefit from the movements they had to carry out, the attitudes they had to adopt? Would these boys be better able to survive than others, or would the society that they constituted be better able to survive? Answer the question seriously: what would these boys have done differently, if this experiment had been carried out, apart from saying a few nice words and performing a few noble gestures; alternatively, what situations would they have encountered that they would encounter again in real life? Our classical works have been made just to be looked at, and not to be used.

['*Gespräch über Klassiker*', BFA 21/309–15.]

Written 1929. Ihering had published a short monograph entitled *Reinhardt, Jessner, Piscator or the Death of the Classics* in 1929. On 28 April 1929 Radio Cologne broadcast a discussion of the issues Ihering had raised, which forms the basis for Brecht's essay. Brecht wrote several versions of this piece, and the version reproduced here is a reconstruction which takes account of Ihering's own notes regarding the broadcast. However, several of the passages Brecht attributes to Ihering were in fact drawn directly from *Reinhardt, Jessner, Piscator or the Death of the Classics*.

The controversy surrounding critical approaches to the cultural heritage had been provocatively sharpened by Piscator's production of Schiller's early play *The Robbers* at the Staatliches Schauspielhaus, Berlin, on 11 September 1926, which Jessner – the artistic director of the Staatliches Schauspielhaus – had commissioned him to produce. Apart from the fact that Piscator had drastically cut and rewritten Schiller's play, conservative critics were outraged by the fact that Piscator had presented Spiegelberg, one of the robbers, as Leon Trotsky. Brecht's discussion with Ihering contains several quotations from and references to Schiller's plays. Wilhelm Scherer, whom Brecht refers to in the context of Goethe criticism, had published a major *History of German Literature* between 1880 and 1883, and is generally regarded as the founder of the positivist school in German literary scholarship.

21

Defence of the Lyric Poet Gottfried Benn

German intellectuals are in a difficult position.

Although the war turned out to be a failure (which wasn't exactly their fault) they have been at the mercy of attacks on people who put their energies in the service of a *hopeless* undertaking. We must not forget that losing this war in no way means that they did no business. It was during the war that *the commodity character of the intellect* was established, in an unbecoming manner. On the other hand, the attitude of German intellectuals in the war proved that when their feelings are engaged in a cause, intellectuals can put their own 'ideas' 'in the service of the cause', as well as the ideas of other intellectuals – for example, dead ones – even, where particular effort is required, with a modest mark-up. They demonstrated that ideas are by no means superfluous just because it is impossible to act according to them; on the contrary, they showed that ideas are very useful if they can provide a justification for action. Harmony can emerge in that way, too. And this is precisely the sort of harmony that pays off.

The above-mentioned certification presented by intellectuals, to confirm that they had made themselves useful in the class struggle, should be taken entirely seriously by the proletariat (of course, whether or not their intellect was up to realising this, intellectuals only made themselves useful in the national struggle, in which otherwise they were of no use, by distinguishing themselves in the class struggle). It is not necessary, for the purpose of evaluating intellectuals, to employ the same intellectuals who have already supported the war effort, although this would be possible too, by simply 'engaging their feelings in the cause' (they are capable of anything when it's a question of having feelings – feeling itself is sufficient reward). Intellectuals can simply be taken to be a single group with a stable composition which, constituted on the basis of material conditions, reacts in an entirely predictable way. Thus, the proletariat may use different intellectuals, but they will work to the same conditions and achieve the same effect.

The function which they might serve (this can be determined purely on the basis of their behaviour during the war) must not be mistaken for a function which, as history shows, the proletariat has already conferred on intellectuals, a quite indispensable function of the utmost importance: that of leadership. (The importance of this function arises from the fact that in historical cases it is at least very difficult to decide whether individuals such as Marx, Lenin, etc., had a function ascribed to them by the proletariat, or whether they, for their part, ascribed a function to the proletariat. Luxemburg gave Lenin, for instance, a black mark for a series of remarks and, more significantly, actions which seem to prove that Lenin, whose usefulness for the proletariat is beyond dispute, tended to the latter viewpoint.) The proletariat proves its strong fighting instincts by treating intellectuals with extreme suspicion, keeping in mind as it does so a series of historical instances of their usefulness. Intellectuals, who obey by giving up their thinking processes and are readily available to the ruling class, are also readily available to the proletariat in a different sense: let the proletariat have the intellectuals who think.

The proletariat's justified suspicion puts intellectuals in a difficult position. They often attempt to merge with the proletariat, and it is precisely this which proves not that there are different types of intellectuals, two types of intellectuals, those who are proletarian and those who are bourgeois, but that there is only one brand of intellectuals, because in the past didn't they always try to merge with the ruling class? Wasn't this the reason why the intellect took on its commodity character?

If intellectuals want to take part in the class struggle, then it is necessary for them to grasp intellectually that their sociological constitution is homogeneous and determined by material conditions. The view they often air, that it's necessary to submerge oneself in the proletariat, is counter-revolutionary. Only evolutionaries believe in overturning the societal order by 'joining in'. Those intellectuals who do join in, for example, because they think it would be monstrous not to join in, play the role of voting fodder in parliamentary democracies, in other words they play an evolutionary role. Real revolutions (as in bourgeois historiography) are not produced by feelings, but by interests.

The proletariat's interest in the class struggle is clear and unequivocal, whereas the interest of intellectuals, which is of course a matter of historical record, is more difficult to explain. The only explanation is that intellectuals can only look to the revolution for a development of their (intellectual) activity. That is what determines their role in the revolution: it is an intellectual role.

The revolutionary intellect differs from the reactionary intellect in that it is a dynamic and, politically speaking, a liquidating intellect.

In a non-revolutionary situation the revolutionary intellect appears as radicalism. Its effect on every party, even a radical one, is anarchistic, as long, at least, as it doesn't manage to found a party of its own or is compelled to liquidate its party.

I am not saying that a revolutionary party might give up its suspicion of real intellectuals during a non-revolutionary situation. Because its liquidations, as long as they cannot be realised, because they don't concern any economic interests [*the text breaks off here*]

['*Die Verteidigung des Lyrikers Gottfried Benn*', BFA 21/337–40.]

Written *c.* 1929. The material presented here forms the opening part of an essay which Brecht did not complete. Gottfried Benn was a leading Expressionist poet and prose writer.

22

Suspicion of a New Tendency in Modern Philosophy

In this respect, it is hard to withhold a certain natural suspicion towards a particular tendency in modern philosophy, that of Unger. It adopts an ambiguous attitude towards Marxism. It tries to persuade Marxism that Ungerian theories are implied by Marxism, but Marxism itself does not draw these implications. The Ungerian tendency draws these implications on a purely intellectual level, however; it skips over things and its effect is absolutely counter-revolutionary; moreover, its views are purely aesthetic, though it tries, of course, to stretch aesthetics as far as possible. Its attitude towards art typifies that of our intellectuals and is therefore not without interest: it is completely influenced by those theories which think art is now bankrupt, and which have had such a big influence on Marxists too. And by art it appears to understand more or less the same artistic trend which it then generalises in a meaningless way. What is clear in all this is that nobody can doubt the ruination of art, if they really take art to be what functions as art at present. But it is interesting to note that precisely those people who overrate creativity in such a ridiculous way (not least because they are suffering from a true-blue Prussian achievement complex) never distinguish the creative from the creative (just as anti-Semites continually take pure Aryans to be Semitic). What these people take to be art, whose in their view typical development they contemplate with such interest, is nothing but the degenerate (incidentally, it is of course the ruling) sub-section of art, whose perspective is purely Romantic. This is the art that is built on pity and longings. These longings are, however, the remnants of anguished pangs of conscience that have no practical effect at all, which certain sated or otherwise impotent pensioners on low incomes carefully preserve for themselves. How ridiculous it is, then, completely to misconstrue the inner purpose of these 'longings' by taking them to be creative, and by suggesting that they should finally be dealt with seriously, not be used any more to produce works of art, but be 'put into action' – not least as these longings constitute long-winded myths, etc., whilst their inner purpose consists solely in trying to evade simple, crude and minimally intellectual measures. This is one of those comical suggestions which, though they lay claim to the designation 'revolutionary', are best judged simply by referring to their *triviality*. From the standpoint of art, what else can these people do but get embarrassed, if they are told that these longings are simply not present in the part of art that's really alive today. It's necessary to deal with this concept of 'creativity' particularly carefully. The activity of great art is reproductive; just as the act of procreation is reproductive, and proves not that something is lacking but that something is present, so too the presence of art proves not that human consciousness contains something inadequate which could somehow be made adequate by the imagination, but that if inadequacy plays a role in this at all, then inadequacy is complete chaos, not a remnant that is still lacking. It is indeed creative to reproduce real chaos, but the process of making art does not tend to shape anew the elements thus obtained according to a new image of the whole, but tends merely to put them together again in the old way. That is how the artist, and through him the spectator made artist, comes to make the pleasure of creation his own, and so art is the perpetually necessary inspection of the creative process, and not the repeatedly undertaken attempt to attain in the imagination a final image inherent in humanity which is not attained by reality (a process which, according to Unger, could then be corrected merely by the words 'in the imagination' being organised out of existence in order that the Third Reich should materialise, which is what this is all about, of course). The Ungerians' view of art differs from a correct view just as their attitude differs from a really philosophical one. Real philosophers have got beyond the stage of wanting-to-attain-something, whenever they began, their activity does not prove the presence of something unattainable.

['*Misstrauen gegen eine Richtung der modernen Philosophie*'*, BFA 21/345–7.]

Written *c.* 1929. Brecht had come into contact with Erich Unger through

Walter Benjamin. Unger was a philosopher and political theorist who argued that philosophy was dependent on economics. He also led a philosophical discussion group whose participants included Brecht, Benjamin and Korsch.

23

Theory of Pedagogies

The Major and the Minor Pedagogy

The Major Pedagogy completely changes the role of acting. It abrogates the system of actors and spectators. It only recognises actors who are simultaneously students. According to the Basic Law – 'Where the interest of the individual is the interest of the state, the gesture which is understood determines the individual's mode of action' – imitative acting becomes a major part of pedagogy. Compared with this, the Minor Pedagogy merely carries out a democratisation of theatre in the transitional era of the first revolution. In principle, the division remains; however, the actors should as far as possible be amateurs (and the roles should be such that amateurs must remain amateurs); professional actors, together with the existing theatre apparatus, should be used in order to weaken bourgeois ideological positions in the bourgeois theatre itself, and the audience should be activated. Plays and production style should turn the spectator into a statesman; that's why one should appeal not to the emotion in the spectator which would permit him to abreact aesthetically, but to his rationality. *The actors must estrange characters and events from the spectator so as to attract his attention.* The spectator must take sides, instead of identifying.

['*Die Grosse und die Kleine Pädagogik*'*, BFA 21/396.]

Written *c.* 1930. Like the following text, this was one of several essays that Brecht produced when working on his *Lehrstücke* between 1929 and 1932. The term 'estrange' is rendered in the German text by '*entfremden*', a term which Walter Benjamin and Brecht pick up again in 1934 and 1935 prior to Brecht's introduction of '*Verfremdung*' in 1936.

Theory of Pedagogies

Bourgeois philosophers draw a major distinction between those who are active and those who are contemplative. Those who think do not draw this distinction. If one draws this distinction, then one leaves politics to those who are active and philosophy to those who are contemplative, whereas in reality, politicians have to be philosophers, and philosophers have to be politicians. There is no difference between true philosophy and true politics. This insight entails the thinker's suggestion that young people should be educated by play-acting, i.e., by turning them into people who are simultaneously active and contemplative, as is suggested in the rules and regulations for the pedagogies. Pleasure in contemplation alone is detrimental to the state; but so is pleasure in action alone. By virtue of the fact that young people, when performing, carry out actions which they themselves scrutinise, they are educated for the state. These performances must be invented and executed in such a way that the state benefits. What decides the value of a sentence, or a gesture or an action, is thus not beauty, but whether the state benefits if the performers speak that sentence, carry out that gesture and proceed to take that action. The benefit that the state is to enjoy could certainly be very much reduced by blockheads, if, e.g., they let the performers carry out only such actions as appear socially minded to them. However, it is precisely the representation of antisocial behaviour by the state's developing citizens that is very beneficial to the state, particularly if that representation is enacted according to exact and magnificent models. The state can best improve upon humanity's antisocial drives – which derive from fear and ignorance – by forcing them out of everybody in the most complete form possible, a form which is almost unattainable by the individual on his own. This is the basis for the idea of using play-acting in pedagogies.

['*Theorie der Pädagogien*', BFA 21/398.]

Written *c*. 1930.

24

On New Criticism

The splitting-off of so-called fine literature, and its separate treatment as 'true literature', has turned literary history into a stomping ground of tastes, and criticism is atrophying into mere description. This bourgeois literary history is one big blurb from which nobody can learn anything.[1] 'Literature' is treated as an autonomous individual, obeying its own laws (which ones?), and maintaining either no relationships at all, or rather vague ones, with other individuals. The idea of its 'organic character', of course, nips any interventionist criticism in the bud. Interventionist criticism is as out of place here – indeed, it is ridiculous – as it would be in relation to a plant; in fact, it is even more out of place, because a plant allows criticism by experiments in cultivation. This 'history' as tradition merely assigns to the writer yellowing standard works of fine literature, instead of orientating him towards *contemporary* works of other literary genres, say those of law, philosophy, history, natural science, etc. That is why it concedes to the writer of fine literature the educational level of the readers of fine literature, a level which is the lowest of all readers. The 'man of letters' need not be acquainted with the achievements of sociology, which compartmentalise public life according to quite unusual, yet infinitely illuminating, perspectives. In his own subject area, he does not have to concede that there is 'progress', i.e., new methods of representation, ignorance of

---

[1] And, of course, no history emerges either; as no use is made of sociology, it is not possible for historians to make use of those works which, in their own age, were utterly dominant thanks to their success and impact, and also influenced those works which then remained, but which also includes [sic] consideration above all of *readers, who are an essential part of a history of literature*! I mean so-called pulp fiction.

which makes all further writing 'old-fashioned'. Construed as a movement, specific to himself, of his hand and his arm, his writing is considered to be beyond influence, peculiar to him (in the sense of ownership and in the sense of strangeness), and criticism here cannot be interventionist, but merely descriptive or retrospectively 'promotional'. As no usability corresponds to value, i.e., as value does not have to be usable, and usable values are never even cited, value is entirely without obligation and has no value itself. The consequences for fine literature itself are dreadful. These are the *consequences of having no consequences.* How is a sentence supposed to have force if, no matter how well it turns out, it can have no consequence apart from the fact that, if they are distanced from their usual mode of thinking, people consider it to be a sentence and 'enjoy' it on that basis. By way of comparison, let us cite the sentences with which physicists communicate their perceptions or record their experiments, or the sentences of lawyers! As every word here has practical consequences, every word is carefully considered. *At the root of every word there is a decision!* And the reader only gains by making decisions! But these are literatures that are intended to be usable.

['*Über neue Kritik*', BFA 21/402–4.]

Written 1930.

25

Ideas and Things

Ideas are Use Objects

Specific ideas (ideologies) are the products of specific relationships insofar as they each produced, or were produced by, the behaviour that was the most opportune. Thus, behaviour largely determined actual utility. It was therefore possible, on the other hand, for all forms of behaviour towards the ideas themselves – such as merely pretending to possess them in the way the faithful do – to be adopted by the various classes according to utility. So, e.g., you had to behave as if God existed. Really having this idea was only useful for particular social strata, etc.

It is quite wrong to consider the sum of all the ideas of a specific class in a specific epoch to be indivisible, even if they once appeared as a whole, hence as more than a sum. Reality itself divides those relationships that did not make ideas useful, by making some ideas last longer than others. So, if the function of an idea has been determined, it can easily be used in today's world – namely, by being reinforced or made conscious in places where it is still facilitated by reality, but is only weakly present in an unconscious way. Ideas are use objects.

['*Vorstellungen sind Gebrauchsgegenstände*'*, BFA 21/406–7.]

Written 1930.

On the Process of Knowledge

In the process of knowledge, apart from organising what has been experienced or is (yet to be) experienced, the intellect also has the function of making events conspicuous, of confronting them with the thought of their negation. The 'that's how things are' is understood *with astonishment* as a 'so things aren't different, then'.

Hence it's almost always the case that truths are only obtained relatively.

Even the statement '*Cogito, ergo sum*' has a dissimilar (and relative) truth. A lot more statements need to be added in order to support it. Being, like thought, is relative and dissimilar (comparative). The statement is only intended to be the foundation stone of an entire building. It does not validate itself.

What does the *cogito* mean? Does it mean: we must doubt everything as long as we have no proof. We must begin by doubting our own person (the thing we are most sure of). We may only believe in it, because we can prove it. Its proof is: it thinks. Is that what the *cogito* means? As many beings exist which (at least comparatively speaking) do not think, these beings could never verify their existence. Thus, the statement means: I am proved by the ego, even if I couldn't think I might still exist, but I couldn't verify that to myself. The verification and the assimilation-of-the-verification is a thought. Has the self-verification of the person succeeded? It has simply been asserted that thought is a kind of being; but there are many more kinds of being.

Doubt really ought to be applied to all things together, because as all things are interconnected, I cannot of course demarcate individual things at all, and basically I don't, of course, doubt things, but only my senses, which communicate things to me in a way which may be inaccurate or false. In reality, however, I do exactly what I cannot do: I doubt one thing more than another, or: I know more about one thing than another, and moreover: I know varying amounts about one and the same thing; that is to say, I can learn more and more about it. And this 'more than' and this 'more and more' are very important operations or categories.[1] So we basically agree with Descartes when he doubts whether he can know things, that is to say, things which are nominalised, fixed and unchanging. However, we don't assume that this depends on the nature of the human mind, but are of the opinion that this sort of thing does not exist in the way that, e.g., Kant claims, if we are to know it, or not know it.

['*Über den Erkennungsvorgang*'*, BFA 21/410–11.]

Written *c.* 1930.

[1]Brecht's footnote reads, 'Operating with these concepts enables us to dissolve Kantian doubt and fructify Cartesian doubt.'

On 'the Thing in Itself'

1 The question about the thing in itself is posed in an era when, on the basis of socio-economic developments, the *utilisation* of all things is set in motion. The question did not, however, aim only to discover new practical uses in things, but also indicated the contradiction of contemplating things only in terms of usability:

things exist not only for us, but also for themselves. Though they are still usable even in this absolute condition . . .

2 We must not forget that the feeling of ownership began to play an enormous role. Feudal property was a consequence of power. Now power became a consequence of property. Even knowledge was power, because it was property or could become property. Bacon, the person who made this assertion, explicitly defined knowledge as 'knowing how to utilise'. People no longer simply took what they needed from things, but once they owned a thing they sought to find new practical uses in it. It was now a case of utilising what others needed. The thing was pressurised enormously into yielding as much as possible.

3 The thing as a commodity, on the other hand, became unusually opaque, all the more so when human beings themselves became commodities in their capacity as workers, with the result that the thing's substantive character began to dwindle. From the observer's point of view, things came into being that were really relationships, and relationships between human beings or things assumed the character of things. It is not possible today for any thing to be named in the way Kant dealt with it: anything other than the Kantian thing is unknowable.

4 Things are not knowable for themselves, because they also cannot exist for themselves.

5 The tree knows human beings to at least the same extent as it knows carbonic acid.

6 For human beings, using oxygen forms part of knowing the tree. The concept of knowledge must therefore be construed more broadly.

7 Epistemology must be, above all, critique of language.

8 Life itself is a process of knowing. I know a tree by living myself.

[*'Über "das Ding an sich"'*, BFA 21/412–13.]

Written *c.* 1930. In this and the next essay, Brecht refers to the eighteenth-century German philosopher Immanuel Kant's doctrine of the thing in itself (*das Ding an sich*), according to which we do not know things as they are in themselves, but perceive them as phenomenal forms only. The slogan that 'knowledge is power' derives from Francis Bacon's treatise *Meditationes Sacrae* of 1597.

Kant's Unknowable Thing in Itself

The distinction drawn in Kant between knowable and unknowable ought to be turned by us into the main object of our critique. It's not without good reason that our critique always applies where the thing in itself causes perceivable phenomena. Shouldn't we simply say that we cannot know anything that we cannot change, nor anything that doesn't change us? Then there always do in fact emerge aspects of a thing which we cannot know (as we cannot or need not change them), so a thing in itself does indeed come into being that is not knowable (as it is not entirely knowable), but this thing in itself, being unusable, is uninteresting, it really does have no impact on the perceiver and, on the contrary, it even becomes (even if never entirely, and so never really perceivably, nevertheless) perceivable where it was not perceivable; in other words, it becomes *more* knowable, in that it is exactly its perceivable aspects, perceivable because they are changeable, which for their part can change the thing (in itself).

['*Kants unerkennbares Ding an sich*', BFA 21/413.]

Written *c.* 1930.

26

Who Needs a World-View?

For these inexpert people who think to no purpose, asserting the dependency of the great intellectual systems of Plato and Kant on economic factors is tantamount to casting suspicion upon them. Apart from the fact that 'economic factors' are being invested with that contempt which they certainly deserve these days – in this contempt is revealed, quite unconsciously, the deep dissatisfaction, untouched by thought, with economic factors that cannot be changed by thought – why do people not see that the dependence on economic factors which we assert was in no way capable of hindering those intellectual systems whose greatness we do not deny? We would go further: even if economic dependence did not produce these ideas, it certainly made them great, that is to say, interventionist. Intervening in what? In economic affairs. Why not prove their greatness with reference to the extent of their intervention?

Depriving thought of any deeper influence means construing it in defeatist terms. In order to grant thought influence – requiring thought to exert influence means making demands of thought – it is necessary, of course, to abandon the idea which has Leonardo painting even without his arms. The idea that someone in chains, muzzled in a hole in the ground in the company of worms, might in no way be prevented from thinking whatever he likes, may well console those who see being in chains as an unalterable destiny. In reality, people muzzled by the economy can only think freely, however, if they can free themselves in thought, that is, from the economy. And they can only do this if their thought changes the economy, in other words, makes the economy dependent on it, and so depends on the economy.

The recognition that thought has to be of some use is the first stage of knowledge.

The majority of those who have reached this stage give up thought (thought which is simply playful) in view of the impossibility of thinking in an interventionist way.

Interventionist thought is not only thought that intervenes in the economy, but primarily is thought that intervenes in thought with respect to the economy.

Kant made it possible for bourgeois science to work in a materialistic way (which is what bourgeois society needed) by allowing it to retain a world-view (which society needed just as much) independently of society and of the results of its work, but by and large this simply gave free reign to materialism, because this same separation of knowledge from faith also separated the sciences from one another, as, of course, they were no longer permitted to pool what they had in common. If the natural scientists had gone into the sociology department next door after work, instead of going to church with the sociologists, then they would have destroyed the bourgeois world-view in theoretical terms as well. By acting the way they did, they destroyed it in practical terms.

Humanity defined in bourgeois terms must give up its bourgeois features if it is to maintain its humanity.

There is a widely held view that the bourgeoisie has lost the strength to establish a real world-view, that this is very bad for the bourgeoisie which is, therefore, eagerly and desperately occupied with achieving a new totality. It is indeed the case that bourgeois science displays tendencies towards this. Everywhere people talk of the great epochs that will lie ahead if physiology and chemistry, or this subject and that subject, finally merged. And, indeed, these tendencies are close to ruining bourgeois science. They are tendencies that originate outside the threatened class position of the bourgeoisie. Unrealisable demands such as these are being made of science from a quite specific quarter.

World-views are working hypotheses. And so, without being particularly damaged in the process, the proletariat may create and employ such a thing; the proletariat's work is important. Such a world-view may also be used by those bourgeois intellectuals who need working hypotheses of a similar kind, but in their case this will certainly be very dangerous.

A Romantic wave which is definitely on the horizon (Voltaire is quite right to speak of an irreconcilable antagonism between Reason and Romanticism) is not the only factor that might compel us to present our studies in a form that corresponds to classical form; the other factor is the necessity of deploying formal qualities as weapons in a hostile environment (at which point one should investigate where quality can still manifest itself as quality, if it is fighting hostile interests). Individual realism, we might note in passing, would hardly be necessary there, as the collusive intent of bourgeois ideologies is directed more towards interpersonal processes. Relationships between human beings are to be disguised, that is to say those relationships which have something to do with social existence. And, what is also to be disguised is the enormous extent to which these relationships are involved in structuring the person. What is needed, then, is a realism of human functions.

Classicism is certainly not, as later observers realise, a particularly high level of perfection within a self-regulating artistic genre, nor is it a mode of expression that merely reflects a self-contained and thus 'classical epoch', in other words, an outcome; no, classicism is something much more intentional (even though it may not necessarily be consciously constructed), and its intentions concerned societal conditions. The attempt to give lasting shape to specific proposals of an ethical and aesthetic nature, and to confer on them a final, definitive character, in other words, the attempt of a class to give permanence to itself and to give its proposals the appearance of finality.

World-view, this remarkably acquisitive, firm structure of moral maxims, perspectives, methods of conduct   [*the text breaks off here*]

The notion that human beings behave differently in different conditions (related to class) presupposes – if it is to be believed – the belief that they behave in a similar way in similar conditions. If they did not do so, this circumstance would no doubt have to be brought about. If it is possible to think of them behaving in a different way (we must do this; it is precisely in the everlasting contradiction thereby produced in the masses that their evolutionary potential resides) then the probability calculus is sufficient, where, formerly, causality was striven for. This is because, from the standpoint of the masses, probability can be almost limitlessly reinforced.

No matter how (by which socio-economic necessities) the separation of the sciences was brought about – it is a creation of capitalism

– it can be evaluated. – Whether it was carried out by capitalism in its constructive phase, or as it went into decline – for us this separation is positive. It will help people to bury capitalism once and for all, and construct socialism. Only their separation enabled the individual sciences to work in a materialist way, and hence to develop methods that really can be used. This separation will not be retained in its mechanical bourgeois form, but once the sciences have mutually pervaded one another, this will not have happened for the purpose that the connoisseurs of a world-view have posited for this pervasion (just as this purpose will not have achieved that pervasion): the Heideggerian bird's-eye view located within the individual will not be the greatest show on earth.

If Planck's constant is no longer much use for our sketch of Being (it may have been partly calculated in terms of the latter, i.e., when it was corrected by empirically perceived reality), then this does not only prove that we need to correct our sketch of Being until Planck's constant fits again; in fact, it is already the case that Planck's constant (which only generates behaviour and wishes to remain anonymous) will render impossible and unnecessary any sketch of Being that has a similar function. No matter what has already changed, or will change in the future, in Engels's statement 'Life is the mode of existence of protein' – the perspective which underlies it can be retained amongst people who, on the basis of a societal order certainly very different from ours, will be able to generate and maintain sufficient insight into themselves through their behaviour.

['*Wer braucht eine Weltanschauung?*', BFA 414–17.]

Written *c.* 1930. This essay is a composite based on a series of individual pages of text whose precise sequence is uncertain. The sections of the printed text correspond to pages of the typescript. Brecht refers implicitly to the German philosopher Martin Heidegger's notion of 'being-in-the-world', as articulated in *Sein und Zeit* (*Being and Time*) in 1927, and his perception of Heidegger may have been influenced by a critical reading group on Heidegger which Walter Benjamin intended to convene in the summer of 1930. Brecht's comments on Max Planck, the founder of quantum theory, reflect his intense interest in sub-atomic physics and the theory of relativity in the early 1930s. The quotation from Engels may be found in *Herrn Eugen Dührings Umwälzung der Wissenschaft* (*Mr Eugen Dühring's Scientific Revolution*).

27

On the Function of Thought

It occurred to nobody to cultivate this authentic philosophy, because its cultivation seemed to be quite impossible in the prevailing circumstances. It seemed to be an undertaking which, for the time being, lacked all the necessary preconditions. Everyone seemed to be waiting for something, in the absence of which any efforts would have to remain pointless. Indeed, what was one to expect a mode of understanding to contribute to clarifying actual human relationships, when it had, for centuries on end, been trained only to disguise such relationships, and moreover, had to be able to disguise something which, for this purpose, it did not even have to recognise itself! Because this was the function which reason had in practical life, this was how the head fed its belly. Or, how was one supposed to adapt to a world that was in no way complete, or come to terms with changeability? It was certainly wise to adopt a particular attitude when receiving a blow that could not be warded off, but what about the blow that could be warded off? Philosophy seemed to be unsuited both to knowing relationships and to changing them, without somehow ceasing to exist because of that. The fact that philosophy still existed in such circumstances was almost the worst evidence against it. It was relatively easy to assert that thought was independent of the ways in which people secured their existence, with and against one another, as long as these ways were reasonably stable, i.e., they didn't seem to change and there was something fateful about them. But now they were changing with every year and every hour, and, where once a statement had sufficed, now a prophecy was needed, just as, during the Inflation, businesses had to build in calculations of the presumed drop in the value of money up to the very day when their assets were realised. And the prophecies kept on being criticised by realities in such a cruel way! You could also pride yourself on the fact that thought was supposed to be independent of the economy, but where was the benefit in the fact that the economy was independent of thought? The economy, that is, was not only independent of a particular type of thought, to be precise philosophical thought, in other words it was something absolute, a thing in itself; it was independent of any thought. The fact that the economy itself was supposed to be independent of the thought of captains of industry, which was not subject to any violent restriction by the state – this was unthinkable, mainly because these few individuals did make profits. Little was known about the circumstances and powers that determined your own fate, but people could be seen pulling the strings everywhere. Were you supposed to assume that these people had no idea? Indeed, they had no idea, and this was the source of their profits. One person could only profit from another person's ignorance, this was the nature of the system. Even for the captains of industry, grasping the whole was neither possible nor necessary, though disguising the parts was. Differences of opinion only existed on the basis of differences of interest, and it was a question of devising not arguments, but threats. Ultimately, all thought was held to be no more than the expression of the persons doing the thinking, with no obligation for everyone else, unless it involved discovering methods of violence. Of course, word soon got out that people only thought in the service of interests, but even in this form, the statement wasn't true. Because large strata of peoples, even with the best will in the world, were incapable of thinking in their own interests; because they were worse at thinking than others, and were in a situation that was worse for thought. These strata were backward, and this backwardness was, of course, exploited, all the more so in that there was of course not really any progress, but simply an advance in exploitation. Basically, in such circumstances, it was the cleverer members of these strata who declared that thought generally was superfluous (in their case it really did lead to nothing!). As the economic process simultaneously brought about so-called rationalisation – a pervasion by reason, which imposed heavy sacrifices on these strata, as they were seemingly excluded from the production process by means of reason – they were now completely against the rational and for the irrational.

['*Über die Funktion des Denkens*'*, BFA 21/418–19.]

Written *c.* 1930.

28

What is Progress?

Is it possible, in the case of a progressive work, to be positive about the form and negative about the content?
Answer: Yes. If, that is, the concept of progress is built into a view of the historical sequence of 'artistic trends' according to which merely action and reaction exist, in other words, purely formal changes, which each assimilate fashionable new material, to be sure, but assimilate no more than is required by the opaque principle of wear and tear, and taking one's turn. Then you have the reactionary sequence of Impressionism being succeeded by Expressionism, and Expressionism by New Objectivity (the heating up of music succeeded by its freezing over) *without the overall function changing or rather: solely in order that the latter doesn't change*. Progress such as this would merely take place in people's brains, which for their part are connected to nothing apart from other brains.

Is progress such as this progress?
Answer: No. Because it is the consequence of *nothing*, and has *nothing* as its consequence. It doesn't derive from a new need, but only gratifies old needs with new stimuli, and so has a purely conservational function. We thus remain trapped in the realm of fashions, artistic trends, novelties and sensations, and unceasing efforts to respond with constantly 'new' stimuli to reactions and

appetites that dwindle increasingly time and again, and if there is no alternative, we even incorporate elements that are as yet unknown 'in this place', because, when 'this place' was occupied, they were unknown in other places too. (Locomotives, engine rooms, airplanes, etc., then serve as a distraction. The better ones are completely negative about content, and present it, or rather carry it off, in Latin.) This sort of progress only demonstrates that something   [*the text breaks off here*]

['*Was ist Fortschritt?*', BFA 21/518.]

Written *c*. 1931. Compare Brecht's previous discussion of Expressionism in no. 4.

29

Dialectics

Dialectic

The fact that socialists, given their experiences, have a very dynamic concept of progress can be explained psychologically. Progress exists in socialism and, without progress, socialism is not possible. This concept of progress is very advantageous in political terms, but it has had detrimental consequences for the concept of dialectic. Viewed from the perspective of progress, dialectic is (has always been) a property of nature, a characteristic which, however, was only discovered by Hegel and Marx. Before this discovery, the world could not be explained and, wherever some aspect of the world had been explained after all, people had simply stumbled on its dialectic without realising and without noticing. What is reflected in the heads of dialecticians, in other words, is simply this thing dialectic, which is the characteristic feature of nature. Made mindful in this way of the peculiarities of earthly phenomena, dialecticians – in an enormous advance on other people – are able to take precautions. The adherents of this simple but inspiring viewpoint lapse into sullen and aggrieved muttering if their attention is drawn to the similarity of their viewpoint with that of some palmists, who believe that they could of course now prevent the imminent events read in somebody's palm, once they had ascertained them. In reality, dialectic is a method of thinking, or, rather, an interconnected sequence of intellectual methods, which permit one to dissolve certain fixed ideas and reassert praxis against ruling ideologies. It may be possible, by making daring deductions, to prove with some success that nature behaves dialectically; but it is much easier to refer to the palpable and indispensable outcomes of dialectical behaviour that have already been achieved, i.e., of applying dialectical methods to societal conditions and occurrences, in other words to the nature of society, our society, in fact. I can imagine that one equals one, and I can imagine that one does not equal one. Is it not enough to say that thinking the latter is more advantageous, namely, if I have to act in a particular way?

['*Dialektik*', BFA 21/519.]

Written *c.* 1931.

Dialectical Critique

If, on the basis of their results, opinions are now to be critically investigated (put into a state of crisis) rather than merely the results of these opinions, then it is essential that the latter also are not examined in a way that suggests we might possibly want to assimilate them. This mode of observation is very difficult to avoid, because the entire structure of the society in which we live is such that we are dependent on assimilating things, and thus on methods that specifically turn all things into objects of assimilation. This approach of ours does things no good. Opinions which are separated from the people who hold them, and thus from the standpoints these people occupy, have absolutely no force any more, and it is mainly because our opinions are removed in this way from specific people with specific standpoints that our opinions have so little influence on our attitude. We merely exhibit them. It is therefore wrong to approach opinions from the position whereby they can be adopted (or rejected) in the above sense. Let us therefore consider people's attitude on the basis of their opinions, and let us remind ourselves that this attitude only agrees with those opinions in a conditional way, which means that we have yet to investigate the degree to which people's actions are beholden to their opinions. Because, at the end of the day, we must get to the point of indicating how people will act when it is a question of changing the world. To that end we must divide them all into groups, and divide them up in such a way that interests become visible which are sufficiently strong and influential to make themselves noticeable, in other words make themselves visible.

['*Dialektische Kritik*', BFA 21/520.]

Written *c.* 1931.

On Dialectic: 6

To be investigated: what assertions (ideas, what intellectual procedure) are needed to act (as a member of what class)?

It is also necessary to seek out the metaphysical element, in every statement. In the statement in question, e.g., it is concealed in the concept of 'necessity'. The 'necessity' of a given historical process is an idea which lives off the conjecture that every historical event must come about on the basis of sufficient reasons. In reality, however, there were contradictory trends that were resolved by argument, and that is much less. Moreover, the aforementioned idea is underpinned by the tacit conviction that, after enumerating all possibilities, motives, dispositions, inclinations, etc., there still exists a necessity as such, a secret power that is not completely expressed in the aforementioned observed and observable events and relationships. Whenever large groups of people, whether individual faces or collectives are visible in them, fight over their interests one against the other and amongst themselves, there initially emerge specific observable outcomes in the form of legal practices, societal customs of every sort, and for these various decisions sufficient reasons can, of course (at least in theory), be discovered; but beyond that, in accordance with old metaphysical tendencies, *another* 'necessity' is often discovered or suspected, a hidden hand: the 'higher power' of religions.

In reality, processes do not reach conclusions. It is observation that requires and imposes conclusions. By and large, of course, decisions are made (and encountered), certain formations change or even lose their functions, qualities decay and the overall picture changes jerkily.

Seek out the situations in which the statements in question might appear. From what quarter might they appear, and for what purpose might they be uttered.

Application of dialectic to destroy ideologies. Axiomatic tables: what are the consequences, what lies behind it.

Asocial behaviour.

['*Über Dialektik: 6*'*, BFA 21/523–4.]

This is one of a series of fragmentary notes on dialectics from *c.* 1931.

30

On the Critique of Ideas

Kant-Goethean aesthetics postulate that the person enjoying art is liberated from his or her interests. That is to say, the person is determined by his or her interests too unequivocally (too firmly) to adopt all the attitudes he or she could adopt (without being determined by interests). Because, in principle, nothing human is alien to human beings. Art allows human beings to act in a universally human way, which they otherwise cannot do. And so it really does allow them to persevere with (their) interests, which are not universally human, namely 'in real life'. The world of the artist thus basically contains everything which is necessary to a world. It can be enjoyed as a whole, and – after individual interests have been given up – it can be enjoyed safely. On the basis of empathy (mimesis), the enjoyer can attain behaviour not conditioned by interests. At any rate, this is what is promised.

This involves a gross deception.

In order to be able, above all, to attain knowledge himself (e.g., of certain events and attitudes), the artist himself must have ideas, quite specific ideas indeed, and, in any case, ideas opposed to other ideas; and, in order to turn his depiction into knowledge, the enjoyer must likewise have interests which are equally specific. These interests which are necessary for the attainment of knowledge give events their *specific* interpretation, however, and rule out many attitudes. It is true that the enjoyer enjoys in art, say, a house which does not belong to him burning down, together with the feelings he would have if he were the owner, but the attitude of ownership is one that serves his interests. And so, interests crop up again in artistic pleasure; indeed, they are what make it possible in the first place. That is the gross deception.

['*Über Vorstellungskritik*', BFA 21/533–4.]

Written *c*. 1931.

31

Theses on the Theory of Superstructure

(*Purpose: the revolutionary significance of superstructural work*)

  1 Culture, in other words superstructure, is not to be regarded as a thing, a possession, a result of evolution, as revenue converted into an intellectual luxury, but as an autonomously evolving factor (ultimately, however, not *only* revenue-creating) and, above all, as a process.

2 One expression of the cultural needs of the masses are the morals and customs which constantly evolve under the pressure of the economy and politics, and which in our day are attaining a revolutionary function with the class-conscious proletariat.

3 Amongst the antagonistic factors that come into being in the womb of a specific society and lead to it being revolutionised, technology plays a decisive role as one of the forces of production. As part of this technology, we must also count the technology of thought, which cannot be restricted without more ado to the area where it initially develops. Dialectical thought, which emerged in the area of the economy and owes its existence to the existence of the proletariat, is spilling over increasingly into other areas, but it remains a proletarian mode of thought.

4 In the age of imperialism, no culture is defined any more in an essentially national way. Even bourgeois culture is essentially international – and how much more is this true of proletarian culture! The cultural institutions of the first proletarian state are not limited by its political boundaries, and, once taken over by the proletariat of bourgeois states, they have a revolutionary effect, precisely because their impact and evolution are being violently impeded. These are not by any means the institutions of a classless society, on the contrary: they are measures taken by the proletariat in the class struggle.

5 The way in which superstructure comes about is: anticipation.

6 What is rational becomes real, and what becomes real is rational.

7 The dialectical infusion of all categories of thought is unavoidable, and every area that has been dialectically infused leads to revolution, *as long as the political dimension is inferred.*

8 It is the duty of dialecticians to dialectically infuse the various areas of thought, and to infer their political dimension.

9 What is 'foreseen' (in both meanings of the word!) for the classless society is real, and it forms part of the superstructure of this classless society, if it is necessary for the latter's emergence and consolidation. People must build the classless society themselves – for the time being, it is itself an anticipation.

10 Superstructure comes about at the moment when it is most needed: when material relationships make it necessary, so that they can change (burst apart!). At the moment of revolution, super-structure experiences qualitative change. Humanity undertakes nothing that it cannot achieve – but it has to undertake everything!

['*Thesen zur Theorie des Überbaus*', BFA 21/570–2.]

Written *c*. 1932. This essay and the one that follows demonstrate the impact of Karl Korsch's work on Brecht in the early 1930s. Brecht first met Korsch in late 1928 or early 1929, and there is some evidence that Brecht and Korsch participated in philosophical discussions led by Erich Unger (see also no. 22). It has also been suggested that Brecht attended lectures given by Korsch at the 'Marxistische Arbeiterschule' (Marxist Workers School) in Berlin from 1929 onwards, and he participated in Korsch's discussion group on Marxist dialectics in 1931. The issue of Korsch's influence on Brecht has been notoriously controversial in Brecht criticism, because it goes to the heart of the key problem in Brecht's work at this time: the precise nature of his Marxism (see Steve Giles, *Bertolt Brecht and Critical Theory*, pp. 81–112). The term superstructure is taken from Marx, and Brecht's theses may be seen as a response to Marx's classic Preface to his *Critique of Political Economy*.

32

Key Points in Korsch, pp. 37 and 54

In order to gain intellectual credibility for their experiments – itself no easy task – the Naturalists excavated pity from the Aristotelian formula for tragedy. But Aristotelian pity is triggered by absolute conformity with natural laws. It is the aspect, turned towards humanity, of consent with those things humanity cannot change. Illicit pity is authorised here. – The interconnection between the tragic and the religious (which also derives from terror) can be seen most clearly in mythologies, which, according to Marx, overcome natural forces in and through the imagination (and, once we have achieved mastery over natural forces, mythologies disappear). In our day, struggling against tragedy, just like struggling against religion, is a revolutionary task, because we have yet to wrest their ideological position from the laws, established by us, which underpin reality. The bourgeoisie is wrong if it believes the proletariat has a tragedy. The tragic does not only characterise a stabilised society, but also presupposes the concepts of high and low. The inescapability which is required to initiate the tragic process of sublimation must be an assertion which is opposed by another assertion (namely that of escapability). The tragic fall presupposes the possibility of its negation. The utterly hopeless fall, in which there is no higher interest, presents, of course no possibility of sublimation. The tragic, like the religious, is a historical phenomenon, interest in it is the yardstick for a society's revolutionary or counter-revolutionary character.

My [view] is: the fate of Rose Bernd, the weavers, etc., can no longer be found tragic, and thus cannot be passed off as tragic either, in an age which can account for these catastrophes in terms of a mere lack of civilisation, for whose remedy it has already worked out eminently practical suggestions. How far the depredation has advanced that comes about through plays like this, or through which plays like this come about, is demonstrated by the idea, alive in some people today, that humanity is well on the way to completely getting rid of the tragic by merely taking civilising measures. Which tragedy? Rose Bernd's? Definitely.

['*Korsch Kernpunkte, S. 37 und 54*', BFA 21/574–5.]

Written *c.* 1932. This essay responds to Korsch's monograph *Key Points in the Materialist Conception of History*, published in 1922. Korsch quotes an extract from Marx's 'Introduction' to the *Grundrisse* on p. 54 of *Key Points* which forms the basis for Brecht's critique of tragedy: 'Is the perspective on nature and societal relationships which underlies the Greek imagination and thus Greek [art] possible in a world of self-acting mule spindles and railways and locomotives and electric telegraphs? [...] All mythology overcomes and controls and shapes the forces of nature in the imagination and through the imagination, and therefore mythology disappears with real control over natural forces. [...] Greek art presupposes Greek mythology, in other words the popular imagination *has already processed nature and societal forms in an unconciously artistic manner.*'

Rose Bernd and the weavers are the protagonists in Gerhart Hauptmann's plays *Rose Bernd* and *The Weavers*, which were classics of German Naturalism.

33

Use of Truth

In an age when capital, in its desperate struggle, is summoning up all its enormous means to stamp as truth any idea it finds useful, truth has become a commodity to such an extent – such a questionable, tricky thing, dependent on buyer and seller, themselves dependent on many things – that the question 'what is true' can no longer be resolved without the question 'whom does this truth benefit'. Truth has entirely become a functioning thing, something which doesn't exist (above all in the absence of people), but which must in each case be created, a means of production, no doubt, but one which is produced!

In view of its enormous use for the prevailing disorder, what are we to make of the metaphysical standpoint that Engels describes thus: 'N.Z.', 8/357.

That context of crises must be generated, and even if nothing else compelled us to give up the metaphysical perspective, it would still be completely justified by the need to arrive at an understanding of this deeper, incurable overall crisis. This crisis certainly demands an activity; it is an activity.

Led by the suspicion that, in this world of commodities, our ideas had long since turned into commodities (they could not remain as goods), let us now investigate these ideas, in particular in relation to their commodity character. For almost too long, when speaking of such things as the new attitude to life, the post-war perspective, the world-view of a new generation, we have let almost all novelty stand as a presupposition, and have used it as such. It's about time we gave substance to these presuppositions. And so, regardless of readers or writers who can only be interested by something interesting, and building solely on bare necessity, new methods for criticising ideas are to be deployed, and new ideas are to be constructed which are legitimised by their usefulness (weapons do not need to be charming for the person who needs them), and their use is to be measured in terms of their power to transform our societal world.

['*Nutzen der Wahrheit*'*, BFA 21/580–1.]

Written *c.* 1932. The Engels citation to which Brecht refers ('N.Z.', 8/357) forms part of an essay published by Georgi Plekhanov in *Die Neue Zeit* (*The New Age*) in 1890. Engels is critical of what he terms the 'metaphysical' view that things and their concepts are intrinsically isolated and independent entities rather than being dialectically interconnected.

34

Einstein–Freud

Einstein assumes that humanity has a dark drive which, embodied from time to time in appalling acts of violence called wars, leads humanity to forget its entire civilisation and besmirch the community which it has taken such efforts to establish. According to Einstein, this drive is unleashed by relatively little printed paper and wild talk. Its outbreak does not require real reasons. As a real, sober, discursory interest in war is not usually visible – how could one suspect a people of thinking that it might improve its material conditions in war? – the reason for war must be sought in the realm of darkness, impulsive, uninterested behaviour.

What prevents Einstein from seeing that the real reasons for war lie in material interests? The answer is as follows: class struggle, of which he is oblivious. What he perceives as the mass of a people's lack of interest in war is the oppressed classes' real disinterest in war. This actual real disinterest of the overwhelming majority of a warring people in war leads Einstein to make the desperate supposition that there are dark and appalling drives whose outbreak does not require any reasons worthy of discussion. In reality, however, it is not the overwhelming majority that determines the destinies of a nation in capitalism; their interests do not form a basis for large-scale campaigns: these masses are compelled to act without reason and 'without interests'. They are in the hands of the leading stratum, subjected to it through violence and ideology, compelled by the force of its organisation as well as by printed paper and wild talk to act as if they, the oppressed majority, had a real interest in war. The readiness to engage in bloody initiatives is not the same as bloodthirstiness; bloodthirstiness is simply its degenerate form. So, real interests are there, but only those of a relatively small stratum, which compels the entire nation to act in a way that serves those interests. The struggle of classes, consequent on the discrepancies between the material interests of the various classes, conceals the true, always utterly real, material reason for war (which belongs to the ruling stratum); on the other hand, class struggle actually provides that reason. As long as the oppressed class cannot get rid of its tormentor, war offers its only prospect for improving its lot – and sometimes even offers it the prospect of getting rid of its tormentor itself. After all, it hopes that it will be able, by and large, to share in the potential booty, even if it is the partner who will, of course, be deceived. (It is encouraged to have such hopes by printed paper and wild talk, and intellectuals are interested – materialistically and idealistically – in printing paper and talking wildly.) Above all, however, that real economic oppression by other competing states which causes wars is felt more painfully and directly by the oppressed class than by the leading stratum itself. The oppressed class can always be persuaded that a major part of its oppression is oppression from abroad. Its readiness to go to the utmost extremes can be explained by its appalling situation. Its situation is always intolerable. It must try any means, and must not shirk any expense, however large it may be. The unceasing, predatory attacks of the ruling class on the ruled produce in the latter a certain nihilism which attracts the attention of intellectuals who no longer notice this constant war.

['*Einstein–Freud*', BFA 21/588–9.]

Written 1933. This essay comments on a pamphlet entitled *Why War?* produced by Albert Einstein and Sigmund Freud. In 1931, the 'Comité permanent des Lettres et des Arts de la Société et des Nations' invited the International Institute for Intellectual Co-operation of the League of Nations to encourage leading thinkers to engage in collaborative projects. Einstein was invited to contact an interlocutor of his own choosing, and he invited Freud to engage in a consideration of the inevitability of war. Einstein wrote a letter on 30 July 1932 in which he posed the question as to whether humanity could be freed from the fate of war, and Freud replied in September of that year. Both letters were published in Paris in March 1933 in *Why War?* and are reprinted in Sigmund Freud, *Civilization, Society and Religion*, The Penguin Freud Library (Volume 12), Harmondsworth, 1991 (pp. 343–62). Brecht's essay responds to Einstein's ideas only; the reference to 'printed paper' relates to Einstein's claim that intellectuals are particularly susceptible to mass hysteria because they work on the basis of printed texts instead of being firmly grounded in direct experience.

Part Three

Nazism and Anti-Fascism 1933–1939

(European Exile)

Introduction to Part Three

The writings in this section and the next date from the period of Brecht's Scandinavian exile. Brecht left Germany immediately after the Reichstag Fire in February 1933, and soon settled in Svendborg, Denmark; but although the subsequent years may appear reasonably settled, in fact Brecht travelled about a great deal throughout the 1930s – to Moscow, Paris, London, amongst others: to promote his plays and organise productions, to participate in political events, to consider alternatives for himself and his family, and generally to maintain and to establish contacts in the literary, cultural and political worlds. These are the years of Fascism in Europe, before the outbreak of war; and it is with Fascism and with the threat of war that the writings of this section are overwhelmingly concerned. Before considering them more closely, however, it is worth making a few general remarks about this period of Brecht's creative, intellectual and political life.

The events of 1933 represented an appalling fracture in the social, cultural and political life of Germany. Brecht's own intellectual and artistic development was violently interrupted, and of the concerns and impulses of the later Weimar years many could never be resumed. The experimentalism of the *Lehrstücke* and the radical Marxist perspectives on cultural theory were, for example, things to which Brecht was not ever fully to return. Moreover, from 1933 until his return to Germany in 1949, Brecht was more or less cut off from the comforts, and the demands, of an established literary scene; in exile, the theatres, the publics, the publishers and so on were a pretty fragmented, endangered, amateur hotchpotch, in comparison with the intense and highly organised cultural life of Berlin in the years before Nazism.

Very broadly speaking, anti-Fascist exile might be said to have had, beyond this very real disjunction, two further consequences for Brecht's thought; and they are somewhat contradictory ones. In the first place, it can be argued that, paradoxically, exile liberated him from the possibly rather narrow exigencies of the life of a successful author in Berlin. Freed from the demands of an immediate 'literary field', Brecht's theoretical speculations took wing. This is particularly noticeable in the writings on theatre, for it is exactly these years, in the near absence of a real theatre, which see the fuller elaboration of the theory of 'epic theatre' in all its details. Nearly one-third of John Willett's collection, *Brecht on Theatre*, is from these six years (1933–9): including the classic texts on Chinese acting, on music in the epic theatre, and the critiques of Aristotle and empathy, and of Stanislavsky (*Brecht on Theatre*, pp. 65–159). In the second place, however, there were at the same time also urgent and very immediate practical concerns. The absence of a familiar public meant that Brecht had to grapple with the problem of how to reach any audience at all; it is, crucially, amidst the ruminations on *Round Heads and Pointed Heads*, one of the very few plays of which he was able to supervise any sort of production in these years, that his theatre-theoretical ideas come back down to earth.[1] Brecht's letters from the period betray the sudden prominence of more mundane practical worries too: where to live, how to maintain contact with friends and colleagues, how to provide for family and associates, and so on. Most importantly, the immediate political struggle in Europe made its own urgent demands for practical responses and real political contributions. There is no point in being a political writer if you cannot keep pace with the political demands of the present. Of course, there are continuities with earlier concerns as well, but it is Nazism, the analysis of Fascism and the deliberations on how the intellectual and the writer should resist that dominate Brecht's writings of the later 1930s: in plays, in poems, and in the essays of this section.

Although we have created a division between the writings on Nazism and anti-Fascism in this part, and those on realism and formalism in the next, this is to some degree artificial. It was the struggle against Fascism and the context of the political role of the

Soviet Union, which gave the debate about the proper artistic means its urgency. The proximity of reflections on theatre aesthetics and the analysis of Fascism is illustrated by the dialogue 'On the Theatricality of Fascism' (no. 51). And there is no real rupture between Brecht's concerns in 'Five Difficulties in Writing the Truth' (no. 39), a classic Marxist contribution to the development of an aesthetics of resistance, and in 'Breadth and Variety of the Realist Mode of Writing' (no. 54). Both are concerned with the 'truth' of literature, and with the capacity of art to contribute to the political struggle, in particular the current struggle against Fascism.

Behind the simple chronological order of the texts of Part Three there is a backdrop of political events. The Reichstag Fire and the move against the political opposition, the Nazi social and economic programme, the anti-Semitic campaign, the murder of Röhm, the Abyssinia crisis, the occupation of the Rhineland, the Spanish Civil War, the Moscow Trials, the Austrian *Anschluss*, the Japanese invasion of China, Scandinavian 'neutrality', the threat of war: these provide both the framework for, and the subjects of Brecht's political essays. But a proper reading requires also a sensitivity to the contexts in which these essays might reach a public. Some of the pieces in this section, notably those about the Soviet Union (nos 47 and 48), were written for private clarification or were perhaps drafts of letters, intended for a small and specific readership. Others are the texts of speeches delivered on large public occasions and subsequently published (the two contributions to the Writers' Congresses in 1935 and 1937, nos 40 and 43). Between these extremes, we have articles for the exile press and a large number of what are apparently unfinished draft articles or speeches, composed with some public in mind. No doubt some things remained unpublished (in many cases until long after Brecht's death) simply because they were unfinished, or because of a lack of opportunities in exile; in other cases, however, Brecht was clearly aware of the need to be cautious, so as not to damage the anti-Fascist front (whatever he thought privately about some of their supposed allies) or, in the case of the thoughts on the Soviet Union, so as not to put himself or his friends in unnecessary danger.

The general outlines of Brecht's analysis of Nazism and of Fascism are quickly sketched. He was determined to reject any notion that this was just some sort of cultural aberration, a sudden outbreak of barbarism, an unmotivated inhumanity. In his speech at the 1935 International Writers' Congress (no. 40) he insisted that a proper investigation of the causes would lead directly to a recognition of the underlying evil: the conditions of property ownership in a capitalist society. In 'Five Difficulties in Writing the Truth' (no. 39) he was even more explicit: Fascism is simply 'the most naked, brazen, oppressive, and deceitful form of capitalism'. This was consistent with the analysis offered by the Communist International in 1933. However, Brecht continued to describe Fascism as a 'late stage of capitalism' even long after that thesis had been modified by the more pragmatically minded ideologues of the Communist Party. Especially after the proclamation by the Moscow-dominated Comintern of a new policy of a Popular Front against Fascism – which, it was hoped, might unite all the opposition forces, including first of all the Social Democrats, and then the bourgeois political parties and even the churches – it was strategically naive to insist so loudly on the capitalist roots of Fascism. Brecht's negotiations with the changing policy of the Comintern reveal some inconsistencies. There are variations between more public and private statements. But his speech at the 1935 Congress, which was a Popular Front event if ever there was one, was, in the context, shockingly outspoken.

There is some evidence of a more Popular Front thinking in the short essay on the League of Human Rights (no. 38) and in the scenes of *Fear and Misery of the Third Reich*, but even here the class analysis dominates – as it does from the first sentences of the 'Unpolitical Letters' (no. 35) to the last essays of the 1930s (e.g. no. 50). Much of the detail of Brecht's observation and critique of Nazism remains persuasive – far more so than either the more dogmatic, but still less consistent, judgements of official Soviet spokesmen, or the baffled mystifications of many non-Communists, such as Thomas Mann, who struggled to explain Nazism in terms of the German cultural 'soul'. Nevertheless, the emphasis on the social and economic unquestionably obscured for him other aspects of National Socialist ideology, above all its racism.

One striking feature of Brecht's response to Nazism is his interest in a critique of Fascist language, above all in his pieces on Nazi slogans and his parallel 'restoration of the truth' behind Nazi speeches (nos 36 and 37). These are demonstrations of textual criticism and discourse analysis as a sort of political behaviour. Language is treated, not as a transparent medium, but rather as a series of ruses which have to be unmasked if we are to get at a different, more 'real' truth. The 'truth' itself (as in 'Five Difficulties in Writing the Truth') is not an idealist absolute, but a contingent category, its value (like that of art in general) dependent upon its 'usefulness' to the revolutionary proletariat, its propagation dependent on cunning. And it is not only the overtly linguistic-critical pieces that express such a mistrust of the discourse of Fascist politics. Brecht's general strategy of deflating Nazi pretensions and the whole satirical thrust of much of his writing at this time are conceived as weapons against the linguistic bombast and propagandistic deceit with which, according to Brecht, Nazism bamboozles the German people, but which is, at the same time, the weakness to be exploited:

Given the immense power of the regime
Its camps and torture cellars
Its well-fed policemen
Its intimidated or corrupt judges
Its card indexes and lists of suspected persons
Which fill whole buildings to the roof
One would think they wouldn't have to
Fear an open word from a simple man.

But their Third Reich recalls
The house of Tar, the Assyrian, that mighty fortress
Which, according to the legend, could not be taken by any army, but
When one single, distinct word was spoken inside it
Fell to dust.

(*Poems*, pp. 297–8)

The large number of satirical pieces (especially nos 35, 41 and 49) leads one also to suspect that Brecht planned, at various times, several different extended works of political satire. The 'Unpolitical Letters', for example, may have been planned as a work of satirical political travel writing (in the style of Heine's 'travel books'), with critical sketches of the attitudes in the countries neighbouring Germany through which Brecht passed in 1933. In the event only the piece on Austria was ever completed, as far as we know. Satire was a mode of writing in which Brecht felt at home. *Round Heads and Pointed Heads* might be described as his first extended work of anti-Fascist satire; the mid-1930s saw the composition also of the series of poems called the 'German Satires' in the *Svendborg Poems*, which have a number of close points of comparison with these prose pieces; and they were followed at the end of the 1930s and beyond by the *Refugee Conversations* and the last of his Scandinavian plays, *The Resistible Rise of Arturo Ui*.

The essays on Nazism, then, are attempts to get a hold on developments in the real political world, by means of description and analysis, and to intervene in the political process by unmasking the contradictions and the cracks in the Fascist world-view and its articulation by the Nazi leaders. They may be understood as an effort of what Brecht called '*eingreifendes Denken*' (interventionist thinking), which should lead on, more or less directly, to action. As such they represent a kind of applied philosophy. To separate the 'philosophical' from the 'political' writings is as misleading as to attempt to differentiate between the aesthetic and the political. The 'Speech on the Power of Resistance of Reason' (no. 45) demonstrates this strand of Brecht's thinking most clearly, and seems to manifest a rather extraordinary, if still cautious, confidence that 'right thinking' might save the world.

It was in this spirit that Brecht took such interest in the many more or less loose alliances and organisations of the anti-Fascists, and participated in congresses and public proclamations. He followed with interest Willi Münzenberg's plan to establish an archive in Paris for the study of Fascism, he was involved in efforts to promote a society for materialist dialectics, he suggested to

Johannes R. Becher that there should be a writers' conference, or an informal academy to edit an encyclopaedia of anti-Fascist linguistic criticism or a dictionary of Fascism.[2] He sought contact, not only with his old friends and political allies, but also, albeit not very successfully, with such international figures as Wells, Shaw, Huxley and Gide. This was a global struggle. And he contributed to the International Writers' Congresses for the Defence of Freedom in 1935 and 1937 (see nos 40 and 43). At the first of these, in Paris, some 250 writers from 37 countries attended, to discuss Fascism, the world economic crisis and the Soviet Five-Year Plan.

It was perhaps Brecht's disappointment at the failures, as he saw it, of these initiatives, which led to the satirical critique of the activities of intellectuals (he called it 'Tuism') which he developed above all in American exile. The intelligentsia had failed to engage in the sort of dialogic-dialectic collective intellectual effort, the interventionist right-thinking, which Brecht had sought to promote.

It is particularly difficult to get a clear picture of Brecht's attitude to the Soviet Union and to Stalin in this period. His early enthusiasm is clear enough; and in later poems and in *Me-Ti* the criticism of Stalin himself, and of Stalinist state bureaucracy, begins to emerge quite strongly. At the time of the purges themselves, however (from late 1936), Brecht was much more restrained, or ambiguous. He visited Moscow in 1935, at the invitation of Piscator, and clearly hoped for a great deal from the contacts he made there. In 1936 he became a nominal editor of the Moscow literary journal *Das Wort* (*The Word*) (with Lion Feuchtwanger and Willi Bredel). This was a loosely Comintern organ, but launched with a more international, Popular Front image. Although it is unclear quite how much Brecht could ever contribute from his distant exile in Denmark, the journal became the site for some of the contributions to the 'realism debate' (see Part Four), and also published Brecht's speech at the Second International Writers' Congress (no. 43) and, in its last numbers in 1938, scenes from Brecht's anti-Nazi cycle, *Fear and Misery of the Third Reich*. As late as 1937, on the twentieth anniversary of the Revolution, Brecht wrote a hymn in apparently extravagant praise of the Soviet Union: 'O great October of the working classes!'[3] He was clearly concerned not to give the enemies of Communism comfort by contributing to the splits on the left; unity in the face of Fascism was all-important. But even in semi-private documents (nos 47 and 48) he seems desperately concerned not to get drawn into anti-Soviet remarks. The effort to make sense of the show trials and executions, even if Brecht may cast doubt on some aspects of the Stalinist campaign, presents a glimpse of the Communist intellectual twisting and turning (his own 'Tuism' in the name of 'dialectics') while refusing to recognise the poisonous rot at the heart of the Soviet system. Nonetheless, we should not doubt Brecht's real consternation at the news which was coming out of Russia. Letters reveal his dismay at the news of the arrest of old friends, Ernst Ottwalt and Carola Neher; and in the context of an appeal to Lion Feuchtwanger for help for Neher, we read the telling request: 'Incidentally, please treat this request of mine confidentially, because I neither want to sow distrust of the Soviet Union nor give certain people a chance of accusing me of doing so.'[4] Other victims of the purges included Brecht's old acquaintances Sergei Tretiakov, Bernhard Reich and Asya Lacis, and his two Comintern contacts Béla Kun and Vilis Knorin. Linked with the purges, and itself shot through with xenophobia, was the increasingly strict imposition of the Socialist Realist aesthetic, blessed by Stalin himself, against which Brecht protested vehemently (in a number of the pieces in the next section); again, he thought it wiser not to publish the more outspoken ripostes at the time. By the time of the arrest of the publisher of *Das Wort*, Mikhail Koltsov, in December 1938, whom Brecht describes in his *Journal* as his 'last Russian connection over there', his private assessment of the situation is bleak: 'Literature and art are up the creek, political theory has gone to the dogs, what is left is a thin, bloodless, proletarian humanism propagated by officialdom.'[5]

There are two other key works from this period, which to some extent overlap with and complement the material in Parts Three and Four. The first is the book of parables and aphorisms, *Me-Ti* (mostly 1935–42), which represents a particularly crucial chapter in Brecht's reflections on Marx, Lenin, Korsch and others, as well as on Stalin and recent developments in the Soviet Union. The second is *The Messingkauf Dialogues*, which he began writing shortly before he left Denmark in spring 1939, and which are centrally concerned with theatre aesthetics. In the context of Nazism, Stalinism and European war, these notebooks and the *Journal*, which he began to maintain conscientiously over this period, became more private repositories for the artistically experimental and politically sensitive thoughts which he continued to develop as he fled through Scandinavia and the Soviet Union to the United States in the years 1939 to 1941.

---

[1] This process is described in *Collected Plays*, vol. 4.

[2] Pieces such as nos 36 and 37 may possibly have been conceived as contributions to such a project; compare, e.g., *Letters*, pp. 136–7 and 189, and *Journals*, p. 31.

[3] Shortly afterwards collected in the *Svendborg Poems*, BFA 12/45.

[4] *Letters*, p. 255; and compare other letters of February and June 1937.

[5] *Journals*, p. 20.

35

Extracts from 'Unpolitical Letters'

After a series of disappointments, caused by enemies within and without, the lower-middle classes of my home country, the numerous cast of small businessmen, shopkeepers, subaltern officers, painters and decorators, students, etc., decided it was time for great deeds. Some of their own people had explained to them that their miserable situation – they were all more or less bankrupt – was the product of an all too materialistic attitude to life; and so they now hoped to construct an existence worthy of a human life by means of a powerful effort of idealism, that is to say, by an unlimited eagerness for self-sacrifice. They did not doubt that something was to be gained from this, for each individual. They recognised that, without leadership, they were just a flock of sheep. 'If we're not firmly bullied, yelled at, slapped across the face, we'll stay as we are, miserable snivellers,' they said, 'it just won't do.' Luckily, a Führer was to hand and they handed power over to him. Every expectation was now directed towards the question, what did he have in store for them? The Führer had so far only mentioned his programme in passing, in part because otherwise unworthy rogues might have pilfered it, in part for other reasons. His followers had not asked him, on the one hand because that might have damaged the Führer principle, on the other because they reckoned: what use is the finest programme if you don't have the power to put it into practice! As soon as the Führer had the power he announced the programme: it turned out to be a very festive programme. To a large, very large, extent it consisted of ceremonies and celebrations, but there were other events as well, of two sorts: above all the unity of the people was to be manufactured. This unity had left something to be desired for a few decades, more precisely a few centuries, since things had not been going equally well for all parts of the nation: some earned too much, others a little and the rest hardly anything. That had caused disunity. It was to be stopped. According to the Führer's grand idea, it was *no longer* to cause disunity. The other, substantial, part of the Führer's programme consisted in draining a few marshes. (Since, unfortunately, there were no marshes in the country, they had to be created first before this great cultural deed could be undertaken.) In addition, in order to give the finances a boost, the houses were to be repaired. The Führer had originally been a house painter, so this idea occurred to him almost naturally; every painter knows that there's nothing so profitable as house repairs. The execution of this vast programme in its three parts demanded, of course, huge efforts on the part of the entire populace, as well as that idealism I mentioned. Without that kind of idealism you cannot embark on programmes like this.

These developments, accompanied by a few little incidents, rendered my own presence in the country problematic. In my nature I am incapable of surrendering myself confidently to great and inspiring feelings, I am not up to energetic leadership, so I began to feel quite superfluous. Asking around in my immediate circle, and on a couple of visits, I became aware that now, as happens from time to time in the life of a nation, a truly great epoch was dawning, where people like me would just mess up the bigger picture. They promised, it is true, to protect me against the rage of the people in a camp specially constructed for the purpose, and even to give me a *völkisch* re-education, but I felt, nonetheless, that such offers were no evidence of a real love for me or for my sort. Besides, I wanted to pursue my studies on human progress and culture, and so I left the country and took to the road.

On my travels I came first to Vienna. [. . .]

At the time everyone was talking about the events in my home country. People reacted with horror to the persecution of the Jews and the book burnings. There was a consensus that a new age of barbarism was approaching. The horrors were the consequences of a despicable warlike spirit which had, in some mysterious way, achieved the upper hand. It was a natural catastrophe, comparable with an earthquake. Some nineteen years previously something similar had occurred, another natural catastrophe; the whole world, at least insofar as it was civilised, had attempted for four long years, not without some success, to butcher one another, following yet again some dark, barbaric urge. Today, as then, the voice of reason, common sense and humanity was drowned out by a terrible, bestial voice, the voice of barbarism. In one part of humanity, perhaps the young, or the uneducated, a quite particularly warlike spirit seemed to slumber, which, awakened, was fit to turn the continent into a slaughterhouse. There were, however, guilty ones. Certain wealthy types and parties had not undertaken enough to banish this spirit and to maintain the rule of the nobler spirit. Their weakness and corruption was generally recognised and deplored. However, even if the consequences of the petty bourgeois revolt were painted in the blackest colours, and a long reign of terror prophesied, people were generally still convinced that now, as in the great war nineteen years ago, a few lone voices of reason in the coffee houses would prevail, the mild, the sublime, the incorruptible voices of humanity. These voices, it was said, could never be fully silenced, not by any earthly power. Some of the owners of such voices had already carefully transported them abroad, so that they could continue to be heard. I myself was recognised by some, and congratulated on my departure. [...]

I should not, however, wish that my, possibly unhappy, depiction [of the dealing in opinions in the Viennese coffee houses] should lead people to conclude that I despise these people. I know very well that their inaction proves little against them, and I don't believe they can be reproached with more than this. The society in which they live does not allow a substantially more useful occupation. Should they be judges and sit in judgement over poor devils who steal bread out of hunger, or doctors who write out useless (if cheap) prescriptions, or architects who build houses in which some human hyena can live in sixteen rooms, or those where twelve people huddle in the kitchen in order to finance that luxury? Some of those who sit here collecting opinions may well have the frailties which are required to occupy public office, and may even be prepared to do the deals which are demanded, it may be but trivial reasons which hold them back; but others here are better people all the same, and even those I've mentioned were prevented by a generous fate from committing real acts of shame. What I objected to in their ideas was, briefly, the lack of prospects. The images these good folk made of reality were perhaps authentic, but they were no help. One might well describe the appearance of these new masters as barbaric, and call that which drove them a dark urge, but what was gained by such explanations? These explanations sufficed perhaps to induce a certain melancholy, but were hardly designed to teach how we should overcome the situation. People may judge me as they will, but in the thought processes of the banished and endangered I increasingly felt the absence of any radical advantage over the thought processes of the banishers and persecutors. Indeed, the one was the raw voice of barbarism, it was raw and stupid, the other was the voice of culture, it was mellifluous but also stupid. The one lot had many weapons and used them, the others had only reason as a weapon, and did not use it. I departed from the land of culture more depressed than I had arrived – from the land of barbarism.

['*Unpolitische Briefe*', BFA 22/11–17.]

This is part of a larger, uncompleted piece (a surviving plan lists eleven parts of which this is a shortened version of just one). Brecht spent some time in Vienna in March 1933 and then moved on to Switzerland and then Denmark. The essay probably dates from the autumn of 1933 and may be one of the first pieces he wrote in Denmark. Many subsequent projects go over similar ground, in terms both of themes and of motifs.

A satirical nickname for Hitler, in reference to his one-time artistic pretensions, was '*der Anstreicher*', the house painter. Brecht makes frequent allusions to this and to Hitler's ability to 'paint over the cracks'. A programme of repairs was indeed a part of the early Nazi work creation programme. The 'marshes' are likewise a recurrent Brechtian image for the economic morass into which capitalism and Nazism led the German people (compare *Round Heads and Pointed Heads*, *Fear and Misery of the Third Reich*, etc.).

36

Fascist Slogans

What Does the Sentence 'Economic Thinking is the Death of All National Idealism' Mean?

1 One has to realise clearly that here the word 'idealism' has nothing to do with the great and ancient doctrine which shows how all real things depend on eternal spiritual laws, nor with the behaviour which strives to change real existence by changing consciousness; instead, the word 'idealism' must be understood here in its vulgar meaning, that used primarily by the petty bourgeoisie. Here it means the will and the ability to subordinate certain material interests to others, mostly described as spiritual but always as 'higher'. Understood in these terms, examples of an idealist would be a national leader who suffers persecution because of an idea, or at least shares out his salary, an inventor who invents something without consideration for his physical well-being, a servant or vassal who, unconcerned with recompense, serves his master out of 'loyalty', a factory owner who ruins himself for the sake of the fatherland, the owner of a large estate who settles poor farmers on his land without demanding any rent, a general who rushes to the front line without being commanded to do so by the rule book, a businessman who makes sure that his customers have money left over for their savings accounts and then, composed and cheerful in the knowledge that he has done his duty, waits for the bailiff. In short, 'idealism' here means the willingness to make sacrifices.

2 If the sentence were '*Economic thinking is the death of all idealism*', then it would, of course, be pointless, for then it would only be a primitive interpretation or paraphrase of the word 'idealism' itself. Then it could only mean 'idealism is when one does not think in material terms', so 'if one thinks in material terms, then one is not an idealist'. The word 'national' gives the sentence its meaning. It means: behaviour directed primarily towards material concerns destroys the kind of idealism (willingness to make sacrifices) which seeks to preserve the interests of the *Volk*.

['*Was meint der Satz "Das wirtschaftliche Denken ist der Tod jedes völkischen Idealismus"?*', BFA 22/57–8.]

The slogan '*Das wirtschaftliche Denken ist der Tod jedes völkischen Idealismus*' appeared in an article entitled 'Adolf Hitler's Answer to Chancellor von Papen' in the Nazi newspaper, the *Völkischer Beobachter*, on 21 October 1932. Brecht was using this and other sources in 1934 as a basis for reworking the language of his play *Round Heads and Pointed Heads* as a critique of Fascist demagogy. In this piece we have rendered the German nationalist term, *völkisch* (i.e., 'pertaining to the *Volk*'), as 'national'.

On the Slogan 'Common Interest Takes Precedence Over Self-Interest'

The slogan 'Common interest takes precedence over self-interest' is now said to have appeared on high denomination banknotes. This is a rumour circulating amongst the people. Of course, no one knows anything about it for certain. No one has ever seen a banknote with a high denomination, so perhaps it is all just a folk tale. If it were true, however, then it would be a great honour for the slogan.

It is one of the National Socialists' most popular slogans, a true feast for the ears. Many people even consider it a genuinely socialist slogan.

In a socialist system there is no contradiction between self-interest and the common interest. There is no fundamental difference between the interests. There are no groups fighting each other with knives because one group can only live well if the other lives badly. In the socialist system, the general public does not build motorways on which only a few individuals can drive, so that expensive motorways are finished whilst cheap cars are not. Nor does the general public drive on these motorways one day after all, namely in tanks, so that a few individuals can make their war profits. In the socialist system, the individual's work benefits both himself and the general public simultaneously, in fact, he helps the public precisely by helping himself. This system is designed so that anyone who helps himself also helps the general public and so that the general public helps itself by helping the individual, and this is precisely what makes it a socialist system. In the socialist system, the slogan 'Common interest takes precedence over self-interest' is therefore surplus to requirements, and what counts instead is the slogan 'Self-interest is the common interest'.

For the popular, honest-sounding, pithy sentence 'Common interest takes precedence over self-interest' is a trickster. It screams incessantly that it is full of the noblest intentions, that its great concern for the general public prevents it from sleeping at night, that it is just not held in sufficient regard, in sufficiently general regard, that everything will turn out well if, at last, it is introduced, namely into high society. It is correct that it has not been introduced into high society, amongst the well-to-do, for they do not take it seriously; there it plays no role, even the Party big shots want nothing to do with it. But even if it were introduced there, still nothing would improve. The many millions of individuals would still have to slave away, until eventually they were herded into the tanks and trenches. People would tell them, possibly for 30,000 years, that this benefits the general public, without them ever discovering who this mystical general public is. Each individual would know, when he looked at his wage packet, that he had not gained anything from all of his long week's work, and when a family received the short official letter saying that their father or son had died in battle, then they would know that he had helped neither himself nor them, but people would still say that the general public had benefited.

So who is this general public, which is supposed to benefit from the individuals, whose public interest is supposed to have priority over their self-interest? Is it perhaps just that bunch of people who spread this slogan, 'Common interest takes precedence over self-interest', and who each year devour 20 thousand million marks out of the 60 thousand million mark national income: the National Socialist Party?

[*Über den Satz "Gemeinnutz geht vor Eigennutz"'*, BFA 22/58–9.]

Written 1934. Possibly a sketch for a planned encyclopaedia of Fascist language. The slogan was used to promote the idea of a *Volksgemeinschaft* (the Nazi 'classless' community of the nation) and was the title of a later speech by Hermann Göring. The phrase actually goes back to Montesquieu. See also no. 40, below.

37

On Restoring the Truth

In times when deception is demanded and errors are encouraged, the thinker strives to correct whatever he reads and hears. Whatever he reads and hears, he says aloud quietly, and as he says it he corrects it. Sentence by sentence, he replaces the false statements with true ones. He practises this for so long that he is no longer able to read and hear differently.

The thinker proceeds from sentence to sentence so that, slowly but utterly, he corrects what he has heard and read in its full coherent form. In this way he leaves nothing out. At the same time, however, he places correct sentences alongside incorrect ones, without concerning himself with their context. He thus ruptures the context of the incorrect sentences, in the knowledge that a context often gives sentences an illusion of correctness, an illusion which comes from the fact that, in context, proceeding from one incorrect sentence, one can still deduce several proper conclusions. The process of deduction is then correct, but the sentences are not correct.

The thinker does not act like this simply in order to establish that deception and errors are being perpetrated. He wishes to master the nature of the deception and of the errors. When he reads: 'A strong nation is less easily attacked than a weak one', he does not need to alter it but to augment it: 'but it attacks more easily'. When he hears that wars are necessary, then he adds under which circumstances they are necessary, as well as: for whom.

1 *General Göring on the triumph over Communism in Germany* (quoted from the *Nationalzeitung*, Basel, 12.12.34)

Verbatim report of the speech	*Restoration of the truth*
It is precisely in an account of the defence against and ultimate triumph over the Communist threat, that the methods of National Socialism, which are opposed to those of Communism in every respect, will be most clearly recognised.	It is precisely in a public representation of the defence against and ultimate triumph over the threat that, under the rule of the working sector of the population, the abuse of property for the purposes of exploitation might be abolished, that the methods of National Socialism, which, since they are mendacious, are entirely opposed to those of Communism, will be most clearly recognised.
The German government must reserve for itself the total freedom	The German government must reserve for itself the total freedom – from the moral demands of other capitalist states and also of capitalist groups at home – to use the
to use the means which it considers appropriate,	means which it considers appropriate, namely means like the arson attack on the Reichstag building designed to imply the guilt of the
and in so doing it can take no consideration of the advice of others.	Communists, and in so doing it can take no consideration of the advice of others.
I refuse to deal yet again with the accusations which have been levied against the	I refuse to deal yet again with the charges which have been levied against the government

government and against me personally in connection with the Reichstag Fire, especially in view of the fact that the High Court of the Reich

has examined the events surrounding the Reichstag Fire with painstaking care and has made its decision.

I characterise the alleged testament
of the former squad leader Ernst
as a crude forgery.

We were completely determined, after our seizure of power

to strike Communism in such a way that it should never again recover in Germany from this blow. To this end we needed no Reichstag Fire.
To implement our measures

and against me personally in connection with the Reichstag Fire, especially in view of the fact that the High Court of the Reich, which has since been relieved of responsibility for such trials, has examined the events surrounding the Reichstag Fire with anguish and has made its decision: that the Communists accused by me did not set fire to the Reichstag and that it could not produce the evidence that we did this ourselves.

I characterise the testament, the authenticity of which has been attested, of the former squad leader Ernst, whom I had shot, as a crude forgery and thereby act in total freedom from all moral demands, using all the means which are necessary to overcome Communism.

We were completely determined, after our seizure of power in the interest of the property owners,
to strike Communism in such a way that it should never again recover in Germany from this blow. To this end we needed a Reichstag Fire.
To implement our measures against the starving

we needed the instrument of a police force which was utterly reliable and as forceful as possible.
I have created this instrument through the reorganisation of the state police and the establishment of the Gestapo.

we needed the instrument of a police force which was utterly reliable and as willing as possible to use force.
I have created this instrument through the reorganisation of the state police and the establishment of the Gestapo, with the aid of the claim that the Communists and Social Democrats were preparing an uprising.

Commentary
As at the Leipzig trial, General Göring argues in connection with the Reichstag Fire that a sensational task is needed to activate the police and, in so doing, confesses openly to his arson. It seems that he must have enemies within the government.

2   *Christmas message of the Führer's Deputy (Hess) in the year 1934*
(quoted from the *Nationalzeitung*, Basel)

Verbatim report of the speech
With justified pride
in the spirit of selfless sacrifice

Restoration of the truth
With pride
in the attitude of the propertied, who have sacrificed a little of that which had been sacrificed to them already by those without property,

and the willingness of our German *Volk*-comrades to help

and in their willingness to appear as helpers to those who are kept by them in misery,

one may say today:
This Christmas and this winter Germany will not let a single

one may say today:
This Christmas and this winter Germany's propertied classes

one of its children go hungry, will not let a single one of those
without property starve
completely.
This is how Germany's
propertied classes behave
the selfsame children, towards the selfsame people,
who just three years ago who just two years ago
were forced into rabble-rousing were forced by their need into
demonstrations demonstrations
against against
Volk, that sector of the population
which exploits the others,
nation, the talk that people would do
well to defend something which
does not belong to them,
and faith, and religion, which sanctifies
the use of property for the
purposes of exploitation
in support of in support of
Bolshevist chaos. a Bolshevist social order in
which the exploitation of man
by man is impossible.

Today they gratefully accept Today they gratefully accept
their their
Christmas gift Christmas gift, without which
they would starve,
from the hands of those who from the hands of those who
were once presented to them as were once presented to them as
enemies. enemies, because they are
enemies.
In reality, however, it was
mainly poor people who made
Hundreds of thousands, indeed the sacrifices. Hundreds of
millions, of German workers, thousands, indeed millions, of
male and female, German workers, male and
female,

who once gave up their hard-
earned pennies for the idea of
an international community of
classes,

sacrifice them today

for a socialism which is eager to
act and to help,

which embraces a nation.

I know that you Germans, at
home and abroad,

do not expect a political address
from me on Christmas Eve;
indeed, that you do not want
that at all.

And I feel far too full of the
Christmas spirit to want to
concern myself today with
everyday politics and statistics.
But I also know that precisely
the German abroad
can receive no better Christmas
joy than to be made conscious
of this: he needs no longer to be

who once gave up their hard-
earned pennies for the idea of a
community of all people,
without distinctions of fortune
or estate, which would extend
to all the countries of the world,
sacrifice them today, although
they are just as hard to earn,
for a state of affairs in which,
for all eternity, there will be the
great masses of those who need
help and for whom all that is
left over are pittances earned
with difficulty by the exploited,
which only embraces the
population of a single country,
but which threatens all other
countries.

I know that you Germans, as far
as you have property at home
and abroad,

do not expect an address on
Christmas Eve about how we
intend to protect your property;
indeed, that you do not want
that at all.

And I have dined far too well to
want to concern myself today
with everyday politics and the
falsification of statistics.
But I also know that precisely
he who has his property abroad
can receive no better Christmas
joy than to be made conscious
of this: he needs no longer to be

ashamed of his German homeland; indeed, he should be proud of it.	ashamed of his German homeland; indeed, he should be proud of it.
And when foreigners come to Germany as guests, they are full of admiration for what has been achieved here in such a short space of time,	And when foreign exploiters come to Germany, they are full of admiration for what has been achieved here in such a short space of time,
not only in the internal and external transformation of the German people, but also in terms of the tangible and evident works,	not only in the internal and external impoverishment of the German people, but also in terms of the tangible and (in the business section of the newspapers) evident dividends,
which have already resulted from the co-ordination	which have already resulted from the theft of the fruits of their labour and the
and reorganisation of the labour power of the *Volk*.	destruction of the social organisation of the larger section of the population.

Commentary

When one has skimmed the speech and the restoration of the truth, reading from left to right, one should recall that the National Socialists needed to praise the Winter Aid Project, and indeed that was very necessary in view of the immense difficulties which are expressed in the right-hand column (in the restoration). Now, reading from the right column to the left, one can study how the individual concerned carried out his task. Then one sees what sort of a man he is, which class he belongs to, which task this class has taken on itself to solve, and how it is solving it.

['*Über die Wiederherstellung der Wahrheit*', BFA 22/89–96.]

Written December 1934. In the left-hand columns Brecht quotes, almost verbatim, the original newspaper reports of the addresses by Göring and Hess. The reference near the beginning of Göring's speech is to one SA-

Gruppenführer Ernst, who is suspected of having been involved in the execution of the Reichstag Fire. The authenticity of his testament is disputed. The Winter Aid was a collection, and subsequently a direct tax, established by the Nazis in 1933 to help the needy. It was later used to finance rearmament.

38

In the Fight Against Injustice Even Weak Weapons Are of Use

In the year following the war I, like many others, thought that institutions like the League of Human Rights were defunct. I did not go as far as some, who accused this organisation of being downright harmful by awakening the illusion that its methods could actually control the monstrous, unnecessary misery which stems from the wrong system of production, and which can therefore only be eradicated if this system is changed completely. I did not want to go this far, but I too believed that pacifism would achieve nothing, for even though it had no prospect of changing the causes, it still undertook to combat wars, which were only consequential phenomena, and to do so directly, with no beating about the bush, but using only the weakest weapons, such as individual conscientious objection to military service. Then, when Germany began to transform itself into a Fascist state, we saw how both the large and small organisations committed to fighting injustice mobilised. I did not go as far as many, who claimed to be observing a wholesale, long-term collapse of the large-scale organisations which aimed to change the social structure completely, but I too saw the tough and important small-scale activities of frequently disparaged organisations like the League of Human Rights, which actually saved many people, which constantly and untiringly exposed injustice with its small voice, and which galvanised many to return to the struggle. So we saw that the fight against injustice must not only be waged in the most ultimate way, addressing all of its causes, but also in the most general way, i.e., using all the means available, even the most feeble. For even worse than the illusion that it is possible to eradicate unnecessary misery without removing its causes is the illusion that we can fight the causes without their consequences, separately, without recourse to the weakest and most feeble of means. I have seen how knowing about these terrible causes actually prevented many people from combating their terrible consequences.

How can someone who places himself in the hands of the police be surprised, they asked, when he is beaten with cudgels, or when injustice triumphs over someone who appeals to courts like ours? They forgot entirely that one does not need to be surprised in order to complain, and that one's own opinions about the police and courts are not shared by everyone else, and that opinions are certainly not enough to change the police and courts. The slogan still applies: he who wants to resist unnecessary misery cannot afford to relinquish even the weakest of weapons.

['*Man muss das Unrecht auch mit schwachen Mitteln bekämpfen*',
BFA 22/61–2.]

Typescript *c.* 1934. The International League of Human Rights was founded in 1898, the German League in 1919. It was criticised by groups on the left for focusing on Utopian aims and individual rights, without concerning itself with the sort of social order which might make those rights meaningful. It was banned by the Nazis in 1933.

39

Five Difficulties in Writing the Truth

Today anyone who wants to fight lies and ignorance and to write the truth has to overcome at least five difficulties. He must have the *courage* to write the truth, even though it is suppressed everywhere; the *cleverness* to recognise it, even though it is disguised everywhere; the *skill* to make it fit for use as a weapon; the *judgement* to select those in whose hands it will become effective; the *cunning* to spread it amongst them. These difficulties are great for those who write under Fascism, but they also exist for those who were driven out or have fled, indeed, even for those who write in the lands of bourgeois freedom.

1 *The courage to write the truth*

It appears self-evident that the writer should write the truth in the sense that he should not suppress it or hush it up and that he should write nothing which is untrue. He should not give in to the powerful, he should not deceive the weak. Of course, it is very difficult not to give in to the powerful, and very advantageous to deceive the weak. Displeasing the property owners means renouncing property. Relinquishing the payment for work you have done may mean relinquishing the work, and rejecting fame amongst the powerful often means rejecting fame in general. That takes courage. Times of the most extreme oppression are mostly times when the talk is often of great and noble things. It takes courage to speak at times like this of such base and petty things as the food and housing of the workers, right in the middle of a mighty hullabaloo that it is sacrifice that counts. When the farmers are being showered with honours, it takes courage to speak of machines and cheap fodder which would make their honoured work easier. When from every radio station the message screams out that a man without knowledge and education is better than a knowledgeable man, then it takes courage to ask: better for whom? When the talk is of perfect and imperfect races, it takes courage to ask whether hunger and ignorance and war do not produce terrible disfigurations. Equally, it takes courage to say the truth about oneself, the defeated. Many who are persecuted lose the ability to recognise their flaws. To them persecution seems the greatest injustice. The persecutors are, by definition, the bad guys; they, the persecuted, are persecuted because of their goodness. But this goodness has been beaten, defeated and frustrated, and so it was a weak goodness, a poor, unsustainable, unreliable goodness; for it won't do to grant goodness its weakness, like rain its wetness. *To say that the good were defeated, not because they were good, but because they were weak, that takes courage.* Of course, in the struggle with untruth the truth has to be written, and it must not be something general, high-flown, or ambiguous. Indeed, this general, high-flown, ambiguous quality is precisely that of untruthfulness. When it is said of someone that he has spoken the truth, that must mean, in the first place, that several, or many, or just one, have said something different, a lie or something general, but *he* has said the truth, something practical, factual, undeniable, which went to the heart of the matter.

It takes little courage to lament in general the wickedness of the world and the triumph of brutality, and to threaten that the spirit will triumph in the one part of the world where this is still allowed. Many take this as their text and make their entrance as if cannons were trained on them, whereas in fact only opera glasses are trained on them. They yell their universal demands into a world of friends of the harmless. They demand universal justice, for which they have never lifted a finger, and the universal freedom to share in the loot which has long been shared with them anyway. They think only that which sounds beautiful can be true. If the truth is numerical, dry, factual, something which requires effort and study, then it is not truth for them, not something which can bewitch them. They only have the outward demeanour of those who tell the truth. The wretched thing with them is: they do not know the truth.

2 The cleverness to recognise the truth

Since it is difficult to write the truth because it is suppressed everywhere, most people think that whether or not the truth is written depends on convictions. They believe that it only takes courage. They forget the second difficulty, that of *finding* the truth. There can be no suggestion that it is easy to find the truth.

First of all it is not even easy to find out *which* truth is worth saying. For example, at this time, in full view of the whole world, one after another of the great civilised states is sinking into the most extreme form of barbarism. Moreover, everyone knows that the internal war, which is being waged with the most terrible means, may turn any day into external war, which may reduce our part of the world to a heap of rubble. That is without doubt one truth, but there are of course more truths besides. Thus it is not untrue, for example, that chairs have seats and that rain falls down from above. Many poets write truths of this kind. They are like painters who cover the walls of sinking ships with still lifes. Our first difficulty does not exist for them, and yet they have a clear conscience. Undeterred by the powerful, but at the same time not deterred by the screams of the ravaged, they dab at their pictures. The non-sensical nature of their actions produces a 'profound' pessimism in them, which they sell for good prices, and which would actually be more justified in others – in the face of these masters and their sales. And yet it is not even easy to recognise that their truths are the sort which concern chairs or rain; they usually sound quite different, just like truths about important matters. For artistic treatment consists precisely in bestowing importance on something.

It is not until you look more closely that you recognise that they are only saying: a chair is a chair, and: no one can do anything to stop rain falling down from above.

These people have not found the truth which is worth writing about. Others in their turn really do concern themselves with the most urgent tasks, fear neither the powerful nor a life of poverty, but they still cannot find the truth. They lack knowledge. They are full of the old superstition, of famous prejudices often beautifully shaped in the olden days. The world is too complicated for them, they do not know the facts and do not see the connections. Apart from convictions, what is needed is knowledge, which can be acquired, and method, which can be learned. What all writers need in this time of complexity and great changes is a knowledge of the materialist dialectic, of economics, and of history. This can be acquired by means of books and practical instruction, so long as the necessary diligence is there. One can discover many truths by relatively simple means, parts of the truth or evidence which leads to the truth. If one wants to search, then it is good to have a method, but one can also find without a method, indeed, even without searching. But with this haphazard approach one will scarcely achieve a representation of truth such that, on the basis of that representation, people will know how they should act. People who only write down little facts are not in a position to make the things of this world manageable. But the truth has only this purpose, none other. These people are not up to the challenge of writing the truth.

If someone is prepared to write the truth and capable of recognising it, there still remain three difficulties.

3   The skill to make the truth fit for use as a weapon

The truth must be spoken because of the consequences which follow from it for behaviour. One example which shows us the kind of truth from which no consequences or the wrong consequences can be drawn is the widespread view that in some countries terrible conditions prevail, which originate in barbarism. According to this view, Fascism is a wave of barbarism which has descended on several lands with the force of a *natural disaster*.

According to this view, Fascism is a new, third power next to (and above) capitalism and socialism; not only the socialist movement, it is argued, but capitalism also could have continued to prosper, had it not been for Fascism. This is, of course, a Fascist claim, a capitulation to Fascism. Fascism is a historic phase which capitalism has entered into, and in this sense it is both new and at the same time old. In Fascist countries capitalism only survives as Fascism, and *Fascism can only be resisted as capitalism, as the most naked, brazen, oppressive, and deceitful form of capitalism.*

How does someone propose to speak the truth about Fascism, to which he is opposed, if he does not propose to speak out against capitalism, which produces it? What are the practical consequences of his truth supposed to be?

Those who are against Fascism without being against capitalism, who wail about the barbarism that comes from barbarism, are like people who want to eat their share of the calf without the calf being slaughtered. They want to eat veal, but they can't stand the sight of blood. They are satisfied if the butcher washes his hands before he brings out the meat. They are not against the conditions of owner-ship which produce barbarism, just against the barbarism. They raise their voices against barbarism, and they do so in countries in which the same conditions of ownership prevail, but where the butchers still wash their hands before they bring out the meat.

Loud accusations against barbaric measures may work for a short time, for as long as the listeners believe that these sorts of measures would be out of the question in their own countries. Certain countries are in a position to uphold their conditions of ownership with less violent measures than others. For them democracy still performs the services for which others have to call on violence, namely the guarantee of ownership of the means of production. The monopoly capitalism of factories, mines and estates creates barbaric conditions everywhere; however, these are not so immediately visible. Barbarism becomes visible as soon as that monopoly can only be protected by open violence.

Some countries which do not yet need, for the sake of the barbaric monopolies, to renounce the formal guarantees of the rule of law, or such comforts as art, philosophy and literature, particularly enjoy listening to their guests when these accuse their homeland of having renounced such comforts, since they will profit from this in the wars which are expected. Are we to say that such people have recognised the truth, those, for example, who demand loudly: an unrelenting fight against Germany 'for this is the true home of evil in this age, the branch offices of hell, the abode of the Antichrist'? We should rather say that they are foolish, helpless and harmful people. For this gossip would lead to the conclusion that the country should be eliminated. The whole country with all its people, for poison gas does not seek out the guilty ones when it kills.

The thoughtless man, who does not know the truth, expresses himself in generalisations, in high-flown and vague language. He blathers on about 'the' Germans, he whinges about Evil, and even with the best will his listener cannot know what to do. Should he decide not to be a German? Will hell disappear, if he is good? The talk about the barbarism that comes from barbarism is also of this ilk. According to this view, barbarism comes from barbarism, and comes to an end by means of civilised behaviour, which comes from education. That is all terribly general, not said for the sake of the consequences for action, and essentially said to no one.

Such accounts show only a few links in the causal chain and depict certain motive forces as uncontrollable forces. Such accounts contain a lot of obscurity, concealing the forces which cause catastrophes. Cast just a little light on the matter, and suddenly human beings appear as the perpetrators of the catastrophes! For we live in an age where man's destiny is man.

Fascism is not a natural disaster which can simply be understood from human 'nature'. But even in the case of natural disasters there are methods of depiction which are worthy of man because they appeal to his ability to resist.

After a great earthquake which destroyed Yokohama, many American magazines published photographs depicting a field of rubble. Underneath was the caption 'steel stood', and indeed, anyone, who at first glance had only seen ruins, noticed – now that the caption had drawn attention to them – that several tall buildings had remained standing. Of all the possible depictions of an earthquake, the ones of unparalleled importance are those by the construction engineers, those which take note of the shifts in the ground, the strength of the tremors, the developing heat, etc., and which lead to constructions which withstand earthquakes. Anyone who wants to describe Fascism and war, the great disasters which are not natural disasters, must produce a practicable form of truth. He must show that these are catastrophes which are brought on the huge masses of working people, who lack their own means of production, by the owners of these means of production.

If one wants to write the truth about terrible conditions successfully, one has to write it in such a way that the avoidable causes of these conditions can be recognised. Once the avoidable causes are recognised, the terrible conditions can be resisted.

4 *The judgement to select those in whose hands the truth becomes effective*

Owing to the centuries-old customs of trading written goods on the market of opinions and descriptions, so that the writer was relieved of the worry over what to do with the written text, the writer had the impression that his client or patron, the middleman, was passing on his written work to everyone. He thought: I speak, and those who want to listen will hear me. In reality he spoke; and those who could pay heard him. What he said was not heard by everyone, and those who did hear it did not want to hear everything. On this subject a lot has been said already, although it is still too little; I only want to emphasise here that 'writing for someone' has turned into simply 'writing'. The truth, however, cannot simply be written; you absolutely have to write it *for someone*, someone who is able to use it. Recognising the truth is a process shared by writers and readers. In order to say what is good, you need to be a good listener and to hear what is good. The truth must be said with calculation and listened to with calculation. And for us writers it is important whom we tell it to and who tells it to us.

We have to tell the truth about the terrible conditions to those for whom these conditions are worst, and we must learn it from them. We need to talk not only to the people who have particular convictions, but also to those people who, by reason of their situation, should share these convictions. And your listeners change continually! Even the hangmen can be spoken to, when the payment for hanging stops coming in, or when the danger becomes too great. The Bavarian peasants were opposed to any revolution, but when the war had lasted long enough and their sons returned home and no longer found a place in the farmyards, then they could be won over for the revolution.

It is important for writers to hit the right tone of truth. Usually you hear a very soft, melancholy tone, the tone of people who could not hurt a fly. Anyone who hears this tone and is in a wretched state becomes more wretched. People who talk like this may not be your enemies, but they are certainly no fellow fighters. The truth is warlike, it does not only fight against untruthfulness, but also against certain people who spread untruth.

5   *The cunning to spread the truth amongst many*

Many, proud that they have the courage to tell the truth, happy to have found it, perhaps tired from the work which it costs to put it in a serviceable form, waiting impatiently for those whose interests they are defending to take hold of it, do not consider it necessary on top of all of this to use especial cunning when spreading the truth. Thus the whole effect of their work often comes to nought. In every age when the truth was suppressed and disguised, cunning was used to spread it. *Confucius* falsified an old patriotic calendar of historical events. He only changed certain words. When it said, 'The ruler of Kun had the philosopher Wan killed because he said this and that', Confucius replaced killed with 'murdered'. If it said that such-and-such a tyrant had been assassinated, he replaced this with 'executed'. By these means Confucius paved the way for a new assessment of history.

Anyone in our times who says *population instead of 'Volk' and land ownership instead of 'soil'* is already denying his support to many lies. He divests the words of their lazy mysticism. The word *Volk* implies a certain unity and hints at common interests, so it should only be used in reference to several *Völker*, for only then is a commonality of interests conceivable. The population of an area of land has different, even opposing interests, and this is a truth which is suppressed. Thus anyone who says 'soil', and describes the fields to nose and eyes by speaking of their earthy scent and their colour, is supporting the lies of the rulers; for what matters is not the fertility of the soil, nor man's love of it, nor his diligence, but instead principally the price of grain and the price of labour. The people who draw the profits from the soil are not those who harvest the grain, and the scent of the clods of earth is unknown on the stock exchanges. They reek of something different. On the contrary, 'landownership' is the right word; it is less deceptive. For the word 'discipline', wherever oppression rules, the word 'obedience' should be used, because discipline is possible even without rulers and so has a more noble quality than obedience. And better than the word 'honour' are the words 'human dignity'. So that the individual does not vanish so easily from our field of vision. After all, we know what sort of lowlife will rush forward to be allowed to defend the honour of a people! And how wastefully those who are well-fed distribute honours on those who, in feeding them, go hungry. Confucius's cunning can still be used even today.

Confucius replaced unjustified assessments of national events with justified ones. In *Utopia* the Englishman *Thomas More* described a country in which just conditions prevailed – it was a very different country from the one in which he lived, but it resembled it closely, except for the conditions!

Lenin, under threat from the Tsar's police, wanted to describe the exploitation and oppression of the island Sakhalin by the Russian bourgeoisie. He replaced Russia with Japan and Sakhalin with Korea. The methods of the Japanese bourgeoisie reminded all the readers of those of the Russian bourgeoisie in Sakhalin, but the work was not forbidden, since Japan and Russia were enemies. A lot of things which may not be said in Germany about Germany may be said about Austria.

There are many kinds of cunning which can be used to hoodwink the suspicious state.

Voltaire fought against the Church's belief in miracles by writing a gallant poem about the Maid of Orleans. He described the miracle which must doubtless have occurred for Joan to have remained a virgin in an army and at court and in the company of monks.

By the elegance of his style and the fact that he described erotic adventures, derived from the opulent life of the rulers, he enticed them into exposing the religion which secured them the means for their lax lifestyle. Indeed, by these means he created the possibility that his works would reach those for whom they were intended by illegal routes. The powerful among his readers encouraged or tolerated the circulation of these works. They thus exposed the police, who defended their pleasures on their behalf. And the great *Lucretius* expressly emphasises his high hopes that the beauty of his verses would aid the dissemination of Epicurean atheism.

A high literary standard can indeed serve to protect a message. Often, however, it also arouses suspicion. Then it may be necessary deliberately to pitch it a few notches lower. That happens, for example, when descriptions of poor social conditions are smuggled into the despised genre of the detective novel at unobtrusive points. Such descriptions might entirely justify a detective novel. Far lesser considerations led the great *Shakespeare* to lower the tone in the speech of Coriolanus's mother, in which she opposes her son who is marching against his home city, a speech which he deliberately fashions so that it lacks force – he wanted Coriolanus to be stopped from carrying out his plan, not by real reasons or by being profoundly moved, but by the lethargy with which he succumbs to an old habit. In Shakespeare we also find a model of cunningly spread truth in Antony's speech at Caesar's corpse. He emphasises unceasingly that Caesar's murderer Brutus is an honourable man, but he also describes his deed, and the description of this deed is more impressive than the description of its perpetrator; the orator thus allows himself to be defeated by the facts themselves; he lends them a greater rhetorical force than he grants 'himself'.

An Egyptian poet, who lived four thousand years ago, used a similar method. It was a period of intense class struggle. With enormous difficulty the hitherto ruling class was fending off its greatest adversary, the section of the population which until then had served it. In the poem a wise man appears at the ruler's court and issues a warning to fight against the enemy within. He describes at length and with urgency the disorder which has arisen as a result of the uprising of the lower classes. The account reads as follows:

'For so it is: the rich are full of complaints and the poor full of joy.
Every city says: let us drive the powerful out of our midst.
For so it is: the public offices are opened and their lists taken away; the
    serfs are becoming masters.
For so it is: the son of a respected man is no longer recognised; the child of
    the mistress becomes the son of her slave.
For so it is: the burghers have been set to work at the millstone. Those who
    never saw the day have emerged into the light.
For so it is: the ebony chests of sacrifice are broken; the precious sesame
    wood is hacked up to make beds.
Behold, the palace has collapsed in one hour.
Behold, the poor of the land have become rich. Behold, he who lacked
    bread now owns a barn; his granary is filled with the goods of another.
Behold, it does a man good to eat his meal.
Behold, he who had no corn now owns barns; he who lived on alms of
    corn now distributes them himself.

Behold, he who had no yoke of oxen now owns herds; he who could not come by animals to pull his plough now owns whole herds of cattle.

Behold, he who could not build a shelter for himself now owns four walls.

Behold, the councillors seek shelter in the granary; he who was barely allowed to rest against the walls now owns a bed.

Behold, he who never before built a boat for himself now owns ships; when their owner comes looking for them, then they are no longer his.

Behold, those who owned clothes are now in rags; he who never wove for himself now owns fine linen.

The rich man thirsts in his sleep, he who once begged him for dregs now has strong beer.

Behold, he who understood nothing of harp music now owns a harp; he for whom no one sang now extols the music.

Behold, he who was forced by poverty to sleep unmarried, now has ladies; those who looked at their faces in the water now own a mirror.

Behold, those in high places in the country run about but have no business to attend to. The great receive no messages. He who was once a messenger now sends out someone else . . .

Behold, there are five men, sent out by their masters. They say: go yourselves, we have arrived.'

It is transparently clear that this is the description of a kind of disorder which must appear to the oppressed as a very enviable state. And yet the poet is difficult to pin down. He expressly condemns these conditions, even if he does so badly . . .

Jonathan Swift suggested in a pamphlet that, in order for the country to achieve prosperity, the children of the poor should be pickled and sold as meat. He made precise calculations which proved that you can save a great deal if you shrink from nothing.

Swift acted as if he were stupid. He defended a particular mode of thinking, which he detested, with great fire and thoroughness, and in a discussion of an issue where all its nastiness would be fully recognisable to anyone. Anyone could be cleverer than Swift, or at least more humane, particularly anyone who until then had not investigated certain opinions with an eye to the consequences which followed from them.

Propaganda for thinking, irrespective of where it occurs, is useful to the cause of the oppressed. This kind of propaganda is very necessary. Thinking is considered base under regimes which serve exploitation.

Whatever is useful for the downtrodden is considered base. Constant worry about filling your stomach counts as base; as does spurning the honours which are promised to those who defend the country in which they starve; doubting the Führer when he leads the way into a disaster; being averse to work which does not nourish its worker; rebelling against the compulsion to senseless behaviour; being indifferent towards the family, whom interest could no longer serve. The starving are cursed as greedy, those who have nothing to defend as cowards, those who doubt their oppressor as those who doubt their own strength, those who want wages for all their labour as lazy, and so on. Under governments like this, thinking in general counts as base and falls into disrepute. It is no longer taught any-where and, wherever it surfaces, it is persecuted. Nevertheless, there are still areas where one can point unpunished to the successes of thinking; namely those areas where the dictatorships need thinking. So, for example, one can prove the successes of thinking in the field of the science and technology of war. Stretching out wool supplies by more efficient organisation and by the invention of wool sub-stitutes also calls for thinking. The deterioration of foodstuffs, the training of young people for the war, all of this calls for thinking: and we are allowed to describe it. Praise of war, that is: of the unconsidered purpose of all this consideration, can cunningly be avoided; so the thinking which issues from the question of how a war can best be waged may lead on to the question of whether this war makes sense and may contribute to the question of how a senseless war can best be avoided.

It is difficult, of course, to pose this question in public. So is it not possible to exploit the thinking which has been propagated, that is to say to shape it for the purpose of intervention? On the contrary.

In a time like our own, in order for the oppression which serves the exploitation of the one (larger) section of the population by the other (smaller) section to remain possible, a very particular kind of basic attitude is necessary in the population, an attitude which must extend into all areas. A discovery in the field of zoology, like that of the Englishman *Darwin*, was suddenly a threat to exploitation; nevertheless, for a while only the Church was concerned about it, whilst the police had not yet noticed anything. The research of physicists in recent years has had consequences in the field of logic, which could be a threat to a series of doctrines which serve oppression. The Prussian state philosopher Hegel, concerned with difficult investigations in the field of logic, supplied Marx and Lenin, the classics of the proletarian revolution, with methods of inestimable value. Developments in the sciences are interrelated but not simultaneous, and the state is unable to keep an eye on everything. The champions of truth can select battle arenas for themselves which are relatively unobserved. Everything depends on the right kind of thinking being taught, a thinking which questions all things and all processes, and is intent on discovering their transient and changeable nature. .

Our rulers have a great aversion to major changes. They would like everything to stay the same, preferably for a thousand years. It would be best of all if the moon stood still and the sun stopped in its tracks! Then no one would ever get hungry and want to eat their supper. Once they have fired, their enemies should not be allowed to carry on shooting, their shot should be the last. A way of thinking which particularly emphasises the transient is a good means of encouraging the oppressed. Also, the fact that in each thing and in each condition a contradiction makes itself felt and grows, that is something which must be used to oppose the victors. This way of looking at things (like the dialectic, the doctrine that things are in flux) can be practised when investigating the subjects which escape the rulers for a while. It can be applied in biology or chemistry. But it can also be practised in describing the fates of a family without arousing too much attention. The fact that each thing depends on many others, which are constantly changing, is a dangerous thought for dictatorships, and it can surface in many guises without offering the police a lever. A complete description of all the circumstances and processes which affect a man who wants to open up a newsagent's can be a harsh blow against dictatorship. Everyone who reflects a little on this will realise why. Governments which lead the masses into misery must ensure that people do not think about the government during this misery. They talk a lot about destiny. This, rather than they themselves, is responsible for the distress. Anyone who tries to find out the cause of the distress is arrested long before he thinks of the government. But it is possible, in general, to counter this talk of fate; one can demonstrate that the fate of man is the work of men.

Again this can occur in a variety of ways. For example, the history of a farm can be told, such as that of an Icelandic farm. The entire village is talking about how this farm is cursed. One farmer's wife has thrown herself down the well, one farmer has hanged himself. One day a wedding takes place, the farmer's son marries a girl who brings a couple of fields into the marriage with her. The curse leaves the farm. The village is unable to agree in its assessment of this happy turn of events. Some attribute it to the sunny nature of the young farmer, others to the fields which the young farmer's wife brought into the marriage and which made the farm viable for the first time.

But it is possible to achieve something even in a poem which describes a landscape, namely if the things created by human beings are incorporated into nature.

Cunning is necessary for the truth to be spread.

Summary

The great truth of our age (recognition of which does not yet achieve anything, but without recognition of which no other truth of importance can be found) is that our part of the globe is sinking into barbarism because the conditions of ownership of the means of production are being held on to with violence. What use is it here to write something courageous which shows that the state into which we are sinking is barbaric (which is true), if it is not clear why we have ended up in this state? We have to say that people are being tortured so that the conditions of ownership will remain the same. Of course, if we say this we lose many friends who are against torture because they believe that the conditions of ownership might also be preserved without torture (which is untrue).

We have to tell the truth about the barbaric conditions in our country, that the measures which will make them disappear can be taken, namely those which change the conditions of ownership.

Moreover, we must tell it to those who are suffering the most from the conditions of ownership, who have the greatest interest in changing them, the workers, and those whom we can bring to them as comrades-in-arms, because they likewise do not have any share in the ownership of the means of production, even though they have a share of the profits.

And we must, fifthly, proceed with cunning.

And we must solve all of these five difficulties at one and the same time, for we cannot investigate the truth about barbaric conditions without thinking of those who are suffering from them, and whilst, always shaking off every last vestige of cowardice, we search for the true causal links with an eye to those who are prepared to use their knowledge, we must think about how to convey the truth to them in such a way that it can be a weapon in their hands, and at the same time with such cunning that this conveyance cannot be discovered and prevented by the enemy.

This much is demanded, when it is demanded that a writer should write the truth.

['*Fünf Schwierigkeiten beim Schreiben der Wahrheit*', BFA 22/74–89.]

Written December 1934, first published in the anti-Fascist journal *Unsere Zeit*, Paris/Basel/Prague, 1935, no. 2–3 (April), pp. 23–35. It was also published as a leaflet to be smuggled into Nazi Germany (some copies apparently camouflaged with the title *Practical Tips for First Aid*). There seems to have been little response at the time, although Walter Benjamin accorded it high praise in a letter to Brecht: '"Five Difficulties in Writing the Truth" has the dry wit and hence the limitless durability of a true classic. It is in a kind of prose which is new to the German language.' In due course it was recognised as one of the most important of Brecht's essays on political aesthetics, and it has established itself as something of a Marxist classic.

Amongst the several references to the language and policies of contemporary National Socialism and of anti-Fascism, it is perhaps worth picking out that Brecht's analysis in section 3 of Fascism as 'the most naked, brazen, oppressive and deceitful form of capitalism' is consistent with the statement by the Communist International in December 1933, that Fascism is 'the open terroristic dictatorship of the most reactionary, chauvinistic and imperialist elements of finance capital'.

Notes on the catalogue of examples are contained in BFA 22/906–9. The 'Egyptian poem' is Brecht's own construct pieced together from six separate 'Admonitions of a prophet' by Ipu-wer (*c.* 2500 BC), and quoted more or less according to the versions in an anthology by Adolf Ermann, *Die Literatur der Ägypter* (Leipzig, 1923). In 1944 Brecht used some of the same material again in the 'Song of Chaos' in *The Caucasian Chalk Circle*.

40

A Necessary Observation on the Struggle Against Barbarism

In order to achieve profits, in our times cereal crops and cattle are destroyed. The destruction of culture has no other purpose.

Comrades, I would like, without wanting to say anything particularly new, to say a few words about the struggle against those powers which are now bent on suffocating Western culture in blood and dirt, or, more precisely, those remnants of culture which a century of exploitation has left us with. I would like to draw your attention to just one single point, on which I believe that clarity must prevail if we are to resist these powers effectively and, most importantly, to the moment of their utter destruction.

Writers who experience the atrocities of Fascism at first or second hand, and who are outraged by them, are not therefore in a position to resist these atrocities simply by virtue of their experience and sense of outrage, without further ado. Some people may believe that it is enough to describe the atrocities, particularly if great literary talent and genuine anger lend the description urgency. And, indeed, such descriptions are very important. Atrocities are taking place. This cannot be allowed. People are being beaten. This should not be happening. What long explanations could be needed? The reader will surely leap up and restrain the torturers. But comrades, explanations are essential.

The reader may leap up, that is not so difficult. But then comes the little matter of restraining the torturers, and this is considerably more difficult. The anger is there, the opponent is clearly identified, but how can he be brought to his knees? The writer may say: my task is to denounce injustice, and leave the question of what to do about it to the reader. But then the writer will make a strange discovery. He will notice that anger, like sympathy, is something quantitative; it is present in this or that quantity and can run out. And the worst thing is: the more it is needed, the faster it runs out. Comrades have said to me: when we reported for the first time that our friends were being slaughtered, there was a cry of horror and many came to our aid. That was when a hundred were slaughtered. But when a thousand were slaughtered and there was still no end to the slaughter, silence descended, and only a few came to our aid. That is the way it is: 'When the crimes mount up, they become invisible. When the suffering becomes unbearable, the screams are no longer heard. One human being is beaten, and the person watching faints. It is only natural. When wrongdoing falls from the skies like rain, no one any longer cries out "Stop!".'

So this is how matters stand. How can they be remedied? Is there no way of preventing man from turning his back on atrocities? Why does he turn away? He turns away because he sees no possibility of intervening. No man lingers in the presence of another man's pain if he is unable to help him. You can fend off the blow if you know when it will strike and where it will strike and why, for what purpose, it will strike. And if you can fend off the blow, if any, even a faint chance of doing so exists, then you can feel sympathy for the victim. You can feel it anyway, but not for long, in any case not for as long as the blows rain down on the victim. So: why is this blow being struck? Why is culture being thrown overboard like so much ballast, those remnants of culture which are left to us; why are the lives of millions of people, of the vast majority of people, so impoverished, denuded, half or completely destroyed?

Some of us are eager to answer this question. They answer: out of brutality. They believe that they are experiencing a terrifying outbreak amongst a large and ever increasing section of humankind, a horrifying phenomenon without discernible cause, which has appeared suddenly and may perhaps, with luck, disappear again just as suddenly, a monstrous emergence of a long suppressed or dormant barbarism, an instinctual urge.

Those who give this answer naturally realise themselves that it does not help very much. And they also realise that it is wrong to give brutality the appearance of a force of nature, of the invincible powers of hell.

So they speak of the neglected education of the human race. Something was left out or could not be done in all the rush. We must make up for it now. Goodness must be brought to bear against brutality. We shall have to summon up the big words, the magic formulae which have helped us of old, the enduring concepts of love of freedom, dignity, justice, whose efficacy is historically proven. And so they employ these great magic formulae. What happens? On being told it is brutal, Fascism answers with a fanatical paean to brutality. Accused of being fanatical, it answers with a paean to fanaticism. Charged with violating reason, it proceeds cheerfully to a condemnation of reason.

For Fascism also believes that education has been neglected. It has high hopes of its ability to influence minds and fortify hearts. To the brutality of its torture chambers it adds that of its schools, newspapers, theatres. It educates the entire nation and it educates it all day long. It has not very much to offer to the vast majority, so the important thing is to educate them a great deal. It cannot provide food, so it has to teach self-discipline. It cannot manage production and it needs wars, so it has to teach physical courage. It requires sacrifices, so it has to teach the spirit of sacrifice. These too are ideals, demands on humanity, some of them are even high ideals, high demands.

Now, we know what purpose these ideals serve, who is doing the educating and whom this education is intended to benefit – not those being educated. How do matters stand with our own ideals, which are so much more humane? They are certainly different, but is it not possible that, when we set up our ideals, we nonetheless have something in common with our opponents? Even those of us who see the fundamental evil in brutality, in barbarism, speak, as we have seen, only about education, only about intervening in people's minds – not about any other kind of intervention. They speak about educating people to be good. But goodness will not come from the demand to be good, to be good under all circumstances, *even the most severe*, just as brutality cannot come from brutality alone.

I myself do not believe in brutality for its own sake. Mankind must be defended against the accusation that it would be brutal even if the rewards were not so handsome; it is a witty inversion when my friend Feuchtwanger says that meanness takes precedence over self-interest, but he is not right. Brutality does not come from brutality, but from the business deals which can no longer be made without it.

In the small country from which I come, less terrible conditions prevail than in many other countries; but every week 5,000 of the best animals reared for slaughter are destroyed. This is a terrible thing, but it is not a sudden outbreak of bloodthirstiness. If this were the case, then the matter would be less terrible. The destruction of animals reared for slaughter and the destruction of culture are not caused by barbaric instincts. In both cases a *part* of the goods, into which so much effort has gone, is destroyed because it has become a burden. In view of the hunger which governs all five continents, such measures are doubtless crimes, but they have nothing to do with wantonness, by no means. In most countries on earth today we have social conditions in which all kinds of crimes are highly rewarded and in which virtues carry a high price. 'The good man is defenceless, and the defenceless man is clubbed to the ground, but with brutality you can procure anything. Meanness is preparing for a 10,000-year reign. Goodness, on the other hand, needs a body-guard, but there's none to be found.'

Let us take heed against simply demanding goodness of people! After all, we too have no desire to demand the impossible. Let us not expose ourselves to the reproach that we, we too, came appealing for human beings to achieve the superhuman, namely to use great virtue to endure terrible conditions which, although they could be changed, should not be changed! Let us not talk only on behalf of culture! Let us have mercy on culture, but let us first have mercy on mankind! Culture will be saved when mankind is saved. Let us not get carried away and claim that man is there for culture, and not culture for man!

Comrades, let us reflect on the roots of this evil!

One great doctrine today, which is taking hold of ever-increasing masses of people on our planet, which itself is still in its youth, teaches that the roots of all evil lie in the conditions of ownership. This doctrine, simple like all great doctrines, has seized the masses of people who are suffering the most under the existing relations of property ownership and the barbaric methods used in their defence. In one country, which makes up a sixth of the surface area of the earth, where the oppressed and propertyless classes have seized power, it is being translated into action. Food is no longer destroyed there, and nor is culture.

Many of us writers who have experienced the atrocities of Fascism and are horrified by them have not yet understood this doctrine, have not yet discovered the roots of the brutality which so horrifies them. For them the danger persists that they will regard the cruelties of Fascism as unnecessary cruelties. They cling to the conditions of property ownership because they believe that the cruelties of Fascism are not necessary for their defence. But if the prevailing conditions of property ownership are to be upheld, then these cruelties are indeed necessary. In this particular the Fascists are not lying, they are telling the truth. Those of our friends who are just as horrified about the cruelties of Fascism as we are, but who want to preserve the conditions of property ownership or are indifferent to their preservation, cannot put up a sufficiently forceful or sustained fight against barbarism, which is so much in the ascendancy, because they can neither name nor help to create the social conditions in which barbarism would be redundant. Those, however, who in their search for the roots of this evil have stumbled upon the conditions of property ownership, have descended deeper and deeper, through an inferno of ever more fundamentally underlying atrocities, until they have arrived at that point where a small part of humankind has anchored its merciless rule. They have anchored it in individual property rights, which serve them to exploit their fellow men and which they defend tooth and nail, and at the cost of a culture which has ceased to offer any defence, or is no longer equipped to defend itself, at the cost of every single law of human co-existence for which mankind has fought so long and so courageously and so desperately.

Comrades, let us talk about the conditions of property ownership!

That is what I wanted to say on the subject of the struggle against the rise of barbarism, so that here too it should be said, or so that I too should have said it.

[*'Eine notwendige Feststellung zum Kampf gegen die Barbarei'*, BFA 22/141–6.]

There are several different drafts and versions of this speech, which Brecht gave at the First International Writers' Congress for the Defence of Culture, in Paris in June 1935. This is the version subsequently published in *Neue Deutsche Blätter*, Prague, 1934–5, no. 6 (August 1935), pp. 341–3. Some 250 writers from 37 countries attended the Congress and there were speeches by E. M. Forster, André Gide, Heinrich Mann, Robert Musil, Anna Seghers, amongst many others. Brecht expressed his dissatisfaction with the conference in a letter to George Grosz: 'We have just rescued culture. It took 4 (four) days, and then we decided that we would sooner sacrifice all else than let culture perish. If necessary, we'll sacrifice ten to twenty million people. [. . .] Fascism was unanimously condemned. What for? For its *unnecessary* cruelties' (*Letters*, p. 208).

His own contribution caused offence above all by its famous penultimate sentence, to liberals for its direct insistence on economics, and to socialists for its failure to recognise the current strategy of the Comintern, who were seeking to propagate a broad anti-Fascist front. Brecht felt he had gained nothing, except further material for his satirical studies of the intellectual in bourgeois society. In §10: 'Common interest takes precedence over self-interest' was a popular saying amongst Nazi ideologues (compare no. 36); Feuchtwanger changes one syllable to create his pun: '*Gemeinheit* [instead of *Gemein*nutz] *geht vor Eigennutz*'. In §11 the 'small country' is Denmark, where Brecht had lived since the summer of 1933.

41

On the Question of Whether Hitler Is Being Honest

1 The question of whether Hitler is honest is often raised, and many people behave as if a lot depended on the answer.

Of course, one might just as well question the honesty of a negro medicine man who pronounces that there will be no more rain until a certain man has been eaten. In general, the medicine man will only be considered dishonest if he has no personal connection with the man he says should be eaten, if they are neither relations by blood or marriage, nor business associates, nor any other kind of enemies. Even then, however, the man in question will not consider him honest, and even if he does, he will be eaten all the same, although no rain may come of it.

The general belief is that one should turn a blind eye whenever someone is striving for high goals. At any time he may say: in order to save the ten thousand of you, right now I need ten people to kill. Of course, the goal has to be really high. The highest goal anyone can name, when he wants to kill someone, is that of saving the fatherland. A lowly goal, in fact the most lowly there is, is money. Now in this lamentably imprecise world there are, however, peculiar combinations. The banker Morgan, for example, saved the fatherland (and earned 200 million dollars); Henry Ford did not save the fatherland (and also earned 200 million dollars). When Morgan sacrificed several hundred thousand human lives and saved the fatherland, there was a by-product: 200 million dollars. When he had earned these 200 million dollars, the fatherland was saved. Ford, on the contrary, earned his money without saving the fatherland, since Morgan had, after all, already saved it when he earned his money. On the other hand, for not saving the fatherland, Ford also did not need 100,000 human lives in order to earn his money. Morgan could not manage to earn his money and save the fatherland without human losses. Ford could not come to us and want to kill 100,000 human beings in order to earn his money, since in his case the fatherland would not be saved if the 100,000 were killed. Were Ford to demand the 100,000 human beings from us in order to earn his money, in our opinion he, in contrast to Morgan, would not be being honest.

2 One ought never to grant one's opponent something which he does not deserve, for example, in order to seem generous and thereby to show that one can beat him at his own game, at a higher level. One must stick to the truth, even when it is improbable. And one ought not to present a falsehood as the truth because at the present time its stigma is not needed at all in order to defeat the enemy. If I begin: Hitler may be honest subjectively, but there still remains . . . , then I have only 'admitted that even I do not dare to dispute Hitler's honesty, I, the opponent'. Certainly, Hitler could be honest and mean well, and yet still objectively be Germany's worst enemy. But he is not honest.

Chauffeur Schicklgruber Holds Forth

When Hitler went against France and undertook the military occupation of the Rhineland he delivered a great speech in which he cried out, sobbing, that he had no country estate and no bank account. This sentence left a deep impression on his hearers.

All around, people saw how Hitler's retinue were thoughtlessly filling their pockets, how governors in recognition of their services granted each other country estates etc., and yet the Führer himself walked off empty-handed? Under his rule a class of robbers had taken over, and everyone had been given the possibility to enrich themselves, but he himself would not accept it? In the face of such ethical stature people's eyes filled with tears.

General Göring, who was, after all, subordinate to the Führer, owned several country estates and laid on banquets like Nebuchadnezzar, and yet his Führer he allowed to wander, with no supper and no roof over his head, through night-time Berlin; God knows if a shelter for the homeless would take him in if he were to say, I am the Führer? Of course he could always, if the worst came to the worst, call up the SA . . .

The Führer of a great Reich should, without doubt, have an income, even if only a modest one. It is quite possible that Mr Hitler does not actually achieve all that much, but what sort of an impression does it give if, as happens in Berlin, the Reich President, who has renounced the salary of a Prime Minister, has to cadge a dime off every porter in order to take a tram?

Many believe, or so I hear, that Mr Hitler does indeed have an income, and quite a decent one too, he just doesn't know it. According to these people, he just thinks he hasn't got a bank account. Is that possible?

I think it is. It is even likely. You only have to ask yourself: how is the Führer supposed to have learned that he's got a bank account? At night he sleeps in the Wilhelmstraße or in his pretty villa in Berchtesgaden, or he lies awake and thinks about how he can keep Germany out of the war: you can't suddenly come and disturb him with the news that he's got a bank account. In the morning he has his breakfast, and at that hour you can't disturb him either, he's got to make himself strong, otherwise we're all for it. And then come the affairs of government: for example, the Führer inspects one of his great building projects. It's well known that his heart is set on a few huge stadia where he can talk to the Germans about all the other things he wants to give them. When he's immersed in plans and projects like that, of course you can't drag him away just to tell him that the money for his beloved buildings is already there. And so it goes on, the whole afternoon and evening, when he visits the Propaganda Minister who tells him in detail what he's doing for Germany and what he has to say in public, in short, does a bit of propaganda . . . If it goes on like this the Führer will never learn that he is provided for, and when he's preparing such an important speech as the one we're just talking about, you can't just shout out the news in the middle. And how are we supposed to know he would talk about it? No one, not even the Führer, has a clue what he is talking about.

All the same, I was kept awake by the Führer's statement that he has no bank account. I even began to understand his own sleepless nights, that he's always telling us about, better. Because it really is a great carelessness to keep so much money at home wrapped up in a sock. It's a habit common amongst the petty bourgeoisie, but it's not a good habit. Although, mistrust of the banks features in the National Socialist Party programme too . . .

It must be a lot of socks. The income of the Führer is no longer so meagre as when he was an army spy in Munich, a miserably paid job (especially miserable when you remember what a hard job it is, winning people's trust, and then betraying them).

You just have to consider the new decree, according to which every couple who marry have to receive a copy of *Mein Kampf* from the community, and you begin to realise what is stuffed in the Führer's money sock. Every year some 700,000 couples get married in Germany. They won't dare offer the Führer less than 50 pfennigs per copy. This little calculation alone demonstrates that at least *his Kampf* was a profitable one.

If the Führer really doesn't have a bank account, not even without being aware of it, and if he keeps his money at home – for he has got a home, surprising though that may seem, a palace in Berlin and an estate in Bavaria – then that is very careless of him. For, even in spite of his Gestapo, one day all sorts of folk might come to visit him on the hunt for his money socks; and what will he live on then? Since he cannot expect to hold on to his office for ever, in these restless times.

[*'Über die Frage, ob es Hitler ehrlich meint'* and *'Auslassungen des Chauffeurs Schicklgruber'*, BFA 22/184–8.]

Spring 1936. These two pieces together provide a response to Hitler's speech to the Reichstag on 7 March 1936, when the German army marched into the Rhineland (demilitarised since the Treaties of Versailles and Locarno of 1919 and 1925). Brecht later turned part of the material into a dialogue for radio broadcast: 'The Führer's Bank Account' (BFA 18/335–7).

The first piece refers to the 'patriotic' achievement of John Pierpont Morgan in extending the American rail network (which cost many lives), as well as the steel and shipping trusts, and compares it with Henry Ford's foundation of the Ford Motor Company (1903). The idea of types of 'productive capitalist' seems to be derived from a piece by H. G. Wells in the *New Statesman and Nation*, London, 27 October 1934, which is in Brecht's personal archive.

In the title to the second piece, Schicklgruber was the name borne by Adolf Hitler's illegitimate father until he was able to prove his real name; to German ears it has a comic Austrian peasant flavour and it was widely used by Hitler's early political opponents.

The satirical tone is reminiscent of Brecht's 'German Satires' from the *Svendborg Poems* of these same years, or of the later play *The Resistible Rise of Arturo Ui*.

42

From the English Letters

People reproach barbarism, because they are not permitted to participate in it. In truth, it is a screaming injustice that some people, just because of the shape of their noses, should not have the right to take part in the exploitation of their fellow human beings, just at a time when exploitation is so in vogue. Are they to be excluded from war profiteering as well, just because their hair is black? What reasons are these to prevent them from feeding off the labours of others. Should only Germans, at the expense of Germans, be allowed to have it so good?

I read Mr Baldwin's most recent speech with some amazement. His Majesty's Prime Minister had to defend their feeble policies in the Abyssinian and German questions. He complained that one could expect no concessions from Mr Mussolini, unless one was prepared to use violence. In his unctuous address there was an unmistakable undertone of 'Didn't I always say so' which I simply could not explain, until I found out that Mr Baldwin is a steel manufacturer. At the end of his speech he remarked that the horizon was dark, but he could now just see some light . . .

*

The attitude of the English middle classes to Hitler is very odd. Generally, they defend him. Some of his enterprises, especially those of a more private nature, are loudly disapproved of. It is held against him that he had his friend Röhm shot, although they also maintain that the fact that he had him shot proves, after all, that he wasn't a friend (because you don't have your friends shot). It is even worse that he was there. From a social point of view, it is quite impossible for a head of state to barge into an old friend's house, pistol in hand, before seven o'clock in the morning, especially if there's an orgy going on. What Mr Hitler was forced to witness at Röhm's place, if Mr Goebbels is to be believed, is, according to local sensitivities, nothing like so bad as the fact that Mr Hitler witnessed it at all. By being there he got caught up in a scandal. Your Englishman does not like it if there's too much about the private lives of his ministers in the newspaper. He was educated in a college, after all, and he knows that you can't just go barging in at any time of day or night, if you want to avoid a scandal . . . On the other hand, your Englishman is used to having to do business with wild natives. Often enough he may have had to force an advantageous deal out of some chieftain, who perhaps has just eaten his uncle. It is perfectly clear that one would not shake the hand of such a man if one could expect no financial advantage. Such considerations have a lot of sense in them; or at least you can see what it is they call sense in this country. Still, it remains a fact, there are things to object to about Mr Hitler. There's a suspicion that he is not a gentleman. On the other hand, they know that a gentleman won't last long in respectable society. If he does last: then he is [not] a gentleman. And Mr Hitler has lasted quite a while. So when you talk about Mr Hitler with the middle classes you quite soon get to hear: OK, so now we've talked about what we don't like about him; let's talk about what we do like. Fine, Mr Miller poisoned his first wife, but now let's talk about something else, namely that he is ready to marry my eldest daughter.

What the English like best about Mr Hitler: the French, they do not like the French.   [*the text breaks off here*]

['*Aus den englischen Briefen*', BFA 22/192–4.]

This typescript dates presumably from the summer of 1936 when Brecht was in London, and is possibly part of a larger plan towards which he was collecting newspaper cuttings.

Stanley Baldwin was British Prime Minister from 1935 to 1937 and leader of the Conservative Party. In 1935 Italian troops attacked Abyssinia (Ethiopia), and in May 1936 Italy declared the annexation of the country; the League of Nations lifted the sanctions they had previously attempted to impose (long since undermined by Germany and others). Röhm was the leader of the SA, killed in June 1934 when Hitler reasserted his control; Hitler accused his one-time ally of having planned a putsch, and of homosexuality and moral degeneracy.

Brecht's image of the English middle classes seems to have been derived in some part from Swiss newspapers, and in particular from a piece in *Der Bund*, Bern, 6 May 1936, which reported the views of H. G. Wells: that, while Mussolini's methods should not be approved, he had brought stability to Italy; German Fascism, on the other hand, was to be condemned for its expansionism and anti-Semitism (compare Wells, *The Shape of Things to Come*, London, 1933). This is not the only place where Brecht engages with Wells's ideas.

43

Speech at the Second International Writers' Congress for the Defence of Culture

It is now four years since a series of terrible events in my country demonstrated that culture, in all its manifestations, had entered a zone of deadly danger. The Fascist revolution aroused, immediately and in much of the world, passionate protests, its acts of violence provoked revulsion. But still the larger picture remained obscure to many of those who were so filled with disgust. Some of the individual events, although they were noticed, were not at all recognised in their essential implications for the survival, or not, of culture.

The monstrous events in Spain, the bombardment of defenceless towns and villages, the slaughter of whole populations, are now opening the eyes of more and more people to the fundamentally no less monstrous, but simply less dramatic, events which happened in my own and other countries, where Fascism fought victoriously for power. They can now discover the terrible common cause of the destruction of Guernica and the occupation of the German Trades Union buildings in May 1933. The screams of those who are now murdered in public squares reinforce the muted, anonymous screams of those who are tortured behind the walls of the Gestapo cellars: the Fascist dictatorships have begun to turn the methods they have used on their own proletariats against the proletariats of foreign countries; they treat the Spanish people as if they were the German or Italian people. When the Fascist dictatorships build up their stock of aeroplanes, their own people get no butter, and those of other countries get bombs. The Trades Unions stood for butter and against bombs, and they were closed down. Who can now doubt the similarity between the way the dictatorships lend each other their military battalions, and the way they stimulate trade in the commodity of labour by providing civilian battalions for finance capital in their so-called 'voluntary' labour programmes?

When the all-out attack was launched against the economic and political status of the German and Italian workforce, when the workers' freedom of association, when the freedom of the press, when democracy was strangled, then culture itself came under all-out attack.

It was not immediately that people saw the equivalence of the destruction of the Trades Unions and the destruction of the cathedrals and other monuments. And yet this was now an attack on the core of culture.

When their political and economic position was wrested from them, the German and Italian people lost any opportunity for cultural productivity – even Mr Goebbels got bored in his own theatres – the Spanish people, however, by defending their land and their democracy with arms, reconquered and defended their own cultural production: with every hectare of land another square centimetre of canvas in the Prado.

If that's the case, if culture is something inseparable from the whole productivity of a people, if one and the same aggressive intervention can rob people of both butter and the sonnet, if culture is something so material, what must be done for its defence?

What can it do itself? Can it fight back? It is fighting back: so it can. And its campaign has several phases. The individuals who are culturally productive distance themselves from the terrible events in their country, in the first instance merely impulsively. But to describe barbarism as barbarism is itself already the first blow. Then they join forces against barbarism, that too is necessary in the struggle. They proceed from protest to appeal, from complaint to a call to arms. They don't just point out the criminal deeds, they name the criminals by name, and demand their punishment. They recognise that the condemnation of oppression must lead in the end to the destruction of the oppressors, that their desire for mercy for the victims of violence must lead them to the merciless pursuit of the perpetrators, that sympathy must become rage, and disgust at violence must itself become violent.

The power of individuals, as of the privileged classes, must be confronted with the power, the uttermost, the shattering power of the people.

For their wars show no signs of ending. The Italian air squadrons, which fell upon luckless Abyssinia, rose up again into the air, their engines still hot, and joined forces with the German squadrons, in order to fall together upon the Spanish people. That battle is not yet over, and already the squadrons of imperialist Japan have taken to the air over China.

We must declare war on these wars, as on every other war of which we have spoken, and our war must be prosecuted as a war.

Our culture, which for so long we have defended only with intellectual weapons, although it was attacked with material weapons, which is itself not just an intellectual, but also, and even especially a material matter, must now be defended with material weapons.

['*Rede zum II. Internationalen Schriftstellerkongress zur Verteidigung der Kultur*'*, BFA 22/323–5.]

First published in *Das Wort*, Moscow, 1937, no. 10 (October). The Second

International Congress for the Defence of Culture began in July 1937 in Valencia and continued in Madrid. Brecht was reluctant to travel to Spain because of the Civil War, and he sent this speech with Ruth Berlau to Madrid. In the event the Congress held a closing ceremony in Paris, and Brecht was able to deliver his speech. The text was published in *Das Wort* along with contributions by many others, including Lion Feuchtwanger, Heinrich Mann, Ludwig Renn, Romain Rolland, and César Vallejo.

In the Spanish Civil War (1936–9) the Spanish Fascists received support from both the Germans and the Italians. On 26 April 1937 German bombers, providing air support for the march of General Franco's troops on Bilbao, destroyed the town of Guernica (this event providing the subject matter for Picasso's great painting). The Prado museum in Madrid houses many of Spain's great art treasures.

The Japanese invaded northern China on 7 July 1937 and provoked the Japanese–Chinese war.

44

Platform for Left-wing Intellectuals

1 The prerequisite of all effective efforts on behalf of culture, whether they be of a literary or of any other kind, whether their desire to civilise is conscious or unconscious, is that they must concern *everyone*, that is: all human beings within their reach, that is how they may exercise influence.

2 We may recognise one of the reasons for the alarming ineffectiveness of our cultural initiatives in the fact that we again issued an all too vague appeal to *everyone*, in the same way as we aimed our work at 'everyone' and intended it to serve the interests of 'everyone'. Developments in Germany teach us that by no means everyone is concerned for everyone else, and that only a very specific class of people, distinguished precisely by this from all other classes, is prepared to represent the interests of *everyone*. This is the class which, under the threat of ruin – or rather because the social order condemns it to perpetual ruin, since precisely this produces the prosperity of the *others* – *must* represent the interests of everyone.

But in order to be able to do so, this class must first be organised and put in a position to act. It is the class of the proletariat.

3 Such a choice of the class which can be mobilised for the interests of *everyone* might be disputed, for it is based on economic criteria. One might want to make the selection on the basis of other criteria, so that this fighting group would be recruited from all social classes. For example, the distinction between the barbaric and the humane has been suggested. We reject this distinction, however, because it does not have any organising power. We prefer to assume that both barbarism and humanity can be produced and organised by humans. If this were not the case, then indeed, only the extinction (the physical annihilation) of whole sections of the population would be able to put an end to barbarism – and it is clear that only the removal of barbarism makes humanity possible: the ideal of an island of humanity surviving in the midst of barbarism is infinitely dangerous. Everyone has always been able to recognise, but recently they have had particular occasion to do so, that barbarism will on no account tolerate such islands, and that it most certainly has the power to annihilate them. The selection of the class which alone can be entrusted with saving the whole of civilisation must be made on economic grounds, because only a class of people constituted in this manner harbours the strength and can be given the organisational form needed to create conditions in which *everyone* has a stake and which can therefore provide the basis for a real culture.

4 National Socialism is also an attempt to produce a universality. It tries to embrace *everyone*, to be precise: in the form of the *nation*. We are not in favour of seeing it simply as a metaphysical phenomenon, of regarding it as a natural disaster, with the timidity and awe with which one greets volcanic eruptions, events which one cannot influence. And which in turn do not have any purpose. However elementary this may be: in order to be able to act, and act we must, we need to regard this phenomenon as a human undertaking, and this is easier if social criteria are used. So we see a petty-bourgeois class, which has seized state power for itself and is striving, by violent means, to unite *everyone* under the banner of a nation. Given the current historical structure of the world economy,

this class sees a unified nation as being in a position to represent the interests of the group of people gathered under its flag, provided that it is equipped to do so in war. The perception that it is possible to use force to dispossess other people and groups of people, to exploit them and to beat them out of the competition etc., is derived from the private sphere of perception of the lower and upper-middle class. Our economy is indeed based on precisely this sort of behaviour.

5 The National Socialist attempt at unification includes the annihilation, exclusion or subordination of those groups of people who are detrimental to national solidarity, the Jews and the workers. A National Socialist Germany is effectively stronger than a Germany which does not believe that it actually has to wage wars, but which clings to a form of economy and society which produces wars. It is also stronger and more logically consistent internally than a Germany which clings to the capitalist form of the economy but, for political reasons, protects its workforce, something for which the economy is not equipped. From the point of view of the existing (capitalist) social order, the National Socialist state is stronger than the liberal one, and it makes no difference here whether the owners of the means of production and of the land govern by direct means, i.e., politically, or indirectly, without visible political power, or even politically ravaged, allowing their economic power to function like a force of nature.

6 Whether one supposes that capitalism wants to preserve its economic power by drawing in the mobilised middle class, or whether one supposes that in National Socialism the middle class establishes itself as the *state* on a capitalist basis, i.e., that a class has, in a manner of speaking, pushed itself between the classes which are engaged in economic struggle against each other, perhaps due to the insolubility of the land issue within this system (the two suppositions are not mutually exclusive) – it is only possible to fight National Socialism by fighting the capitalist economic system. Only the working class can be a comrade-in-arms in the fight against National Socialism. To fight Fascism and to want to preserve capitalism is impossible: this would mean returning capitalism to a

weaker position which it had already abandoned as untenable. It is not in its nervous liberal form, which tends to relent to the 'black-mail demands' of its proletariat, but now only in its most brazen and brutal state form that capitalism can attempt to withstand the crisis, which has indeed now been stabilised. Within the shortest possible span of time the entire bourgeoisie will have to realise that Fascism is the best form of capitalist state in this epoch, just as liberalism was the best in the previous epoch. Fascism can only be resisted by those who renounce private ownership of the means of production, and everything which goes with it, and who want to fight together with the class which fights most passionately against private property.

7 Hitler is completely right to describe Marxism, the other far-reaching attempt to unite *everyone*, as the enemy of the National Socialist attempt at unification. But of course it is not the Marxist doctrine which is the reason for the disunity, but rather the cause of this doctrine: an economic and political system which uses the want of the many for the advantage of the few; for capitalism does not survive in spite of the want of the many, but rather as a result of their want; capitalism would not be improved through *general* well-being, but rather it would be destroyed.

8 The most dangerous, the only real enemy of Fascism is, as Fascism itself knows, Communism. It is not a question of assessing whether Communism is now indeed strong enough: what matters is to strengthen it. After Fascism, and in this too Fascism is right, can only come Communism, nothing else. Culture will have fallen, or will stand with it.

['*Plattform für die linken Intellektuellen*', BFA 22/326–9.]

Typescript from *c.* 1937. Probably conceived in relation to the speech Brecht delivered at the Second International Writers' Congress for the Defence of Culture (above).

45

Speech on the Power of Resistance of Reason

In view of the stringent measures, both methodical and violent, being taken against reason by the Fascist states, it seems appropriate to ask whether human reason will be in any position to resist such a violent assault. It is, of course, not enough to fall back on optimistic generalisations, like 'in the end reason will always triumph', or 'the human spirit demonstrates its greatest freedom in violent adversity'. Such assertions are themselves hardly reasonable.

In fact, the human capacity for thought can be damaged to a surprising degree. This is true of the rationality of individuals and of whole classes and peoples. The history of human rationality has great periods of partial or total infertility, examples of appalling regression and decay. Given the right means, apathy can be organised on a grand scale. Mankind is just as capable of learning, in the right conditions, that two and two makes five, as that two and two makes four. The English philosopher Hobbes remarked, back in the seventeenth century, 'If the rule that the angles of a triangle together add up to two right-angles were to contradict the interests of commerce, then the men of commerce would set to and burn the geometry textbooks.'

One must assume that individual nations never produce more reason than they can use (if more were produced, it would simply not be used), but that they often produce less. So if we cannot give a specific use for reason, a quite specific and immediate necessity for the maintenance of the status quo, then we cannot claim that reason will necessarily survive the current period of severe persecution.

When I say that reason has to be necessary for the maintenance of the status quo if we are to give reason any decent chance, then this is something I have thought about carefully. There are good reasons why I don't say, reason should be necessary for the *transformation* of the status quo. Just because reason is necessary in order to improve the appalling status quo, does not, in my opinion, mean that we can hope reason will be summoned into being. Appalling conditions can persist for an unbelievably long time. One should say: the worse the conditions, the less reason there is, rather than: the worse the conditions, the more reason is produced.

Nevertheless, I do believe, as I've said, that as much reason is produced as is necessary for the maintenance of the status quo. So the question arises, how much reason is that? For, once again, if we ask how much reason will be produced in the near future, then we have to ask how much of that reason will be necessary to maintain the status quo.

One can hardly doubt that conditions in the Fascist countries are appalling. The standard of living is falling, and they need, all of them, wars in order to keep going. But one should not assume that the maintenance of such poor conditions requires especially little reason. The rational effort that needs to be employed here, and which must be produced in an almost uninterrupted stream, is substantial, even if it is of a particular variety.

One might say: it must be a crippled rationality. It must be a rational capacity which can be regulated, more or less mechanically increased or diminished. Reason must be able to run far and fast, but it must be possible to whistle it to heel. It must be able to whistle itself to heel, to intervene against itself, to destroy itself.

Let us investigate the sort of reason which is required. The physicist must be able to construct optical instruments for war which permit him to see into the distance, but at the same time he must be able *not* to see threatening developments in his immediate environment, for example, in his university. He has to construct defences against the attacks of foreign nations, but he is not permitted to think about what is to be done against the attacks on himself by the authorities. The doctor in his clinic seeks treatments for the cancer which is threatening his patient; but he is not permitted to seek treatments for the mustard gas and bombs which threaten him in his own clinic. For the only treatment against gassing would be a treatment against war. The brain workers have to continue to develop their logical skills all the time in order to work on their specialist questions, but they have to be able *not* to apply these logical skills to the fundamental questions. They have to make sure that war is terrible, but they have to leave the decision, war or peace, to people of clearly lesser intelligence. In these fundamentals they have to observe the use of methods and theories which, in their own spheres of knowledge (like physics or medicine), would be positively medieval.

The quantity of reason which the ruling classes need in order to continue their business is not just something they can freely decide; in a modern state the quantity is substantial, and it becomes even more substantial if business has to be continued by other means, in other words by war. Modern warfare devours a huge amount of reason.

The introduction of the modern primary school did not come about because the then ruling class, out of idealism, wanted to perform a service for reason, but because the education level of the broad mass of the population had to be raised in order to service modern industry. If the education of the working class were to be scaled down too much, industry would not be able to keep going. So, whatever might seem desirable to the ruling classes, for whatever reasons, it cannot be scaled down too much. One cannot conduct a war with illiterates.

So if the quantity of rational effort required is not simply up to the ruling classes to decide, then nor can this requisite and guaranteed quantity of reason be unproblematically translated into the quality of reason which the ruling classes would prefer.

The vast spread of reason brought about by the introduction of the primary schools did not only raise the performance of industry, it all raised the level of demands and expectations, in every respect, within the broad masses of the people. Their claim to power rests firmly on the foundation of education. One can establish a general principle: the ruling classes demand, for the purposes of the oppression and exploitation of the masses, such great quantities of reason, and of such quality, that oppression and exploitation themselves are threatened. By cool calculations such as these, one may arrive at the conclusion that the attacks on reason undertaken by the

Fascist governments will turn out, once again, to be so much tilting at windmills. They are *compelled* to preserve great quantities of reason, indeed, even to develop them themselves. They may curse at rationality all they will. They may present it as a sickness, they may denounce intellect as bestial; but even for the speeches in which they do this they need radio transmitters (themselves products of rational endeavour). In order to maintain their rule, they need just as much reason amongst the masses as is necessary to overcome their rule.

['*Rede über die Widerstandskraft der Vernunft*', BFA 22/333–6.]

Typescript dated by Margarete Steffin to November 1937. Brecht treats a similar theme in a scene of *Fear and Misery of the Third Reich* and again in *Life of Galileo*. The Hobbes quotation appears not to be genuine; Brecht may have known Hobbes by way of Descartes.

In this essay Brecht makes extensive use of the German word *Vernunft* and its derivatives, which may cover a range of meanings in English: reason (the power of reason, not in the sense of a cause), sense (good sense, common sense, sensible), rational thought, rationality, even intelligence. See also the next essay.

46

Speech on the Question Why Such Large Parts of the German People Support Hitler's Politics

Intelligent foreigners often remark: it is unthinkable that such large parts of the German people would support Hitler's politics, if there were not something sensible in it for them. Clearly these people only say this because they have such a high opinion of the rational good sense of the German people, for they themselves don't consider this politics to be at all reasonable.

The question, what is there that's reasonable in Hitler's politics, can be answered if you make a clear distinction between the act of comprehending an untenable position which demands urgent measures, and the act of discovering what those measures should be; and if you treat both acts as proofs of good sense. This distinction can be made, and it is often made. There is nothing particularly sophisticated about it. There are scientific studies of great value, in which certain matters may be opened up to new understanding, although no measures are proposed or, perhaps, even false measures are proposed. Medicine, for example, is quite familiar with work the value of which is correctly to describe certain illnesses, although the cures proposed may be quite wrong. Indeed, it may be understood as an act of intelligence to define a real problem at all, and to demand its solution; that requires intelligence, even if the solution is itself unintelligent.

In the two areas implied by its name, National Socialism has, beyond question, tackled real problems in Germany, and with great energy. After the war, German industry – which before the war had been, in accordance with the whole economic structure of the country, dependent on imperialist advances – was developed, with the help of other countries, so unrestrainedly that its imperialist political drive could only be intensified. The unhappy Treaty of Versailles did away with the German army, but left German industry intact, even strengthened by various other profitable contracts; and, in so doing, the Treaty perpetuated, indeed intensified, the necessity for an army. It is clear that Germany today, by its acts of violence, threatens the peace of Europe, but it is just as clear that it is not just the raging stream which commits violence, but also the bed which contains the stream.

There is enough logic in Hitler's remarks about the national state of emergency in Germany, even if the remarks themselves are riddled with grammatical and other errors, and even if the measures he proposes are so fateful: enough logic that one can grasp why his politics in this respect have the power to interest large parts of the German people.

The attempt to discover logical elements in Hitler's politics – that is, elements which are more or less convincing and have something to do with real needs in Germany – becomes rather more intrepid if we turn to his views on social matters. At the latest, three years after his coming to power it became clear to most people that the work creation programme was a contribution to war; the numerous attempts at a planned economy openly served the preparations for war. The disadvantages for Hitler which might follow from this recognition were widely overestimated. Admittedly, many now recognised that this sort of work creation would slide eerily over from the feeding of people to the feeding of cannons. And yet the whole way the social issue was approached achieved a certain sort of logic; the basic fault of all measures used to alleviate real social need was further obscured. The treatment of social problems was justified by the necessities of war, and so the larger truth was hidden again from view: namely that wars are only necessary if effective social measures are not employed. And if we allow that that large part of the German people which accepted National Socialism happily, or at least uncomplainingly, was able to discover in it something logical, reasonable, then our critique must start here.

Only a nation with a particular social structure has need of war. The Russian example demonstrates that the ownership and development of a large industrial sector does not by any means entail wars with other nations. Only if the interests of particular property-owning classes are valued above the interests of the overwhelming majority of the people does an imperialist politics of war become necessary. The businessmen profited demonstrably more from the German programme of work creation than did the workers. War itself is a business, even a war which is lost.

Today the extraordinary number of projects and enterprises itself lends National Socialism the appearance of a logic which has to be taken seriously. An extraordinary amount of rational effort is invested, simply because it has been forcibly invested, in all this planning and organisation on such a grandiose scale. The outsider will be less easily impressed by this appearance, but even he will not have an easy job, as the many examples of foreign observers prove, to recognise the nonsensical and ultimately deeply purposeless nature of all these measures. And this phenomenon is a consequence of the fact that here problems are being tackled in such an utterly wrong way, although they are indeed real problems which require logical thought and real solutions, if the whole continent is not to collapse into misery and barbarism.

['*Rede über die Frage, warum so grosse Teile des deutschen Volkes Hitlers Politik unterstützen*', BFA 22/338–40.]

Written 1937.

In another essay written at about the same time, 'Fascism and Youth' (BFA 22/348–50), Brecht acknowledged the impact of Nazi propaganda on young people, but insisted: 'It is of great importance what is said to young people, but it is not the crucial thing. Of crucial importance is where they are, in social terms, when they are addressed. Cut off from the processes of production, liberated from the need to earn a living, they are exposed to a propaganda, the impact of which can only be diminished within the sphere of social production. [. . .] National Socialism has the opportunity to influence young people as long as they are young. When they get older they enter the sphere of production, they gather in the factories and offices, and take an active role in the massive schooling of outlook and the apprenticeship in the social life of the nation, a schooling and apprenticeship which generate powerful ideas contrary to those of National Socialism. Rather paradoxically, one might say, that it would be the best chance for National Socialism if it had to do only with the young, if there were no adults at all, i.e., if there were no production and no struggle for profits in the capitalist manner.'

47

On My Attitude to the Soviet Union

For many intellectuals the struggle against the Soviet Union goes under the slogan *For Freedom!* They point accusingly at the great unfreedom in which both individuals and the mass of the workers and peasants allegedly live in the Union. The oppression is said to be the work of a number of powerful and violent people, at whose head stands just one man, Joseph Stalin. The word goes around and this image is propagated, not just by Fascists, bourgeois democrats and Social Democrats, but also by Marxist theorists who stand in honest opposition to the Fascists, bourgeois democrats and Social Democrats. These theorists give voice to the feelings and opinions of a great many intellectuals. If their opponents, the Fascists, bourgeois democrats and Social Democrats, were to describe them as allies, they would contest that they are engaged in a struggle against the Soviet Union; they would say that they are just against the 'conditions in which the Soviet Union currently finds itself', against a number of powerful and violent people there, against one man, Joseph Stalin. But if the Soviet Union were to get involved in a war, this distinction would make great difficulties for them, for they would only be able to defend the Soviet Union conditionally, only if it were to split itself from Stalin, and they could not welcome a victory of the Soviet Union if that was a victory under Stalin, in other words, in their opinion, a victory for Stalin. Nor can they deny that the preparation of war against the Soviet Union is made easier by their arguments, which are 'only directed against Stalin'.

The main reason why their arguments make the preparation of war against the Soviet Union easier is that the opponents of the Soviet Union can say, on the basis of their arguments: what you want, you socialists, has been realised in Russia. You shouted about freedom. You said what had to be done to achieve freedom. Well look, it has been done, and now you say yourselves: that's not freedom. Where they have done exactly what you propose, there is no freedom. You have upturned the whole economy, you have changed all the conditions of ownership. You always preached that there would only be freedom when the economy was upturned and private ownership abolished, and now that's happened, and there's still no freedom.

When they hear that, the anti-Stalinists do not answer directly; instead they turn, furiously, on the 'Stalinists' (since for them everyone who is for the Soviet Union these days is a Stalinist, that is: paid, or oppressed, by Joseph Stalin) and say: there you have it. Thus far   [*the text breaks off here*]

['*Über meine Stellung zur Sowjetunion*', BFA 22/297–8.]

Unfinished typescript of *c.* 1937. The reference to anti-Stalinist theorists may refer to Leon Trotsky, or possibly also to Karl Korsch and Fritz Sternberg (compare Part Two). The terms of this debate amongst European left-wing intellectuals were established to some degree by André Gide's disillusioned report *Retour de l'U.R.S.S.* (1936) and by Lion Feuchtwanger's riposte *Moskau 1937*, in which he is critical of the Stalin cult but far from dismissive of political progress of the Soviet Union.

48

On the Moscow Trials

As far as the discussion of the trials is concerned, to adopt an attitude in opposition to the government of the Union, which is staging these trials, would be quite wrong – since this would automatically, and in no time at all, be transformed into an attitude of opposition to the Russian proletariat, which stands under the threat of war from global Fascism, and to the process of the construction of Russian socialism. The trials have demonstrated with total clarity, even in the minds of convinced opponents of the Soviet Union and of their governments, that there is an active conspiracy against the regime, and that these nests of conspirators have not only committed acts of sabotage internally, but have also had dealings with Fascist diplomats regarding the attitude of their governments to a possible change of regime in the Union. Their politics was grounded in defeatism and had the spread of defeatism as its object. The accused, insofar as they present political arguments, all confess to doubts about the possibility of the construction of socialism in one country, to firmly held beliefs about the endurance of Fascism in other countries, and to the notion that it would prove impossible, without capitalism, to develop economically the undeveloped territories at the margins. In the meantime, the psychological aspect of the trials has, more and more, become a political matter. Sympathetic intellectuals are honestly shocked by the confessions. They think it impossible that the accused, who are known as great revolutionaries, should confess to such crimes as industrial sabotage, espionage (for money!) and murder (especially that of Gorky!), unless they had been subjected to some sort of inhuman 'pressure' by the investigating authorities. Especially since the latter are almost unknown, as far as their own revolutionary past is concerned. There is as little evidence for, as against, the existence of such pressure. The case for is made by pointing out that the confessions exceed by far the sensible and likely level of mis-demeanours, and that they presuppose a degree of remorse which itself implies a full awareness of one's own false notions. So the question arises whether we can conceive a political frame of mind which might motivate the deeds to which the accused have con-fessed. A frame like this is indeed possible and imaginable. The essential fundamental assumption of such a conception would be: an unbridgeable gulf between the regime and the masses; and, in order to motivate a politics like that of the accused, this gulf would have to be understood, not just as a gulf between an elevated body of functionaries and the masses of the workers and peasants, but as a gulf between these masses and the Communist Party as a whole (for the Party apparatus alone would hardly be able to bring about the loss of every war). Such a development can, in turn, only be con-ceived on the basis of the emergence of unreconcilable differences of interests on the part of workers and peasants. One would have to assume the utter impossibility of the control of production by the workers, and so the impossibility of the control of the army by the workers. If one were to assume this impossibility, one might be tempted into a politics of sabotage: in order to unmask the Utopianism of the experiments currently in progress, before the proletariat was utterly enfeebled. In terms of a policy towards the outside world, one would have to be prepared for confessions of the sort which have been heard in these trials. The whole framework is almost what we have come to expect of a Social Democrat. Just as such a train of thought is imaginable, so too we can easily conceive that it may be false. Especially since social life, on the basis of the violent progress and extension of production, is changing so very rapidly. Co-operation with capitalist general staffs, which is such an incriminating charge against a revolutionary, might turn out to be 'merely' co-operation with individuals in the pay of foreign authorities: that, ultimately, makes no difference, either for the accused or for the prosecution. They find themselves surrounded by every rabble with a passing interest in such defeatist notions. There is no point in even entering into the question of whether the Soviet Union, in its present condition, is able, while unmasking and denouncing life-threatening conspiracies, at the same time to meet the demands of bourgeois humanism. In the course of the great Revolution, Lenin himself, when he insisted on the necessity of terror, protested time and again against the purely formalistic demand that a humanism be implemented, which could not meet the actual social circumstances and was in effect counter-revolutionary. That is not an argument for physical torture; it is quite wrong to assume that, and also quite unnecessary to assume it.

In the matter of the trials, the mood in Scandinavia, not only amongst the intellectuals but also to a great extent amongst the working classes (who are guided by social democracy), is deeply opposed to the Union. Everyone's interest is once more concentrated on the psychological, on the plausibility or implausibility of the *confessions*.

People react like this: if I were to hear that the Pope had been arrested for stealing a sausage, and Albert Einstein for murdering his mother-in-law as well as for the invention of the theory of relativity, then I would expect the two gentlemen to deny the charges. If they confess, then I have to assume they have been tortured. I do not mean to say that the charges are similar to my caricature, but that's what it feels like here. What we have to do is to make them comprehensible. If the politicians accused in the trials have descended to the level of common criminals, then this has to be explained to Western Europe as a political career; that is to say: their politics has to be shown to be one which leads to common crimes. We have to make visible, behind the actions of the accused, an imaginable political concept which would lead them into the morass of common criminal acts. And, of course, such a concept is easily described. It is defeatist through and through; it is, metaphorically speaking, suicide motivated by the fear of death. But it is illu-minating to consider how it came into the heads of these people. The immense natural difficulties in the construction of a socialist economy, alongside the rapid and serious exacerbation of the condition of the proletariat in several large European states, induced panic. The political idea behind this panic can be traced back to political attitudes which are evident in the history of the Bolsheviks. I am referring to Lenin's attitude in the Brest-Litovsk question and in the question of the *New Economic Policy*. Of course these attitudes, as justified as they were in 1918 or 1922, are now completely anachronistic, counter-revolutionary, criminal. They are neither necessary, nor even possible. In just the few years since the concept has come into being, the anachronistic nature of the concept has revealed itself even to those who did the conceiving. They cannot uphold their own opinion any more, they reckon it to be a criminal weakness, an unpardonable betrayal. A false political concept has led them deep into isolation, and into common criminality. All the vermin, domestic and foreign, the parasites, professional criminals and spies have lodged with them: they formulated their goals in common with all these rabble. I am convinced that this is the truth, and I am convinced that this truth must sound plausible, even in Western Europe, even to readers who are our enemies. The vulture is no pacifist. The receiver is all in favour of bankruptcy. The politician who can only be helped to power on the back of defeat, is all for defeat. He who would be a 'saviour' must be concerned to engineer a situation in which he can save, in other words a bad situation.

In contrast, the following account is implausible: that, already during the Revolution, agents paid by capitalism insinuated themselves into the government of the soviets, with the intention of reintroducing capitalism to Russia, by whatever means. This account sounds implausible because it lacks the element of development, it is mechanical, undialectical, rigid.

That is my opinion about the trials. Sitting in my isolation in Svendborg, I am relaying it only to you; and I should be grateful if you would tell me whether such an argumentation seems to you, in our current situation, politically correct or not. In Copenhagen there has been some unrest because of the resignation from the Party, which I've heard about, by the Dutch writer Jef Last. He is said to have hinted at a similar attitude on the part of Malraux, of whom he is a good friend. Do you know anything about this?

['*Über die Moskauer Prozesse*'*, BFA 22/365–9.]

This is a typescript, corrected by hand, from the spring of 1938. It was cut into pieces in order to rearrange the sections, and is presumably the draft of a letter. Other correspondence from this period refers to the Moscow Trials, though nowhere at such length and so explicitly (compare *Letters*, nos 305, 328, 375 and others).

The trials had begun in August 1936, but it was a while before international concern became widespread. Brecht refers here to the trial against an 'anti-Soviet, right-wing Trotskyite bloc' in March 1938, in which politicians like Bukharin, Rykov and Jagoda were condemned (and immediately executed). The accusations of conspiracy with Fascist diplomats, espionage, defeatism and so on were common to all the trials. It was Genrich Jagoda who was accused of involvement in the murder of the great Soviet writer Maxim Gorky.

In the negotiations over the Treaty of Brest-Litovsk in 1918, Lenin overruled a majority in the Party leadership and agreed to the Soviet Union's concession of sovereignty over Poland and Lithuania. The 'New Economic Policy' was similarly forced through in the face of opposition within the Party.

Jef Last and the French novelist André Malraux, like many other intellectuals and writers, left the Communist Party and turned against the Soviet Union in the wake of the Moscow Trials and, subsequently, the German–Russian pact of 1939.

49

The Greatest of All Artists

'Stammtischlein, deck dich!'

The little old continent is being shaken once again by the marching step of mass armies and the din of threatening speeches. Its peoples listen in to what the leader of the second German Republic, the Bayreuth Republic, has to say to them. He has moved the annual festival to Nuremberg, and it is there he is currently speaking. The subject of his first speech is: culture.

As he has already repeatedly mentioned, he is building a thousand-year Reich complete with every accessory, including culture. Of course, he has his own opinion on the subject. The most important thing is art and he is an artist himself: according to his Propaganda Minister, the greatest. He is not due to speak to the Workers' Front until tomorrow and then he will be, in truth, a worker, but today it is the turn of culture and art, and so he was, in truth, a painter. His talent was not recognised, the Jews never gave him a chance, because he wasn't sufficiently decadent, so he had to take a detour and fight the Jews, and various other people besides. But he has remained an artist, he likes talking about art, especially now that no one can stop him any more, not even the generals. He claims that all 'respectable epochs' have produced art.

He only touches on science. Scientists are the people who produce *Ersatz*. They use wood not just for tables, but also for the food on the tables. The technicians win the great art prizes for building military roads and bomber planes. But he only touches on this. Nor does he talk about the second greatest artist after himself, Schacht (he hasn't won a prize; in fact, he has even had the occasional failure recently; he is currently experiencing a lull in his creative activity).

Of all the arts, his least favourite is literature. He does not even mention it. He demands of music, which he cannot live without, that it leave out the words. It doesn't need words. The listener can make them up himself. Music must manage with sound alone. After all, even as a speech maker, he just about manages with sound alone. In any case, when words start creeping into music, then all hell breaks loose. Used without due care, words result in meaning, and then one just has to intervene. But music is an art and should not demand intervention, but empathy. He notes with pleasure that good pitch and reason are rarely united in *one* body. Nice people, musicians, they can stay as they are. This time he does not waste many words on painting. He already said last year what there was to say. Art criticism has been abolished (by the way, even his festivals no longer have anything to fear from it, no one could, for instance, pass criticism on what he is saying now!), and the doctors have stepped into the critics' shoes. Instead of tearing things to shreds, they opt straight away for sterilisation. That'll make people think twice about whether they want to continue painting in the wrong way!

Back in the past, they even misappropriated war! Nothing is sacred to them. But let us move on to architecture.

Architecture is his favourite among all the arts. No words.

No words *and* it looks good. Stone like that can last millennia. And it keeps its mouth shut. His Minister for Road Construction, the prize-winning artist, reports that all his digging has created a bigger dust storm than three (or is it four?) Egyptian pyramids. The pyramids were also built in a respectable epoch. That was work creation on the grandest scale! His own work creation project is three (or is it four?) times greater, in this one area. And besides, he is building all these barracks, gigantic buildings. Later generations will stand before them and marvel, just as we stand before the medieval cathedrals. What actually gets built depends on the age; now barracks (and ministries) are being built. Churches are no longer being built, the people are not to be trusted with them. They would just use them to read out words.

Yes, the future will have something to say about his buildings. That is for certain. His tone is upbeat. As for the sentence to end all sentences, 'What an artist perishes with me!', he doesn't seem to have started the rehearsals for that one yet.

['*Der grösste aller Künstler*', BFA 22/469–70.]

A response to the 10th NSDAP conference in Nuremberg, September 1938, first published in the exiles' journal *Die neue Weltbühne*, Prague/Zürich/Paris, no. 38, 22 September 1938.

The motto is an ironic variation on the magic spell of the fairy tale *Tischlein, deck dich!* (*The Little Table*) from the Grimm brothers' collection. A *Stammtisch* is a table for regulars in the pub; Brecht implies that this is about the level of Hitler's opinions. The reference to the 'Bayreuth Republic' is a play both on the Weimar Republic and on the love of the Nazi leadership for Wagner (whose festival takes place in Bayreuth). As a young man, Hitler was twice refused admission to the Vienna Academy of Art. One of the constant endeavours of Nazi industrial science was to discover substitutes ('*Ersatz*') for products which were scarce or which might not be available to Germany in time of war. In 1938 Goebbels awarded the National Prize for Art and Science to the minister in charge of the road-building programme, Fritz Todt, as well as to the Volkswagen manu-facturer Ferdinand Porsche and the aeroplane manufacturers Willy Messerschmitt and Ernst Heinkel. Hjalmar Schacht was president of the Reichsbank and Economics Minister. The quotation in the last lines is from Suetonius's account of the death of Nero.

The satirical tone compares again with the 'German Satires' in the *Svendborg Poems*.

50

Why are the Petty Bourgeoisie and Even the Proletariat Threatening to Turn to Fascism?

Because the approaching world war throws up the national question, that of defending the nation against impending military and economic incursions. Because Social Democracy sacrifices the nation (in order to save business, although it is common knowledge that when the nation is sacrificed, so is business). Social Democracy preaches neutrality in war, forgetting that you can only enforce neutrality from a position of strength, not weakness. It does not give the nation the strength to enforce its neutrality (by forging powerful alliances, steeling the will to self-defence, creating independent markets, etc.). So certain sections of the population demand to be subordinated to the strong nation next door as a *consequence* of Social Democratic policy, i.e., they turn to Fascism.

Because Social Democracy has no vision of the future. Neither in foreign, nor in domestic affairs. It is unable to fill the Scandinavian idea with social content, unable to establish socialism on a broad basis for the whole of Scandinavia. Where domestic affairs are concerned, you only need to look at the Social Democrats' attitude towards the question of overcrowding in the medical profession, for instance! As if there were too many doctors! As if there were enough doctors! Where do they think the young people, whose careers are being blocked, will turn?

Because Social Democracy does not propagate socialist ideals and does not implement the socialist programme. It is not enough to provide advantages for the middle classes and the proletariat through the hard labour of politics, unless the entire system of production is transformed. Socialism is not about distributing goods, but about producing them. Production must be expanded, planned, freed from the need to squeeze out surplus value and profits. The only match for Fascist ideals are socialist ideals, the genuinely socialist ones. You do not win by hiding your good qualities. The proletariat and the middle classes would not fear the socialist ideals if they were explained to them, for they have nothing to fear from them, on the contrary.

Because Social Democracy always backs away from the Communists, when they propagate socialist ideals, denouncing them as Utopian and as a danger to the working and middle classes; because Social Democracy itself thus produces a fear of Communism and, with it, of socialism too!

Because property (in its present, individual form) is protected better by Fascism than by Social Democracy; for the socialists can only protect – and increase – property in its socialist form.

In order to fight Fascism, instead of fighting Communism they need to create their own battle formations which will match and surpass those of the Fascists. They need to propagate their own socialist ideals, spreading the word that they are useful, superior and progressive, and proving all this by their actions. They need to have a grand programme for foreign and domestic policy which will open up a prospect for the future (Scandinavian unification and a socialist economy). They need to forge external and internal alliances, i.e., unite Sweden, Norway and Denmark at the same time as uniting the workers, peasantry, intelligentsia and small retailers. (E.g., show that the prices of agricultural produce can only rise if workers' wages rise too etc.)

['*Warum droht die Abwanderung kleinbürgerlicher und sogar proletarischer Schichten zum Faschismus?*', BFA 22/587–8.]

Typescript *c.* summer 1939. This was presumably produced in the same context as Brecht's work on the one-acter *How Much Is Your Iron* (see *Plays 4*). Brecht is concerned with the conduct of the Scandinavian governments in relation to the offer of a non-aggression pact with Nazi Germany. In the end Denmark, under enormous German pressure, signed the pact, while the other Scandinavian states asserted their 'neutrality'.

51

On the Theatricality of Fascism

THOMAS   We were talking recently about how one might achieve a sort of theatre in which the representations of human social existence might give the spectators the key by which to master their own social problems. We were looking for an ordinary event from everyday life, which wouldn't normally be described as theatrical because it isn't played out amongst artists and doesn't pursue any artistic purpose, but which nonetheless involves the use of artistic, theatrical methods, and is at the same time a demonstration designed to give the spectators the key with which to master an unclear situation. We discovered a little scene at a street corner, in which the eyewitness of a traffic accident demonstrated the behaviour of those involved to passers-by. In the mode of acting employed by our street-side demonstrator we foregrounded some features which might be of value for our theatre. Now let us consider another sort of theatrical presentation, again one which is neither by artists nor serves any artistic purpose, but which is staged in a thousand variations and repetitions on the streets and in assembly halls. Let us consider the theatricality of the way in which the Fascists present themselves.

KARL   I suppose these reflections are intended also to serve the theatre, and I must confess, that makes me uncomfortable. How am I to turn my mind to the theatre when life is so terrible? Living, by which I mean to say staying alive, has itself become an art these days; who can then afford to reflect how art is to be kept alive? In times like these even the sentences I have just spoken begin to seem cynical.

THOMAS   I understand your sensibilities. But we had agreed that the theatre we envisage should be able to further precisely that art of living. When we speak of the theatricality of the oppressors, of course we speak as experts in the theatrical, but we speak also as the oppressed. In view of the misery which man is inflicting on mankind, we have to speak of the services which our art may render to the rapists. What we intend, by means of our art, is to wage war on the exploitation of man by man. In that case we must investigate precisely what means we employ; and we may best observe these means where they are not used by professional artists for artistic purposes. After all, we ourselves don't wish to employ our professional artistry just for artistic purposes.

KARL   Do you mean to say the theatre does not only imitate events from social life, but also the manner in which such events themselves are imitated 'in life'?

THOMAS   Yes, that's precisely what I mean. And now I suggest we investigate how the oppressors of our times make theatre – not in their theatres, but on the streets and in the assembly halls, as well as in their private homes, diplomatic offices and conference rooms. And by 'making theatre' we understand this: that they behave not just as their immediate purposes demand, but rather that they act consciously in the eyes of the world, and try to impose their immediate tasks and purposes on a public, as if they were reasonable and exemplary.

KARL Let's anticipate the little dramatisations which are so characteristic of National Socialism. I mean how they lend a theatrical expression to otherwise unremarkable circumstances. The Reichstag Fire is a classical example. Here the point is to dramatise the danger of Communism and develop it into an 'effect'. The 30th of July offers another example: when the Führer, in person, entrapped a few homosexuals in flagrante, and a scarcely developed political countermovement was elaborated into a real, acute and three-dimensional conspiracy. But from there we can move on to the more immediately stagy. There is no doubt that the Fascists behave in an exceptionally theatrical manner. They have a particular feel for it. They speak themselves of *Regie* [direction, stage management], and they've adopted a whole range of effects directly from the theatre, the lights and the music, the choruses and the surprise twists. An actor told me years ago that Hitler even took lessons with Fritz Basil, an actor at the court theatre in Munich, not only in elocution but also in comportment. He learned, for example, how to step out on stage, the hero's walk, for which you straighten your knee and set the whole sole of your foot on the ground in order to appear more majestic. And he learned the most impressive way to cross his arms, and studied how to be casual. There's something ridiculous about that, isn't there?

THOMAS I wouldn't say that. It's true, it constitutes an attempt to dupe the people, since they're supposed to think that a strange behaviour which has been laboriously learned comes naturally to a great man, that it's a born expression of his greatness and his exceptional nature. Besides, he was imitating an actor who, when he himself appeared on stage, provoked amusement amongst the younger spectators because of his affectation and pomposity. That may well be ridiculous, but the man's general intention, to improve himself by copying others, is not ridiculous – even if his choice of models was. Think of the countless perfectly sensible young people, not in the least inclined to deceit, who attempted, at around the same time, to imitate screen heroes. Here too there were poorly chosen models, but there were good models too. I propose we don't linger too long over Hitler's attempt to acquire an impressive, 'star'-like appearance, but that we turn instead to a consideration of the theatrical elements which he, and the other heroes of his type, didn't borrow directly from the theatre, even if the theatre of our time does use them. I would like to investigate the *representative* nature of his behaviour.

KARL   Yes, let's do that. Let's observe him as he makes his entrance as the great example to us all! The very model of the German, the inspiration for our youth!

THOMAS   I didn't just mean that. That aspect is obvious. That is still a part of being impressive. There's the Siegfried model, slightly modified to incorporate a certain 'man-of-the-world' air, you can most easily make a study of it in those photographs where he's bowing (to Hindenburg or Mussolini, or to some high-society ladies). The role he constructs (the friend of music, connoisseur of great German music; the unknown soldier of the world war; the joyful donor to political causes, the conscientious citizen of the *Volk*; the dignified mourner, with stiff upper lip) is an individual one. In contrast to the Roman dictator he is clearly disdainful of physical labour. (The former likes to present himself building walls, ploughing fields, driving, fencing.) Our man prefers the attitude of inspecting. There is a remarkable photograph of his arrival in Italy (Venice). Mussolini is evidently showing him the town. The house painter is playing the part of the preoccupied, hard-working travelling businessman, who happens to be, at the same time, a *fine connoisseur of architecture*, incidentally also the fact that he has to avoid wearing a soft hat, sun or no sun. On a visit to the aged and infirm Hindenburg in Neudeck the camera captures him playing the *jovial house guest*. His host and his host's grandson, in contrast, are unable to forget the camera, and seem out of place in the scene. Of course, he has many functions to satisfy, and he doesn't always manage to shape his role in a truly unified way. The representation of the scene in which the Führer contributes his few pennies to the

Winter Aid Programme is more successful. He has been given a couple of notes, and one of them is folded so it can be pushed into the collecting tin. Yet he manages to show a *Gestus* which is perfectly petty bourgeois: he seems to be fishing a coin out of a purse. At a commemoration of the Battle of Tannenberg he is the only one who manages to express an even half-genuine respect for the fallen of 1914, even though he has to carry a top hat in his lap! That is exemplary in the best sense. But let's go further. Let us observe, above all, the manner in which he acts on the occasion of his great speeches in preparation, or justification, of his acts of butchery. You understand, we must observe him where he's concerned to induce a public to empathise with him and to say: yes, that's how we would have acted too. In short, where he presents himself as an ordinary *human being* and seeks to convince the public that his actions are simply human, and to persuade them, quite naturally, to applaud him. That makes for very interesting theatre.

KARL   Indeed, and it is very different from the theatre of the witness of our accident at the street corner.

THOMAS   Very different. You could even say, it's very different precisely in that it has much more to do with the theatre which we normally get to see on the stage. For there it is again, that empathy of the public for the protagonists that we tend to think of as the most essential product of art. There's that feeling of being swept along, that transformation of the spectators into a unified mass, which we demand of art.

KARL   I have to say, this turn in your argument alarms me. It seems you want to associate the production of empathy, come what may, with the performances of that dubious man, just in order to bring empathy into disrepute. It is, of course, correct that he proceeds from that sort of empathy, but the same could be said of some outstanding people.

THOMAS   That's quite right, but if empathy is getting disreputable surely he, rather than I, must be made responsible. We won't get much further if we allow our observations to be ruled by the fear of what might follow from them. Let us study fearlessly (or even in fright) how the subject of our deliberations makes use of the artistic means of empathy! Let us see what artistic turns he employs! Consider, for example, how he speaks in public! In the course of speeches which are meant to pave the way for, or to explain, state actions, he submits himself, in order to facilitate empathy, to intensely personal feelings, feelings which are readily accessible to the private individual. In themselves, speeches by politicians are not impulsive, spontaneous outpourings. They are much revised and reworked from all angles and prepared for a particular date. When he steps up to the microphone, the orator feels neither especially courageous, nor especially angry nor especially triumphant, nor anything else. So generally the speaker is content to read out his speech in a serious tone of voice, to lend his arguments a certain urgency, and so forth. The house painter and his like proceed quite differently. First of all, by all sorts of tricks, the expectation of the audience – for the people must become an audience – is aroused and provoked. Word gets around that no one can predict what the speaker will say. For he doesn't speak in the name of the people, and he doesn't say simply what the people have to say. He's an individual, a hero in the drama, and it's his purpose to make the people (or rather the audience) say what he says. Or more precisely, feel what he feels. So it all depends on the fact that he himself feels, intensely. And in order to feel intensely the house painter speaks as a private individual, to private individuals. He picks fights with individuals, foreign ministers or politicians. He gives the impression that he's involved in some personal dispute with these people, because of the way they are. He loses himself in furious tirades like some Homeric hero, insists on his innocence, implies that he can only barely stop himself leaping at his opponent's throat, addresses him directly, flings challenges at him, ridicules him, and so on. In all this, his audience follow him emotionally, they participate in the speaker's triumphs, adopt his attitudes. Without doubt, the house painter (as some call him, since he can only daub whitewash over the cracks in a building that's ripe for demolition) has taken up a theatrical method, by which he can persuade his audience to follow him almost blindly. He induces everyone to abandon their own points of view, and to adopt his, the protagonist's viewpoint, to forget their own interests, and to pursue his, the protagonist's interests. He involves his audience in himself, implicates them in his movements, lets them 'participate' in his troubles and his triumphs, and dissuades them from any criticism, even from a fleeting glance at their surroundings from their own viewpoint.

KARL   You mean, he doesn't work with arguments.

THOMAS   That's not what I mean. He uses arguments all the time. His pose is as 'one who argues'. He loves to hang a 'because' on the end of some sentence which is actually perfectly complete as it stands and which he's just uttered as if it were an incontrovertible, incontestable truth, and then to pause, and then produce reasons. It's like he's tossing a handful of 'reasons why' in the wake of his assertions, reasons which he just happens to have to hand. Some of what he tacks on after such a 'because' is not really a reason at all, it's just labelled a reason by the gestic emphasis it's given; sometimes he promises, to himself, as it were, in his excitement, three reasons why, or five, or six, evidently without having first worked out precisely how many he actually has. So he discovers the number he's promised, or not, as the case may be, sometimes it's one too few, or one too many. What matters to him is to induce in the empathising public the attitude of 'one who argues', one who employs arguments, or more exactly, one who looks for arguments.

KARL   And what does he achieve by this?

THOMAS   He manages to make his behaviour take on the appearance of being determined, so to speak, by natural law. He just is as he is – and everyone else (empathising with him) is as he is. He cannot be otherwise than he has to be – and everyone else can't be otherwise either, they have to be as they are. His followers even say of him that he follows his path like a sleepwalker, or as if he had already passed that way before. So he takes on the appearance of a natural phenomenon. To resist him is simply unnatural, and in the long run impossible. He has weaknesses, but only because mankind, of whom he is the outstanding representative, has weaknesses, and they are the weaknesses that everyone shares, unavoidable weaknesses. 'I am simply your voice,' he likes to maintain, 'the commands that issue from me are nothing else but the commands you call out to yourselves.'

KARL Of course, I can appreciate the danger of empathising with him; he is, after all, leading the people on a dangerous path. But it seems to me that is not your only point, that it *may* be dangerous to empathise with a protagonist (as it is dangerous to empathise with this one), but rather that it *must be* dangerous, quite irrespective of whether he's leading you on a dangerous path or not. That's right, isn't it?

THOMAS Indeed. If only for the reason that the establishment of empathy makes it impossible for the person who falls under its spell to recognise whether the path is dangerous or not.

KARL So when does the establishment of empathy not work? After all, we know that there are great masses of people who observe the house painter distantly and coldly and don't for one moment adopt his standpoint.

THOMAS He must fail to establish empathy with those whose interests he perpetually damages, as long as they are able continually to call to mind the whole of reality, in all its variety, and to see him as just a small part of it.

KARL And only they are able truly to perceive the laws by which his appearance and his behaviour are governed?

THOMAS Yes.

KARL So, they don't empathise with him, because they recognise that their interests are different from his. But surely they might well empathise with someone else who could represent their interests?

THOMAS Of course they might do that. But then they would be equally unable to perceive the laws which govern the appearance and behaviour of this other person. You might say: but he is leading them on the right path, how can it be dangerous to follow him blindly? But that would be a completely mistaken understanding of a 'right path'. A right path can never be followed on a harness. The life of man does not consist in going somewhere, but in that he walks at all. The concept of the right path is less appropriate than the right way of walking. The most amazing capacity of mankind is criticism, it has added most to the goods of happiness, improved life the most. Whoever empathises with someone, and does so completely, relinquishes criticism both of the object of their empathy and of themselves. Instead of awakening, they sleepwalk. Instead of doing something, they let something be done with them. They are those with whom others live and from whom others live, not those who truly live themselves. They have only the illusion that they are living, in reality they are vegetating. They are, so to speak, passively lived. That is why the theatrical presentation offered by Fascism is not a good example of theatre, not if we expect of it representations which might give the spectators the key by which to master the problems of social existence.

KARL   It is hard to agree with this conclusion. It adds up to a rejection of a practice of theatre which has been exercised for thousands of years.

THOMAS   So do you suppose the practice of the house painter is new?

['*Über die Theatralik des Faschismus*', BFA 22/561–9.]

Corrected typescript from May 1939. According to notes by Margarete Steffin, Brecht and Hermann Greid (an actor and director who was also in exile) discussed *Verfremdung* and the artistic tradition in Lidingö at this time. The topic also crops up in the plans for *The Messingkauf Dialogues* at around the same time, but this piece was never reworked for the *Messingkauf*. The reference to the 'everyday event' at the beginning is to *The Streetscene*, where Brecht develops ideas of the epic by means of a practical example (*Brecht on Theatre*, pp. 121–9).

The (true) anecdote about Hitler's 'acting' lessons is wonderfully exploited in *The Resistible Rise of Arturo Ui*, scene 6. The Battle of Tannenberg was one of the early German successes which became the occasion for yearly celebrations. There are numerous photographs of Hitler, giving speeches, visiting Mussolini, and so on, amongst Brecht's papers. On Brecht's disparaging description of Hitler as 'the house painter', compare note to no. 35.

52

The Last Word

The first country which Hitler conquered was Germany; the first people whom he oppressed were Germans. It is incorrect to say that German literature accomplished an *exodus in toto*. It is correct to say that literature was driven out of the German people. Chinese poetry is the oldest surviving example of the lyric form, and occasionally, as a mark of respect, certain princes forced each of the better poets to leave the provinces where their poems were too popular. Li T'ai-Po was exiled at least once, Tu Fu at least twice, Po Chu-yi at least three times. This shows that setting down roots in one place was not the main aim of this literature, nor was this art simply concerned to please. Yet the kind of attention, indeed, the degree of honour conferred by the state on contemporary German literature in the form of its complete expulsion, has virtually no precedent in the history of literature: the Fascists' respectful bows consist in kicks. I hope that German literature will prove itself worthy of this extraordinary level of attention. Some writers have proudly quoted the biblical verse 'In the beginning was the word'. The most important of all words seems to me – The Last Word.

['*Das letzte Wort*'*, BFA 22/455.]

Typescript *c.* 1938. Brecht makes similar remarks in poems of this period, and in an open letter to Karin Michaelis of 1942 (BFA 23/9).

Part Four

Realism and Formalism 1938–1940

(Denmark–Sweden–Finland)

Introduction to Part Four

As we saw in Part Two, by the early 1930s Brecht had begun to develop aesthetic categories anticipating his later theory of *Verfremdung*. Similarly, he had also formulated the core precepts in his critique of realism, notably in his 1931 monograph *The Three-penny Lawsuit*. His primary target was that photographic approach to representation which took a realist text to be a direct copy of reality as it presents itself to our senses. But in the modern world of advanced capitalism, Brecht maintains, it is increasingly not the case that a simple reproduction of actuality, such as a photograph of the Krupp munition works or of a power station belonging to the General Electric company, can really say anything significant about reality. The reason for this is that human relationships have become reified, so that they are only visible to us in the outward form of the factory, for example. At the same time, social reality as such has become functional and abstract. While the expressive theory of art had assumed that the author's individual experiences were the touchstone of reality, Brecht suggests that any notion of art based on 'experience' is now obsolete, because reality construed as a totality of structures and relations lies beyond direct, immediate experience.[1]

It therefore follows that a new type of art is needed if aesthetic production is to have any cognitive value – a new art whose pedagogical and realist dimensions anticipate Brecht's much quoted characterisation of realism in 'The Popular and the Realistic' in 1938:

Realistic means:
revealing the causal complex of society/unmasking the ruling viewpoints
as the viewpoints of the rulers/writing from the standpoint of the class

that has in readiness the broadest solutions for the most urgent difficulties besetting human society/emphasising the factor of development/ concretely and making it possible to abstract.[2]

From Brecht's point of view, authentic art must aspire to the conditions of veracity of the natural and social sciences and emulate their procedures. At the same time, his reconceptualisation of realist representation is indebted to the anti-illusionist and defamiliarising artistic techniques of modernism. It is this synthesis of Marxist socio-economic theory and modernist aesthetics that constitutes a defining feature of Brechtian realism from now onwards.

The determining context for Brecht's subsequent essays on realism and formalism, written between 1938 and 1940, was the impact of the work of Georg Lukács, the most influential Marxist critic of the day. Lukács had written three seminal essays in Marxist aesthetics, dealing with the respective merits of realist and avant-garde modes of writing. The first of these, 'Greatness and Decline of Expressionism' (1934), formed the backdrop to an intense and acrimonious debate on Marxism and modernism conducted in the pages of *Das Wort* (*The Word*) in 1937–8, to which Lukács contributed 'Realism is at Stake' (1938). In the interim period he had published the most cogent and compelling account of his views on these issues in 'Narrate and Describe' (1936). Although Brecht's response to these essays was intensely critical of Lukács's theoretical and historical approach to realism and modernism, there are also crucial similarities in their positions. Lukács would have had little difficulty in broadly assenting to Brecht's specification of realism in 'The Popular and the Realistic', not least because he shares the view that realist writing must go beyond a photographic reproduction of actuality, so as to uncover contradictory currents of historical development at work beneath the visible surfaces of social life.

At the same time, Lukács could not have accepted Brecht's advocacy of abstraction, for two main reasons. First, he would have been highly critical of Brecht's structuralist approach to social analysis, with its focus on functions and relations, because Lukács consistently emphasised the importance of the actions of individual agents. Second, whilst Lukács insists that the reader must feel at home in the authentic realist narrative, secure in its illusory projection of life in all its breadth and wholeness, sharing in the experiences of the characters from whose standpoint events are being narrated, Brecht's new art of cognitive realism is radically anti-empathetic. Instead of motivating action in terms of the individual's character or inner life, cognitive realism is to concentrate on the typical external behaviour of figures performing specific functions. It does not seek to establish a bond of identification between audience and work or audience and author, but wishes instead to enable its audience to derive causal relationships inductively from the behavioural attitudes presented in the work, and thus to make abstract judgements. The audience must be given the opportunity to adopt a critical perspective on the political and economic relationships that underlie observable social reality. Only then will it be possible for the audience to see that human beings are conditioned by specific societal relationships, yet also capable of changing them.

The texts in Part Four are presented as follows: first, a broad selection of Brecht's essays on modernism, realism and formalism from 1938–9; second, his most substantial essay on realism, 'Notes on the Realist Mode of Writing', written in 1940; and finally, his account of the crime novel, produced contemporaneously with the essays on realism and formalism.

Brecht's intervention into the debate on formalism immediately questions the hackneyed and confused premises that underlie it. The term formalism had come to be used in orthodox Marxist circles in a decidedly pejorative fashion in order to condemn purely formal or stylistic modes of innovation associated with modernist art. In his 1938 essays on Expressionism (no. 53), Brecht points out that this approach ultimately misconstrues the relationship between form and content, which in his view is dynamic and symbiotic. If seeking new forms for an unchanging content exemplifies formalism, Brecht continues, then so does retaining old or supposedly universal forms when confronted by new content. In other words, if the social environment constantly changes, then so must artistic form. Brecht's argumentation derives directly from Marx's view that, in order to be authentic, a form must be appropriate to its content. What this means for Brecht is that artistic form must be radically historicised, so that one can no longer speak of aesthetic structures and techniques which are universally valid. Furthermore, nor does it make sense to praise the content of a work and reject its form, or vice versa: any critique of an artwork's politics must engage with its formal dimension, just as formal analysis must be politically grounded. Indeed, Brecht suggests that his own adoption of traditional and conventional forms in his early works had hampered his own ideological and intellectual development. By the same token, narrative techniques developed to represent early nineteenth-century industrial capitalism, which were entirely valid in their own day, cannot simply be taken over by writers attempting to come to grips with the complexities of advanced capitalism in the twentieth century.

This contention is at the heart of Brecht's critique of Lukács. Lukács had recommended contemporary realist writers to adopt the representational techniques of the early nineteenth-century novel, notably as exemplified in the work of Balzac. For Brecht, however, Lukács's recommendation is both anachronistic and dogmatic: one cannot take the formal procedures associated with one realist writer or one particular period of realism and present them as the uniquely valid mode of realist writing. Instead, Brecht calls for an expanded and expansive view of realism, which focuses on the variety of ways in which realist writers may influence reality by producing accurate reproductions of reality. The most striking instance of Brecht's more comprehensive approach to realism is his proposal, in 'Breadth and Variety of the Realist Mode of Writing' (no. 54), that the Romantic poet Shelley is a greater realist than the realist novelist Balzac. This is because Shelley's class sympathies lay with the lower orders of society, and because he better enables his audience to draw abstract conclusions. Nevertheless, this does not mean that contemporary realist writers should now take Shelley as their model: their relationship to the great realists of the past should be eclectic and pragmatic.

Brecht's own specification of realism highlights its sociological and epistemological dimensions. The primary aim of realism is to display causal structures at work in society, and Brecht welcomes *any* formal devices or techniques that will enable the writer to achieve that aim, irrespective of whether they have been categorised as realist or modernist. At the same time, Brecht is by no means uncritical of modernism, and he is particularly scathing about avant-garde painters who construe modernist abstraction as an end in itself. While he shares the view that making strange is a legitimate aesthetic tactic, he insists that the process of estranging objects and experiences in order to enable the audience to 'see differently' must be embedded in a specific social or political strategy. 'Seeing differently' must be the precursor of 'seeing correctly', just as ostensibly realist depictions must be checked against the realities they purport to represent. At the same time, realist writers must speak not to some self-regarding artistic elite, but to the people. Clearly, this entails that realist writing must be comprehensible to the people, but Brecht does not construe this requirement as a populist or demagogic speaking down to them. Realism does not involve pandering to pre-existing prejudices and preconceptions, and instead must present new social and political insights in an innovative but appropriate fashion.

Brecht's strategic perspective on realism also conditions his attitude to the cultural heritage and the artistic techniques that might be adopted by writers committed to socialism. In the essay 'On Socialist Realism' (no. 55), he now accepts that contemporary socialists must engage productively with the great achievements embodied in the cultural heritage, even though they were engineered by social classes hostile to the proletariat; nevertheless, he also argues that this engagement must be critical, pragmatic and, where necessary, iconoclastic. Appropriation of the cultural heritage by contemporary socialist writers should be determined by the imperatives of their political struggle rather than embody the misplaced humanist reverence he attributes to Lukács. And, when this principle is applied to Socialist Realism, once again it militates against a unitary or dogmatic view of the writer's role and of the techniques writers must adopt. Brecht rejects the neo-Stalinist view, predominant in orthodox Marxist circles at the time, that socialist content should simply be transposed into bourgeois form. But socialist writers cannot blithely incorporate the technical devices associated with nineteenth-century realism, because the ideological underpinnings of those devices are incompatible with an authentic Marxist critique of contemporary capitalism. The bourgeois realist novel had concentrated on representing psychologically complex individuals with whom the reader is encouraged to identify, but this mode of writing has been rendered obsolete by the emergence of mass politics, and thanks to the structural complexities of societies in a radical and advanced stage of modernisation.

Brecht's most substantial account of realism at this time, 'Notes on the Realist Mode of Writing' (no. 58), elaborates on many of the issues discussed in Brecht's shorter essays from 1938 and 1939, but also yields further insight into his historical analysis of realism in the context of his more general views on aesthetic theory. Brecht insists that restrictive notions of art must be abandoned, in favour of a more expansive conception of art. He therefore rejects a series of propositions characteristic of modern aesthetics, namely that art can only deal with universal features of human nature; that creation in art is deeply and intensely personal, so much so that technical considerations of, say, narrative structure are inimical to art; that originality in art is grounded in the artist's unconscious, just as the insights embodied in art transcend those generated by the intellect; that art must be strictly demarcated from science. For Brecht, on the other hand, a comprehensive conception of art should include the arts of engineering, of medical surgery, of lecturing and public speaking. Similarly, artists are enjoined to produce representations of reality which are as useful and as practicable as those of scientists.

Contemporary artists are confronted by a major dilemma, however, in that, like contemporary physicists, they must represent forces which underlie actuality and are not immediately visible to us. But, in depicting such hidden realities, they run the risk of lapsing into modernist subjectivism when moving beyond the realm of phenomenal experience. Brecht's solution to this dilemma is to propose that art must be firmly grounded in social science, which identifies and explains political and economic processes that are hidden from view. Realist writers must concentrate on revealing the dynamic forces that underpin everyday social life, and base their texts not on intuition, but on the careful study of the laws of nature and society. They must then expose the contradictions that emerge when new dynamic forces come into conflict with pre-existing patterns of belief and modes of action.

Brecht's emphasis on dynamism and contradiction also comes into play in his historical account of realism. Following the tradition of Marxist orthodoxy that extends from Mehring to Lukács, Brecht argues that the key factor in the emergence of realism was the self-portrayal of the rising middle class in the eighteenth century. Indeed, he asserts that truly creative realism can *only* be developed in collaboration with rising social classes capable of intervening in social institutions and resolving economic and political problems posed by the dynamic development of productive forces. At the same time, Brecht continues to maintain that the societal function of realism alters, that it is historical and relative. Even within the confines of a rising class, the practical benefits of realist works vary considerably, depending on which particular class tendencies a writer represents. And a writer with less progressive social opinions – Balzac, as opposed to Dickens, for example – may nonetheless generate more insight into capitalism by revealing societal contradictions that impel the reader to make abstract judgements with a view to influencing society.

Brecht's essay 'On the Popularity of the Crime Novel' (no. 59) imputes a similar position to its readers, whose responses are said to be logical and intellectual rather than intuitive and emotive. The crime novel abandons the introspective psychology associated with traditional literary genres, adopting instead an externalist approach to the representation of character. Characters are developed from their actions, rather than vice versa, and the reader is required to assume the analytic persona of the natural scientist, drawing abstract conclusions from evidence, instead of identifying with complex personalities. Brecht identifies clear parallels between the techniques of the crime novel and the working methods of scientists. Both identify and collate facts, develop hypotheses, test those hypotheses experimentally, and expose previously unknown causal relations. At the same time, however, the rationality and intellectuality of the crime novel set it apart from everyday life. Whereas the crime novel is a haven of neat and orderly thought processes and clear-sighted decision-making, everyday life is messy, complex and inconclusive. While strict causal laws function satisfactorily in the crime novel, in everyday life we are confronted by probabilities and uncertainties. Yet it is precisely this disparity between the crime novel and everyday life that accounts for its popularity in the contemporary era. For, as Brecht stridently observes, 'We undergo our life experiences in a catastrophic form.' The crime novel provides us with the intellectual training we need in order to reconstruct the hidden patterns of an ostensibly chaotic world.

---

[1] See *Brecht on Film and Radio*, pp. 164–5; the entire text of *The Threepenny Lawsuit* occupies pp. 147–99.

[2] My translation differs somewhat from previous versions, but is a more accurate rendition of Brecht's text. 'The Popular and the Realistic' is translated in *Brecht on Theatre*, pp. 107–15.

53

The Expressionism Debate

The Expressionism Debate

At the moment, people are talking about Expressionism again.

And so we have that neat and tidy Marxist analysis which, with an alarming orderliness, puts artistic trends into certain pigeon-holes that already contain political parties, where Expressionism, e.g., is assigned to the USP. Something heavy-handed and inhuman is at work here. An order is being created not through production, but through elimination. Something is being 'reduced to its simplest formula'. Something that was alive, was wrong. I always remember with a mixture of pleasure and horror (which shouldn't exist, should it?) the joke in a satirical magazine, in which an aviator pointed at a pigeon and said, pigeons, e.g., fly incorrectly.

Several age cohorts of artists went through an Expressionist period. This artistic trend was contradictory, erratic, confused (it even made a principle of this), and it was full of protest (mainly that of powerlessness). Its protest was aimed at the nature of artistic representation, at a time when what was represented itself invited protest. Its protest was loud and unclear. The artists continued to develop, in various directions. The artistic judge said of some of them 'they became something despite Expressionism', and of others 'they came to nothing because of Expressionism'.

What is it about this artistic judge that annoys me? It's the fact that I can't get rid of the feeling that his opinion is this: we mustn't get carried away. What he means is this: the Expressionists have simply relocated their passions, instead of getting rid of them altogether. But what he says is this: we mustn't get carried away. I myself was never an Expressionist, but artistic judges like this annoy me. There's a confusion in the debate concerning formalism. One person says 'you people are only changing form, and not content'.

The others have the feeling that you really are sacrificing content to form, and to conventional form, moreover. There's one thing, you see, that many people do not understand: holding on to the old conventional forms, when confronted by the constantly new demands of the constantly changing social environment, is also formalism.

Can we subversives really come out against experimentation? What, 'we shouldn't have taken up arms'? It would be better to explain the disadvantages of a putsch by explaining the advantages of a revolution. But not the advantages of evolution.

Turning realism into a formal issue, linking it with one, only one form (and an old form at that) means: sterilising it. Realist writing is not a formal issue. All formal features that prevent us from getting to the bottom of social causality must go; all formal features that help us to get to the bottom of social causality must be welcomed.

If you want to speak to the people, you must be understood by the people. But that, again, is no mere formal issue. The people don't just understand the old forms. In order to reveal social causality to the people, Marx, Engels and Lenin resorted to very new forms. Lenin didn't just say different things from Bismarck, he also spoke in a different way. He wanted to speak neither in the old form nor in a new one. He spoke in a form that suited.

The mistakes and errors of some Futurists are obvious. They put an enormous cucumber on an enormous cube, painted the whole thing red and called it *Lenin's Portrait*. What they intended to say was this: Lenin shouldn't resemble anything that has ever been seen anywhere before. The picture was supposed to remind people of nothing they recognised from the bad old days. Unfortunately, it didn't remind them of Lenin either. That is a terrible thing to happen. But that still doesn't put those artists in the right whose pictures now do indeed remind us of Lenin, but whose style of painting reminds us in no way of Lenin's mode of struggle. That is also obvious.

We must fight against formalism as realists and as socialists.

['*Die Expressionismusdebatte*', BFA 22/417–19.]

Written 1938.

Brecht's interventions in the Expressionism debate were not published at the time, and the majority of them did not appear until ten years after his death in his two-volume *Schriften zur Literatur und Kunst*, edited by Werner Hecht (Aufbau, 1966). His comment on the relationship between Expressionism and the USP is based on claims made by Georg Lukács. Lukács had maintained that, towards the end of World War I, Expressionism had become the literary ideology of the USP or Unabhängige Sozialdemokratische Partei (Independent Social Democratic Party). The USP had been founded in 1917 as an anti-war party, recruiting from across the political spectrum of the majority Social Democratic Party. The USP achieved major electoral successes in the immediate post-war period, but went into sharp decline after its left wing left the party to join the German Communist Party in December 1920. The remainder of its membership merged with the Social Democratic Party in September 1922. Recent scholarship has cast considerable doubt on Lukács's claims: see Richard Sheppard, 'Artists, Intellectuals and the USPD 1917–1922. Some Preliminary Reflections', *Literaturwissenschaftliches Jahrbuch*, 32 (1991), pp. 175–216.

Practical Thoughts on the Expressionism Debate

The debate about Expressionism, organised by *The Word*, has very quickly turned into a battle with the slogans 'Up with Expressionism' and 'Up with Realism'. Old wounds are erupting, new ones are being made, outdated hostilities between friend and foe are being pursued, people are beating their breasts, or each other's. Nobody, apparently, can be convinced of anything but their own viewpoint. Up to now, everything has been in a state of wonderful disarray, i.e., the parties are not making easy compromises, but are rearming with all their might. Somewhat dejectedly, two spectators stand on the field of battle, the *writer* and the *reader*. The latter has read and seen the things about which the battle is raging, while the former still has things to write. He watches this total rearmament with hunched shoulders, he hears the knives being sharpened.

The *reader* (and the *viewer*, to the extent that pictures are concerned) is remorseful too. His pleasure in looking at a Chagall, a pleasure which he clearly recollects, has just been exposed as being sinful. The matter is aggravated by the fact that, at the time, he didn't finish reading a novel that was declared to be exemplary, and he knows even now that he won't summon up the moral strength to have another go at it. Still, horses are not in fact blue, it was quite right for that to be denounced in the debate.

Remorsefulness produces gallows humour. In the case of a strong constitution, doubt. Maybe the battle lines haven't been drawn quite correctly? In such a case, disarray roughly similar to ours would arise. E.g., if the 'Up with Expressionism' party contained a series of realists, and the 'Up with Realism' party contained a bunch of bashful types who actually just wanted to 'express' themselves. Toller's *Transformation* was an Expressionist play, and it showed many people all sorts of aspects of reality that they didn't know about or only half knew. It didn't show everything by any means, and not everything it showed was true to reality. But maybe Mann's *Joseph* novel doesn't contain the whole of reality? Nor does his *Buddenbrooks*. And, is the *Joseph* novel really written with much more popular appeal than *Ulysses*? I have heard quite intelligent readers praise Joyce's book for its realism. Not that they praised the way it's written as such (some spoke of affectation), but it did seem to them to have a realist content. People will probably call me a compromiser if I admit that *Ulysses* made me laugh almost as much as *Schwejk*, and usually people like me only laugh at realist satires.

Lukács has, as it were, wiped the floor with my friend Eisler (who will strike few people as a pale aesthete) because he supposedly did not display the prescribed reverential emotion when acting as executor for the will of the cultural heritage. He rummaged around in it, as it were, and refused to take possession of *everything*. Well, maybe as he is an exile he is not in a position to lug that much around with him.

There must be some misunderstanding here.

There are enough people who are strictly and consistently against realism. E.g., the Fascists. They have an interest in reality not being depicted as it is. And the whole of capitalism shares this interest with them, even if it advocates it in a less drastic form. George Grosz didn't take many fewer formal liberties than Franz Marc. Mr Hitler thundered on about the fact that the horses in Marc were not like they are in reality, but he wasn't as loud in maintaining that the middle class in Grosz are different from how they are in reality. Grosz had taken a few more, different, liberties.

We must not spend too much time on formal issues. Or else we must be precise and say something concrete. Otherwise, we will become formalists in our role as critics, no matter what vocabulary we make use of. Our contemporary storytellers become distraught if they have to hear too often that 'our grandmothers could tell stories in a completely different way'. Maybe the woman was a realist. Assuming that we are realists, too, would we then have to tell stories in exactly the same way as our grandmothers? There must be some misunderstanding here.

Do not proclaim with an expression of infallibility that there is only the one true way to describe a room, do not excommunicate montage, do not put *interior monologue* on the Index! Do not strike the young people dead with the old names! Do not permit artistic technique to develop until 1900, but not from then onwards! What is it with this Balzac, who was without doubt a great writer and a pretty good realist? *Old Goriot* has a great plot compared with Flaubert's *Sentimental Education*, which is also a significant realist work, but other works by Balzac have weaker, less memorable, less plot-like plots. *The Wild Ass's Skin* is symbolist, this writer's mode of writing changes constantly, and Taine thinks, even though he admires him enormously, that he could not write at all, which is unforgivable for a Frenchman! Amongst other things, Balzac constantly interpolates dozens of pages of self-contained treatises about themes that 'have absolutely nothing to do with the issue'! He is a realist, he works with every means to get a hold on reality. And at the same time, let us not forget, his literary competitors force him to make astonishing deviations of Romantic and other sorts. Being advised to 'Stick to Balzac' is like being advised to 'Stick to the sea'!

As long as we do not have a scientifically based definition of *realism*, it may be better, i.e., more practical, i.e., more encouraging for realist writing, to speak of realists and their method of influencing reality by means of accurate reproductions of reality.

We will then be concerned not so much to restrict the number and types of these methods as, rather, to expand them. In that way we will encourage invention instead of discouraging it. We will put a price on truth, and allow any elbow room that's needed in order to attain it. In short, we will act as realists.

The Marxist classics paid considerable attention to, and gained attention for, old *Hegel*'s statement that truth is concrete. It has demonstrated a quite extraordinary explosive force, and will continue to do so. No realist should disregard this statement in the context of the meaning it has been given in the Marxist classics. Realism, with which the literature of the anti-Fascists stands or falls, should not be reduced to the status of a formal issue. You should also be a realist (and not only 'be for realism') in your role as a critic. You should say: this and that scene, in this and that novel, does not correspond to reality because . . . or: the behaviour of worker x in situation y does not correspond to the real behaviour of a worker with the traits in question, because . . . or: the treatment of tuberculosis in this novel gives quite the wrong idea, because in reality . . . It is quite correct that, when it is being described, too few aspects can be attributed to an issue, with the result that it no longer makes a realistic impression. This can be demonstrated concretely, with reference to individual cases. On the other hand, works that cannot extract any new aspects from reality are hardly great realist works: no realist is content to repeat continually what people already know; that does not display a living relationship to reality. That, too, can be demonstrated concretely, with reference to individual cases. A realist writes in such a way that he can be understood, because he wants to have a real impact on real people. What is comprehensible, and what is not, can be demonstrated concretely, with reference to individual cases. (Not only, e.g., those things are comprehensible which have already been understood.) A realist who concerns himself with art (e.g., as a critic) allows art a certain amount of elbow room so that it can be realist. He grants art a right to humour (over- and understatement), imagination, and joy in expression (in new expression too, in individual expression). He knows that you find that in real artists.

Realism is not a formal issue. You cannot take the form of one single realist (or of a limited number of realists) and call it *the* form of realism. That is unrealistic. Proceeding in that way would lead to the conclusion that *either* Swift and Aristophanes *or* Balzac and Tolstoy were realists. And, if you take the form of a dead writer, to the conclusion that no living writer is a realist.

So are we giving up on theory? No, we are building it up. We are preventing ourselves from obtaining a theory that consists of a mere description and interpretation of existing works of art, from which purely formal guidelines are derived. For the works that are yet to be created. We are preventing a formalist mode of criticism. Realism is at stake.

['*Praktisches zur Expressionismusdebatte*', BFA 22/419–23.]

Written 1938.

Ernst Toller's play *Transformation*, premiered in 1919, was one of the most important plays in post-war Expressionist theatre. Brecht had published a scathing review of *Transformation* and other Expressionist plays in 1920, in an essay entitled 'Dramatic Paper and Other Items'; compare also nos 4 and 5.

Brecht's interest in Jaroslav Hašek's novel *The Adventures of the Good Soldier Schwejk* dates back to 1928, when it was produced by Erwin Piscator in dramatised form at the Piscator-Bühne.

Franz Marc was a major early Expressionist painter, best known for his non-naturalistic use of colour in paintings such as *The Red Horses* and *Blue Horse I* (both 1911).

Brecht adopted Hegel's dictum that 'truth is concrete' as a motto which he pinned to the wall in his study in Svendborg.

The final sentence of Brecht's essay sardonically quotes the title of Lukács's essay 'Realism is at Stake', translated as 'Realism in the Balance' in Ernst Bloch et al., *Aesthetics and Politics* (Verso, 1977), pp. 28–59.

54

Breadth and Variety of the Realist Mode of Writing

Prologue

Several journals, amongst them *The Word*, have recently published extensive discussions which, for all the diversity of their standpoints, nonetheless displayed some unity about the fact that in order to obtain literature which intervenes in society, it is necessary to combat certain purely formalist trends. The attempt was made to establish how far specific formal elements weaken the impact of literary works, and transmit a false image of reality. As the discussion was, for the most part, conducted at a somewhat general level, and the specifics remained rather vague, many readers gained the impression that it was a question of completely rejecting the deployment of new forms, and ending discussion about this. Of course, that is by no means the only opinion. Even if the beginnings of a Marxist aesthetic existed, in addition to the beginnings of Marxist literary research, a Marxist aesthetic would not declare the evolution of artistic forms to be over and done with. The numerous submissions of lyric poetry to the editorial board of *The Word*, e.g., show that detailed examinations of lyric forms are very necessary. The following brief study is intended to help us reach an agreement about one of the many areas.

['*Weite und Vielfalt der realistischen Schreibweise (Vorspann)*'*, BFA 22/423.]

Written 1938. This text was originally intended to form the Introduction to the next essay.

Breadth and Variety of the Realist Mode of Writing

Recently, thanks probably to several essays which were particularly interested in a specific realist mode of writing, that of the bourgeois novel, concerns have been expressed on the part of readers of *The*

Word that this magazine wanted to assign too narrow a space to realism in literature. It may be that, in a few discussions, the realist mode of writing was characterised in far too formal terms, and that many a reader therefore came away with the idea that what is being proposed is that a book is written in a realist way if it is 'written in the same way as the bourgeois realist novels of the last century'. Of course that is not being proposed. Realist writing can only be distinguished from non-realist writing by being confronted with the very reality it deals with. There are no special formalities that have to be observed. It may be a good idea to introduce to the reader at this point a writer from the past, who wrote differently from bourgeois novelists and yet must still be called a great realist: the great revolutionary English poet P. B. Shelley. If it were the case that his great ballad *The Mask of Anarchy*, written immediately after the bourgeoisie's bloody suppression of riots in Manchester (1819), did not fit the usual descriptions of a realist mode of writing, then we would need to make sure that the description of the realist mode of writing is indeed changed, broadened and completed. Shelley describes how a terrible procession makes its way from Manchester to London:

> I met Murder on the way –
> He had a mask like Castlereagh,
> Very smooth he looked, yet grim;
> Seven bloodhounds followed him:
>
> All were fat; and well they might
> Be in admirable plight,
> For one by one, and two by two,
> He tossed them human hearts to chew
> Which from his wide cloak he drew.
>
> Next came Fraud, and he had on,
> Like Eldon, an ermined gown;
> His big tears, for he wept well,
> Turned to mill-stones as they fell,

And the little children who
Round his feet played to and fro,
Thinking every tear a gem,
Had their brains knocked out by them.

Clothed with Bible, as with light,
And the shadows of the night,
Like Sidmouth next, Hypocrisy
On a crocodile rode by.

And many more Destructions played
In this ghastly masquerade,
All disguised, even to the eyes,
Like Bishops, lawyers, peers or spies.

Last came Anarchy: he rode
On a white horse, splashed with blood;
He was pale even to the lips,
Like Death in the Apocalypse.

And he wore a kingly crown;
And in his grasp a sceptre shone;
On his brow this mark I saw –
'I AM GOD AND KING AND LAW.'

With a pace stately and fast,
Over English land he passed,
Trampling to a mire of blood
The adoring multitude.

And a mighty troop around,
With their trampling shook the ground,
Waving each a bloody sword,
For the service of their Lord;

And with glorious triumph, they
Rode through England proud and gay,
Drunk as with intoxication
Of the wine of desolation.

O'er fields and towns, from sea to sea,
Passed that Pageant swift and free,
Tearing up and trampling down
Till they came to London town;

And each dweller, panic-stricken,
Felt his heart with terror sicken
Hearing the tempestuous cry
Of the triumph of Anarchy.

For with pomp to meet him came
Clothed in arms like blood and flame
The hired Murderers, who did sing
'Thou art God and Law and King.

'We have waited weak and lone
For thy coming, Mighty One!
Our purses are empty, our swords are cold,
Give us glory and blood and gold.'

Lawyers and priests, a motley crowd,
To the earth their pale brows bowed,
Like a bad prayer not overloud
Whispering – 'Thou art Law and God.'

Then all cried with one accord
'Thou art King and God and Lord;
Anarchy, to Thee we bow,
Be Thy name made holy now!'

And Anarchy, the Skeleton,
Bowed and grinned to every one,
As well as if his education
Had cost ten millions to the Nation.

For he knew the Palaces
Of our Kings were rightly his;
His the sceptre, crown and globe,
And the gold-inwoven robe.

In this way, we follow the procession of anarchy towards London, and see great symbolic images, and know with every line that reality is having its say here. Not only is murder given its true name here, but also that which called itself law and order is unmasked as anarchy and criminality. And this 'symbolist' mode of writing did not in any way prevent Shelley from becoming very concrete. His flight did not soar up too high above the ground. His ballad goes on to speak of freedom, and this comes about as follows:

> 'Rise like Lions after slumber
> In unvanquishable number,
> Shake your chains to Earth like dew
> Which in sleep had fallen on you –
> Ye are many – they are few.
>
> 'What is Freedom? – ye can tell
> That which slavery is, too well –
> For its very name has grown
> To an echo of your own.
>
> ''Tis to work and have such pay
> As just keeps life from day to day
> In your limbs, as in a cell
> For the tyrants' use to dwell,
>
> 'So that ye for them are made
> Loom and plough and sword and spade,
> With or without your own will bent
> To their defence and nourishment;
>
> ''Tis to see your children weak
> With their mothers pine and peak
> When the winter winds are bleak –
> They are dying whilst I speak;
>
> ''Tis to hunger for such diet
> As the rich man in his riot
> Cast to the fat dogs that lie
> Surfeiting beneath his eye;

''Tis to let the Ghost of Gold
Take from Toil a thousandfold
More than e'er its substance could
In the tyrannies of old –

'Paper coin, that forgery
Of the title deeds, which ye
Hold to something from the worth
Of the inheritance of Earth;

''Tis to be a slave in soul
And to hold no strong control
Over your own will, but be
All that others make of ye;

'And at length when ye complain
With a murmur weak and vain,
'Tis to see the tyrants' crew
Ride over your wives and you –
Blood is on the grass like dew.

'Then it is to feel revenge
Fiercely thirsting to exchange
Blood for blood, and wrong for wrong –
Do not thus when ye are strong.

'Birds find rest, in narrow nest
When weary of their winged quest,
Beasts find fare, in woody lair
When storm and snow are in the air;

'Horses, oxen, have a home
When from daily toil they come;
Household dogs, when the wind roars
Find a home within warm doors;

'Asses, swine, have litter spread
And with fitting food are fed;
All things have a home but one –
Thou, o Englishman, hast none!

'This is slavery – savage men
Or wild beasts within a den
Would endure not as ye do –
But such ills they never knew.

'What art thou, Freedom? o, could slaves
Answer from their living graves
This demand, tyrants would flee
Like a dream's dim imagery.'

A lot can be learned from Balzac – assuming that we have already learned a lot. But poets like Shelley must be assigned an even more visible place than Balzac in the great school of realists, as Shelley better enables us to make abstractions than does Balzac, and is not an enemy of the lower classes, but their friend. We can see from Shelley that the realist mode of writing does not mean giving up imagination or true artistry. Nor does anything prevent the realists Cervantes and Swift from seeing knights fight windmills, and horses found states. It is not the concept of narrowness that is appropriate to realism, but the concept of breadth. Reality itself is broad, varied, contradictory; history creates and rejects models. The aesthete may, for example, want to lock up the moral of the story in the events depicted and ban the writer from pronouncing judgements. But *Grimmelshausen* refuses to be banned from moralising and abstracting, so does Dickens, so does Balzac. Tolstoy may make it easier for the reader to empathise; Voltaire makes it more difficult. Balzac constructs with tension, conflict-ridden; Hašek constructs without tension, and with very minor conflicts. External forms do not turn you into a realist. And there is also no infallible prophylactic: fresh artistry turns into putrid aestheticism, flourishing imagination into barren obscurantism, often in one and the same writer; we cannot warn people off artistry and imagination just because of that. Thus, realism degenerates into mechanical Naturalism, again and again, in the most important realists. Advising people to 'Write like Shelley!' would be absurd, as would advising people to 'Write like Balzac!'. Those advised in this way might express themselves, here, in images snatched from the lives of dead people, and speculate, there, on psychological reactions that no longer obtain. But, once we see the variety of ways in which reality can be described, we see that realism is not a formal issue. Nothing is worse when proposing formal models than proposing *too few* models. It is dangerous to link the great concept of realism to a few names, no matter how famous they may be, and to subsume a few forms into the one true creative method, even though they may well be useful forms. We must interrogate reality about literary forms, not aesthetics, not even the aesthetics of realism. The truth can be withheld in many ways, and it can be told in many ways. We derive our aesthetics, like our morality, from the needs of our struggle.

['*Weite und Vielfalt der realistischen Schreibweise*', BFA 22/424–33.]

Written 1938.

Shelley's poem *The Mask of Anarchy* was published in 1819 in the wake of the Peterloo massacre in Manchester on 16 August 1819. Brecht provided his own translation of *The Mask of Anarchy*, which was prepared in collaboration with Margarete Steffin. He also used Shelley's ballad as a model for his poem 'Freedom and Democracy' (1947).

Note Concerning 'Breadth and Variety of the Realist Mode of Writing'

I wrote this short essay because I have the impression that we are specifying in too formal a way the realist mode of writing which we need in the struggle against Hitler, with the result that at the enemy's front line we run the risk of getting embroiled in squabbling about form. I cannot believe, deep down, that Lukács really wants to propose just one single model for the realist mode of writing, that of the bourgeois realist novel of the last century, a model which I am not alone, amongst anti-Fascist, Communist fighters, in finding inadequate for literature. It is absolutely essential for us (and without a public, embittering, *time-consuming* dispute) to construe the concept of realism more broadly, more generously, in fact, more realistically, and not to let the problem of writing the truth about Fascism degenerate into a formal problem. Individual works must be assessed according to how far they have grasped reality in a concrete instance, and not according to how far they correspond in formal terms to a proposed model of a historical type. So I suggest that the question of broadening the concept of realism for our journal, with its broad anti-Hitler front, should not be made the subject of a new debate. A debate of that sort might only exacerbate unbearably any oppositions that do exist; which we must definitely avoid. I have therefore chosen to express my views in a positive fashion and have written in such a way that the issue can therefore be left at that (this issue took on a really vicious form in the last issue of *International Literature*, where Lukács denounced 'certain dramas by Brecht' as formalist without giving any evidence).

['*Bemerkung zu: "Über Weite und Vielfalt der realistischen Schreibweise"*'*,
BFA 22/433–4.]

Written 1938.

Brecht's comment on Lukács refers to the latter's 1938 essay 'Marx and the Problem of Ideological Decline'.

55

Socialist Realism

Transition from Bourgeois to Socialist Realism

The bourgeois realist novel, whose study is currently being recommended to socialist writers, contains a lot that needs to be learned about. We find in it a technique which permits the representation of complicated societal processes. This technique enables us to come to grips with the differentiated ('rich') psyche of bourgeois human beings. The refusal of these writers to express too much of their own opinions, in favour of the broadest possible *display of great masses of material*, furnishes the reader with rather rich images of an epoch. The opinions they refuse to express are bourgeois. The images are, of course, by no means complete, and the bourgeois viewpoint is, of course, generally maintained. We can put it this way: the representation hardly permits the formation of a non-bourgeois, i.e., anti-bourgeois, opinion either. This is one of the reasons why it is so difficult for socialist writers to take over technical devices from bourgeois realists. Technique is not, of course, something 'external', something that can be moved out of the ambit of tendentiousness. The socialist writer is not inclined just to leave the reader with masses of material to be used as raw materials for any old abstractions. No matter how deeply socialism 'has become second nature' to the socialist writer, and even if the limits which the bourgeois mode of production (and not just the mode of literary production) impose on the bourgeois writer no longer seem to 'apply' to him, his political consciousness will nevertheless be much more alert, the world will seem to him much more to be in the throes of stormy development, he will plan much more, because, of course, planning is exactly what socialism has brought into the mode of production. Careful criticism of bourgeois realism establishes that, in decisive points, this mode of writing fails as far as the socialist writer is concerned. The bourgeois novel's entire technique of empathy has reached a mortal crisis. The individual in whom empathy is generated has changed. The more clearly people understand that the fate of humankind is humankind, and the more clearly class struggle is recognised as the dominant factor in the causal nexus, the more fundamentally the old bourgeois technique of empathy fails. It shows itself more and more to be a historically conditioned technique, no matter how loudly it cries that, without it, art and aesthetic experience are absolutely impossible. We retain, of course, the task of representing complicated societal processes; empathy with a central individual has reached a crisis point precisely because empathy paralysed that type of representation. It's no longer simply a question of the novel providing us with sufficient real motives for the psychological movements of human beings; to us, the world seems to have been inadequately reproduced if it only appears in the mirror of the hero's emotional dispositions and reflections. The entire social causal complex can no longer be used as a mere stimulant for mental and emotional experiences. This is not in any way to deny the value of representing psychological processes, or even individuals, and the reader's mental and emotional experiences will, of course, remain. The issue here is as follows: the old technique has reached a point of crisis precisely because it did not allow a satisfactory depiction of individuals in the class struggle, and because these mental and emotional experiences do not insert the reader into the class struggle but lead him out of it. The transition from the bourgeois realist novel to the socialist realist novel is not a purely technical or a purely formal question, even though this transition involves a quite extraordinary transformation in technique. A mode of representation cannot simply remain untouched *in toto* (as 'the' realist mode), nor can the bourgeois standpoint, say, just be exchanged with the socialist (i.e., pro-letarian) standpoint. It is not enough to produce empathy with the proletarian rather than the bourgeois: the entire technique of empathy has become dubious (in principle, it's entirely conceivable that you could have a bourgeois novel which encourages empathy with a proletarian). Studying the bourgeois realist novel is very valuable – if we embark on the above-mentioned difficult investigations.

['*Übergang vom bürgerlichen zum sozialistischen Realismus*', BFA 22/460–2.]

Written 1938.

The doctrines associated with Socialist Realism emerged in the Soviet Union from 1928 onwards. The term was invented in 1932, but was not fleshed out until the 1934 All-Union Congress of Soviet Writers, in particular by Maxim Gorky and Andrei Zhdanov, the Secretary of the Communist Party of the USSR. Key features of Socialist Realism – later decried by T. W. Adorno as 'Boy-meets-tractor literature' – included typicality, optimism and revolutionary romanticism. Socialist Realism came to be designated as the only artistic style appropriate in a socialist society. See John E. Bowlt (ed.), *Russian Art of the Avant-Garde. Theory and Criticism* (Thames and Hudson, 1988), pp. 265–97.

On Socialist Realism

The slogan *Socialist Realism* is meaningful, practical, productive when it is specified in terms of time and place. It means that, where socialism is being constructed, the writer supports this construction, and researches and represents reality to this end, as, according to *Bacon*, we control nature by subjecting ourselves to it. The watchword means that, where people are fighting for the construction of socialism, the writer supports this fight, and researches and represents reality to this end. The slogan makes possible excellent criteria, criteria which are not located in the aesthetic, formal realm (does the writer support the construction of socialism, the constructors of socialism, the struggle for socialism, and does he grasp reality or just produce illusions, oversimplify what needs to be done, etc.?). If we are already at the point of constructing socialism – which itself, of course, means a constant fight against its enemies – then, no doubt, yet other criteria must come into play, criteria of an aesthetic, formal nature; because there is no doubt that the construction of socialism involves the expansion of the arts, the development of artistic productivity on the broadest basis. This is where the question of the cultural *heritage* arises; we have to grapple with cultural records passed down to us, records of a culture ruled by a different, hostile class, but which embraces, nevertheless, simply everything that has been produced; we have here before us the final stage that was reached under bourgeois rule and control, but which represents, nonetheless, the latest stage that humanity has reached. It is clear that grappling with the records of bourgeois culture in the period of struggle that precedes victory is different from doing this when victory has been won, in a situation where the battles that still remain can be fought from a position of superiority, where the entire economic and political substructure of culture is being turbulently transformed in the direction of socialism.

It would be a terrible diminution of the great slogan *Socialist Realism* if, say, people mechanically duplicated the Stalinist slogan of nationality politics, *socialist content, national form*, and proposed as a slogan something like *socialist content, bourgeois form*. In nationality politics, the slogan *national form* is thoroughly revolutionary. It means unshackling shackled nations, awakening the productive forces of backward nations, it meant that oppressed nations could hear socialism being talked about in their native language, it unshackled cultural forces. The slogan *bourgeois form* would simply be reactionary. It would merely signify the banality of *new wine in old bottles*. Stalin's clever attitude towards Mayakovsky, a wrecker of form of the first order, and his interesting comment that creative poets should be engineers of the soul, ought of themselves to warn our critics against making such generalisations and distorted transpositions. Indeed, the essays of various of our critics derive their characteristic quality of being so obviously beyond time and place from the fact that their criteria are obtained from here, there and everywhere, and not simply from the struggle. Study with *Balzac*, fine, but to what end? The question is justified: but it would hardly be raised in the case of Mayakovsky. If *formalism* means constantly seeking new forms for content that never changes, then retaining an old form for a new content is also a sign of formalism. Our critics must study the conditions of struggle, and develop their aesthetics from those conditions. Otherwise, their aesthetics are of no use to us, because we are in a state of struggle. I myself, e.g., started in all areas of literature and theatre with old, conventional forms. In lyric poetry, with the song and the ballad. In drama, with the five-act milieu play. In the novel, with the plot tied together in a variety of ways. But the struggle caused me to reach out for new forms. The old mode of writing hampered me in the struggle. I have studied many modes of writing, me of all people, but I cannot understand any remarks about modes of writing that do not take account of the needs of the struggle. And why should it be different for other people? I believe I can see very well which advantages are offered to our struggle by the bourgeois novel of the last century; as far as possible I learned from this. But I also see the disadvantages, and they are enormous. This leads to a complicated attitude towards the realists of bourgeois literature. I acknowledge them, I love some of their works, I learn from them, I am concerned to attain the standards of a general nature which Western humanity has achieved in them. But we also need to get beyond these standards. This is not simply a question of poetic force. It also depends on whether we can do justice to the conditions of *our* struggle. The formal principles that we can derive from the standard works of bourgeois realism, of capitalist and imperialist realism in literature, those principles are fundamentally inadequate. The historical, transitory and unique character of this mode of writing will dawn on anybody who is fighting for socialism. The capitalist and imperialist character of this 'content' permeates this 'form'. Our critics must realise that they are engaging in *formalist criticism* as long as they don't understand the need, or refuse, to deal with formal questions in a way that takes account of the conditions of our struggle for socialism.

['*Über sozialistischen Realismus*'*, BFA 22/463–5.]

Written 1938.

The slogan 'socialist content, nationalist form' is contained in a speech delivered by Stalin in 1936. Writing in *Pravda* in 1935, Stalin had described Mayakovsky as the most talented poet of the Soviet era. The phrase 'engineers of the soul' occurred in a conversation between Stalin and Gorky in 1932.

56

The Struggle Against Formalism

Glosses on a Formalist Theory of Realism

Anybody who does not define realism in purely formal terms (as what was taken to be realism around the 1890s in the realm of the bourgeois novel) can make all manner of objections to narrative techniques such as montage, interior monologue or estrangement, but they can make no objections from the standpoint of realism. You can, of course, have interior monologue that is to be designated formalist, but you can also have interior monologue that is realist, and, with montage, you can represent the world in a distorted and also in a correct fashion, there's no doubt about that. When dealing with purely formal questions, we should not speak in the name of Marxism without having second thoughts. That is not Marxist.

We must not confuse montage with that technical clumsiness by means of which lengthy sections of 'theoretical' material are inserted into quite conventional narrative, opinions of the writer, leading articles, descriptions, which are immaterial to the narrative. Montage has absolutely nothing to do with this artistic error.

The suggestion that we should study the novels of Balzac and Tolstoy is not a bad one. These writers really do develop some very important techniques for realist representation. (Incidentally, it's an almost incomprehensible logical error blithely to accuse someone who suggests making a selection from the representational methods of other writers of wanting to shred the works in question; nothing at all is done to those works. Historical research, of course, has to consider them as wholes, it does not construe them as a heap of technical methods, that is obvious. But the writer who is studying techniques approaches the works of previous generations and other classes from a different perspective, that is also obvious.)

['*Glossen zu einer formalistischen Realismustheorie*', BFA 22/465–6.]

Written 1938.

The Struggle Against Formalism in Literature

The struggle against formalism in literature is of the greatest significance, and is in no way just a 'phase' we're going through. This struggle must be fought out in its full breadth and depth, specifically not just 'formally', so that literature can fulfil its societal function. When making efforts to liquidate empty forms and meaningless talk, it is important that forms are at no point acknowledged or rejected separately from their societal functions, or in isolation from these.

What is formalism?

Proletarian writing is making great efforts to learn formal lessons from old works. That is natural. It is recognised that preceding periods cannot simply be skipped over. The new must overcome the old, but it must contain within itself the old that's been skipped over, it must 'sublate' it. People must recognise that a new type of learning is around now, which is critical, transforming and revolutionary. The new exists, but it emerges from struggle with the old, not without the old, not from thin air. Many people forget learning, or treat it with contempt, as a formal issue, and some people treat the critical dimension as a formal issue, as something obvious.

This leads to funny attitudes. People praise the content of a particular work and reject its form, other people do the opposite. Material and content are confused with one another, the author's convictions contradict the convictions of his material.

Realism is equated with sensualism, even though there are, of course, quite unrealistic sensualist works, and quite realistic unsensualist works. Many people think that a graphic description can only be produced on a sensualist basis, and they call everything else reportage, as if vivid reportage might not also exist. 'Composition' is made out to be a purely formal concern. When some people condemn montage, they come into very dangerous proximity to Blood and Soil, and a disreputable metaphysic of organicism, because they haven't, in fact, investigated montage; they haven't demarcated its sphere of influence, or taken note of its achievements. People try to combat aestheticism with a purely aesthetic vocabulary, intent only on using forms to breathe down formalism's neck. Literature simply has the duty to be literature. It is the writers' duty to improve their forms.

You cannot properly understand non-Euclidean geometry if you haven't studied Euclidean geometry. But non-Euclidean geometry presupposes both that you know Euclidean geometry, yet, at the same time, misunderstand it to a certain extent.

Changes that are not changes at all, changes 'in terms of form', descriptions that only reproduce externalities and do not equip us to form judgements, ceremonious conduct, acting so as to come up to form or preserve form, creations that only exist on paper, lip-service – that is all formalism. When concepts occur in literature, we should not move too far away from their meaning in other spheres. Formalism in literature is something literary, but it's not simply literary. Nor can we, e.g., be precise about realism unless we think about realism, realistic action, judgements, realists in other spheres.

It's not bad, not entirely bad, to refer to an inability to do something as giving rise to new movements, e.g., to say that epic theatre emerged thanks to the incapacity of some dramatists to produce real, genuine theatre of the usual sort. This incapacity is still with us. If we think of painting, then the first judgement made about recent painting, that of the Impressionists, for instance, was that they simply couldn't paint. And this was an expert judgement, this was the voice of the experts. Painting was something quite specific, something fixed, which required training of a specific type, and not simply the application of paint to canvas; anybody who was not capable of this quite specific skill, practised by many people since times of old, simply couldn't paint. The Impressionists answered insult with injury, saying that the good people who didn't understand their pictures couldn't see. The dispute lasted quite a while, and as they aged the Impressionists had the opportunity to become acquainted with the products of people about whom they could only say that they had no idea of painting. In the end, this game became so well-known that the most stupid philistines began to speculate in painting, only buying such paintings as they did not like, because they were the ones that quite obviously had a future. Not every artistic movement has a popular phase, but each one has an unpopular phase. Not every artistic movement has an unpopular phase, but quite a few have a phase that then becomes very popular. Not everything that comes from the people and is directed at the people is equally popular. These are truisms, but there are also falsisms, against which no other counter-arguments can be presented. If certain people see new forms, then they bellow accusingly 'formalism!', but they are themselves the worst formalists, worshipping the old forms at all costs, people who only look at forms, only pay attention to them, and only make them the object of their enquiry. The inability to do something, the inability to do something specific, really is a precondition for being able to do something else.

I cannot, e.g., represent the rise of a class from the perspective used by Balzac to represent the career of a young bourgeois, because I would need to represent the career of a young proletarian, but the rise of his class is reflected in his career just as precisely as the rise of the bourgeoisie is reflected in the career of a bourgeois. For some people, what goes on in the oil industry is somehow not quite human, a love story has to be introduced or some other 'purely' human conflict. In this way, the major phenomena of the contemporary era fail to become objects of literature, as do the major events. If I say, I cannot, then I am being somewhat imprecise, I have to say I cannot any longer, in other words write in the old way. I could do that once, when I started. Four-act play with simple plot, passionate conflict, etc. That play (*Drums in the Night*) was very successful, and I'm sorry that it was written by me of all people. Its political mistakes, and the shortcomings of its world-view, were inseparably linked to its normality, its four-actedness, simple plot, etc. A person with such views could not have written any other play but this, and had to have this success. A pity that this person was me of all people. So, my inability to write a normal drama was not hereditary, I acquired it, not without effort, and at a high price. I don't need to say that in those days I took my appreciative audience to be 'the people'. The supporters of normal dramatic writing, incidentally, are not always entirely satisfied with their creations, at least not with those of their colleagues, the other supporters of normal dramatic writing. Of course, they praise the latter's normality, but they feel something is lacking. The naturalistic dimension, e.g., is fine and can stay, but the language ought to be rather more elevated, unnaturalistic. The characters are well-drawn, but so damned straightforward, i.e., it's not the draughtsmanship that's primitive, but only what emerges from it. The plot carries them along, but not in the right direction. The passion is significant, but it is not ignited by quite the right issue. The whole thing is lively, but life is different. It's not just the sequencing of episodes, but, unfortunately, it is only an episode. You are really involved in the whole thing, but what have you actually experienced when you've finished? In short, it's good that people can write this way, but actually people need to be able to write in a different way. This type of self-criticism is excellent, but it mustn't be too formalist, and not just for form's sake.

['*Der Kampf gegen den Formalismus in der Literatur*'*, BFA 22/488–92.]

Written *c.* 1938.

Brecht's observations on reportage are a response to Lukács's essay 'Reportage or Composition', published in 1932, which was heavily critical of the reportage style of writing associated with avant-garde left-wing novelists in the late 1920s and early 1930s.

The slogan Bood and Soil was associated with Nazi painting, and implied a direct link between the natural world and national identity. The comment on Balzac's depiction of a young bourgeois refers to Eugène de Rastignac in *Old Goriot*.

Brecht's play *Drums in the Night*, set during the Spartacist uprising in Germany soon after the end of World War I, was premiered in 1922 and won the Kleist Prize.

Our Struggle Against Formalism

Our struggle against formalism would itself very quickly turn into hopeless formalism if we were to commit ourselves to specific (historical, transitory) forms.

One example: in the reality of high capitalism, we find not only the desire of capitalists to neglect the full development of human capacities, but also their practice, which does, in fact, cripple humanity, make it one-sided, empty it out, etc., in other words leaving crippled, one-sided, emptied human beings in its wake. We cannot simply accuse a writer who depicts such people of supporting this desire of capitalists, or of himself 'treating' his people like a capitalist. The struggle for full humanity does, of course, reawaken humanity in those who struggle, but this is a complicated process, and it occurs only in those who struggle. A writer who might endeavour merely to evaluate human beings differently from the way capitalists evaluate them, and therefore depicted human beings as being 'well-rounded', 'harmonious', 'psychologically rich' – such a writer would be a bad formalist. Balzac's technique cannot turn Henry Ford into a personality of Vautrin's ilk, but, even worse, nor does it allow us to represent the new humanity of the class-conscious proletariat of our era. *Upton Sinclair*'s technique is not too new, but too old for such tasks. It involves not too little Balzac, but too much.

We are making a grave error if we confuse efforts to teach people to enjoy Balzac with efforts to establish regulations for the construction of new, up-to-date novels. In the first case, it is necessary to grasp Balzac's novels as a whole; we must be able to empathise with his times, we must view his novels as self-contained, well-rounded and *sui generis*, and we must not criticise them in detail or pass judgement on finer points. If we wish to extract construction regulations from these novels, then we also need to put in place a certain empathy with their times, but we must also let technical considerations play their part. We transmute ourselves into critics, we read as design engineers.

['*Unser Kampf gegen Formalismus*'*, BFA 22/492–3.]

Written *c.* 1938.

Upton Sinclair was well-known for his documentary style of writing, and was one of the novelists criticised by Lukács in 'Reportage or Composition'.

57

On Non-representational Painting

I see that you have removed the motifs from your pictures. Recognisable objects don't occur in them any more. You reproduce a chair's sweeping curves, rather than the chair; the redness of the sky, rather than the burning building. You reproduce a mixture of colours and lines, rather than a mixture of things. I must say that this surprises me, basically because you say you are Communists, people who seek to transform our uninhabitable world. If you were not Communists, but were instead subservient spirits to those in power, your painting would not surprise me. Then your painting would not seem to me to be inappropriate, indeed, it would even seem to be logical. This is because things (which human beings are also a part of) as they are now mainly awaken strong feelings of aversion, mixed with thoughts that criticise them, and want them to be different. If painting were to reproduce things in a recognisable way, then it would get caught up in this dispute of feelings and thoughts, and if you were subservient spirits to those in power, then it would be clever of you to make things unrecognisable, because there are, after all, things that are in a pretty bad way – which may lead to accusations being made against your patrons. If you were subservient spirits to those in power, then you would be well advised to fulfil your patrons' desire for rather imprecise, general, somewhat non-committal depictions. It is those in power who like to hear sayings such as 'you must enjoy work for itself, no matter what its fruits are, how it proceeds, or why it is being done', or 'a forest is a pleasure even to someone who doesn't own it'. And it is only those who are ruled who cannot enjoy the most beautiful landscape, as they are roadworkers who have to break rocks in it, and on whom powerful emotions like love are lost, as their living conditions are too appalling. As painters and subservient spirits to those in power, you could proclaim that the most beautiful and most important feelings are produced by lines and colours (so that anybody can enjoy them, as the lines and colours of everything, even of the most expensive things, can be had for free). And, as painters to those in power, you could drag all the objects out of the world of feelings, all tangible assets, everything that is essential or substantial. As painters to those in power, you would not need specific feelings, such as anger at specific injustices or desire for specific things that are being withheld, nor feelings connected with knowledge that provoke feelings which might change the world or change things in specific ways; you would only need quite general, vague, unnameable feelings which are available to everybody, to thieves as well as to people who have been robbed, to oppressors as well as to the oppressed. Then you paint something red and indeterminate, e.g., and some people cry at the sight of this red and indeterminate thing because it reminds them of a rose, while other people cry because it reminds them of a child covered in blood who has been torn to bits by flying bombs. Then your task is done, you have produced feelings by means of lines and colours. – It is evident that in our world of class warfare, motifs, all the objects that can be recognised in pictures, must spark off the most varied feelings. When the exploiters laugh, the exploited cry. The poor, who lack a kitchen chair, do not lack of colour and form. The rich, who have a very nice antique chair, do not see it as something to sit on but as form and colour. We Communists see things differently from the exploiters and their subservient spirits. But our seeing things differently is focused on things. Things are at stake, not eyes. If we want to teach people that things should be seen differently, then we must teach this with reference to things. And we don't, of course, just want people simply to see 'differently', we want them to see in a quite specific way, a way which is different, not only different from every other way but correct, i.e., appropriate to the thing. We want mastery over things, in politics and in art, we don't simply want 'mastery'. Suppose somebody came along and said, 'I have mastery.' Wouldn't everybody ask, 'Over what?' I can hear you say, 'With our tubes of oil paint and our pencils, all we can do is reproduce the colours and lines of things.' That sounds as if you are modest people, honourable people, averse to any pretence. But it sounds better than it is. A thousand examples have demonstrated that it is possible using tubes of oil paint and pencils to state, reveal and teach more about things than just aspects to do with line and colour. Bruegel also only had tubes of oil paint and pencils, and he also reproduces the colours and lines of things, but that's not all he reproduces. The feelings he generates derive from his relationship to the objects which he reproduces, and that is why these are specific feelings, which can change the relationship which the viewer of his pictures has to the objects represented. Nor should you say, 'There are a lot of good things in art that weren't understood in their own day.' It does not follow from this that things can only be good if they were not understood in their own day. Point to your own pictures, show us instead how in our day human beings are like wolves tearing each other apart, and then say, 'That won't sell these days. Because these days, the only people with money for pictures are wolves. But things won't always be like that. And even our pictures will contribute to things not always being like that.'

['*Über gegenstandslose Malerei*', BFA 22/584–6.]

Written *c*. 1939.

Critical discussion of abstract art had featured in the Expressionism debate in 1938, but the non-representational type of art referred to by Brecht is particularly associated with the non-objective work of the Russian Suprematist Kasimir Malevich, and his classic painting *White on White*.

The work of Bruegel made a profound impression on Brecht in the mid-1930s: compare *Brecht on Theatre*, pp. 157–9.

58

Notes on the Realist Mode of Writing

1   *Realism and technique*

In comparison to literature, other arts, like music and the plastic arts, have a more liberated and more natural relationship to their technique. Musicians and painters like to discuss their technique, they develop technical terms, they require specialised study. Writers are much more inhibited and secretive in this respect; even if they have really become quite realistic in relation to lots of things, they still do not like to discuss their own technique. Although writers commonly understand 'art' to involve something quite specific, indeed, all too specific and restricted ('you can't call that art', 'in art everything is quite different'), this area itself is nonetheless rather obscure and vague, no matter how alien it claims to be in relation to other areas, or how much it supposedly differs from them.

It would be much more useful if the concept of 'art' were not construed too narrowly. When defining it, we should feel free to draw on such arts as the art of surgery, of university lecturing, of mechanical engineering and of flying. In this way we would run less risk of talking nonsense about something called 'the realm of art', something very narrowly delimited, something that permits very strict, albeit very obscure, doctrines. According to such doctrines, certain things do form part of the realm of art, and certain things do not. Art has its own domain. It gets linked to a fair number of features in the absence of which it supposedly is not art. A piece of writing is art only if it, e.g., infects all its readers with one and the same emotion; if it is not the case that all its readers (irrespective of which class they belong to) react in the same way, namely in the same way and equally strongly, then it simply is not art. Where science gains admission, art does not. Art does not have to answer to science. Skill only counts as 'art' when applied to specific areas, and whatever else may change in the world, these areas never change. 'Art' is fundamentally bound to deal only with things which are invariably 'eternal'. The variable drives of human beings are not worthy of being dealt with by art. In the theatre, the actor's art involves getting the spectator to empathise; if the actor aims to do something else, then no matter how much skill is displayed in what he does, it is just not 'art', etc., etc.

It's not as if writers did not also intentionally use technique in their art, but their technique is isolated from other techniques in a peculiar way; it is non-communicative, it has an entirely private character, it supposedly or even really is not transferable, it is a personal style, so that if a new mode of representation is taken over by another writer then this is branded as unoriginal. From this point of view, to talk about the structure of a novel or a play in such a technical way is as absurd as talking about the structure of a horse would be (which, incidentally, science would be prepared to do if needs be). In short, there is something mysterious in the relationship of literary artists to technique.

2 *The superstition of artists* is an interesting relic in our scientific age. Science itself, of course, is by no means as free of superstition as it pretends. Where scientific knowledge is inadequate, scientific faith is produced, which is always superstition. Science also is too

closely connected to a class which profits from knowledge only in quite specific areas, and from ignorance in many others. Nevertheless, it is astonishing to what extent art has guaranteed itself a right to superstition, and that art has surrounded itself with such a thick bulwark of superstitious fog. In those areas where it may and, indeed, must fight against superstition, science has given way to art, at its urgent request, and (without its instruments and methods) views art as a sanctuary of illusions whose necessity dimly dawns on it, given the nature of our social order. Science, however, which has established itself in the area of art itself, has established itself in an area where the class that tolerates it profits from superstition, and not from knowledge. As we have said, artists are terrified of science, though their terror also occasionally passes itself off as 'shy' admiration. The old picture at Sais, that work of art which clerics withhold from the view of 'mortals' in the myth, must no doubt have been a realist work of art. Artists are generally afraid of losing their originality by coming into contact with science. If they were to check out their originality, then they would recognise that it is a pretty mundane affair, and they would not very much like the place where that certain something originated if they were to set eyes upon it. The eternity of their feelings has only been around for a few decades, and many of their 'thousand-year-old drives' were drummed into them by their schoolteacher with his cane. What speaks out of artists is not so much the voice of their God as the voice of a few exploiters, so maybe it is the voice of their God after all. The 'pious awe' with which writers refuse to observe the origins of their ideas and feelings becomes understandable once we reveal those origins, and their concern that they would not be able to write any more if they 'knew too much' is not entirely unjustified, because it is much more difficult to make credible lies that you no longer believe in yourself. The proposition (to be read in any newspaper) is that it is best for artists to draw on the unconscious. It may well be that artists in our day, if they switch off their intellect or restrict it to a purely artisanal role, may occasionally blab out some truth; that sheds a clear light on their intellect. And it's not a particularly good indicator for a societal order when only the immature and the drunk speak the truth, or are at least prepared to speak it. The bad thing is simply that artists mostly draw only errors and lies from their unconscious. They only withdraw what was deposited into it, and while the withdrawal is unconscious, the deposit was usually very conscious. Those who advocate the theory of the unconscious triumphally indicate that art cannot 'be calculated', and cannot be produced mechanically at a drawing board. This is a platitude: every natural thought process comprises a playful dimension, it has multiple connections, and is slippery, emotional and speedy. Many unconscious operations are indeed carried out here. But that's not what our 'back-to-the-unconscious' theorists mean. They crudely advise against using the intellect and refer us to the rich treasure of unconscious knowledge, which simply has to be richer than the paltry muck heap of conscious knowledge they have organised. It's the old clerical thesis, directed towards the ill-nourished (who, however, feed the clerics), that their Father will feed them even if – or particularly if – they don't think. Besides, science itself has also felt this 'pious awe' at particular times – at a time when, from its current perspective, it wasn't yet science. You can read up on how great this awe was for the first anatomists; for a long time, after they had ceased to be in awe of God, they had to be in awe of the police. Now there can be hardly any doubt that there are such things as crises of production, which are somehow related to scientific efforts on the part of artists. In our day, some lyric poets forgot how to sing when they read *Kapital*. And even Schiller and Goethe had their scientific periods, when the artistic stream 'flowed more thinly'. It's just that contact with science produced crises only to the extent that, because of them, contact with reality ensued. Our lyric poets lost their voice, not so much because of the book *Kapital*, but because of capital itself. And a crisis shows, not how independent of reality art is, but how much art depends on reality. Our artists have stopped seeing in their class what it is not (and have stopped showing it), and they have stopped seeing (and showing) anything at all. Their eyes are not microscopes through which you see everything you put under them; you see only specific things, or nothing. These seers are easily gripped by panic, by the fear that their object was on the surface of the microscope, and not beneath it. The danger which is suspected, and often comes to pass, is located in the leap from one class to another. The writer who switches from one class to another emerges not from nothingness into something specific, but from something specific into something specific. He emerges, educated and, indeed, perfected in the means of expression of a class amongst whose enemies he would like to be counted from now onwards. He has studied its arts, even its unsavoury ones; he is a master at gratifying its vices. It is easy for him to prove that two times two makes five; now he's had enough of that, but how do you prove that two times two makes four? And, as Lenin says, actually he's always had to show that two times two makes a shoe brush! An enormous confusion arises not just in his thoughts, but in his feelings too. He knows that he has advocated the unnatural, but that came naturally to him. From now on, it comes unnaturally to him, naturally. If he feels anger, he must check whether anger is called for, he must view with mistrust his sympathies and his idea of justice, freedom and solidarity, and he must view all his impulses with suspicion. His situation is made harder rather than easier due to the fact that the new world is not completely different from the old one. In a certain sense, both classes live in one and the same world. Particular feelings and thoughts are only false in the old world, rather than simply not existing there. For these people the moment when the scales fall from their eyes may be (but isn't always, by any means) the moment when they see best, but it is hardly the moment when they show things best. Let us return to those artists whose pen or paintbrush is guided by as yet unknown forces. We know that our best painters, for instance, are not only not dissatisfied if their pictures do not resemble the reality they depict, but indeed are dissatisfied insofar as they do resemble reality. They feel that they ought to give us more than mere copies. The thing before them disintegrates into two things for them, one which is present and one which is to be created, one which is visible and one which is to be made visible; something is there, and there is something behind it. They are still haunted by primeval images, Plato's Ideas, which Bacon secularised in his 'Idols'. Modern science evolved by presenting a critique of ideas, which it treated as images or copies produced by human beings. As far as art is concerned, we can assume that, to every new optical utilisation of a thing, there corresponded a general societal utilisation. It really was the case that all sorts of stuff was hidden behind things. Not only processes like electrical or microbiological ones, whose law-like regularities had to be ascertained before things could be manipulated, but also societal processes, which were no less decisive in determining how things might be influenced. The artists' uneasiness was understandable. But the artists' consciousness is still conditioned in many ways by much earlier, more primitive ideas. We find ideas about creativity reminiscent of those which Lévy-Bruhl discovers in primitive communities; there, worlds are created in the 'imagination', in 'the artist's worlds', and people 'live' in them. Enemies are said to be killed if you shoot at copies or images of them. These ideas crop up, of course, almost inseparably entangled with later ones. The first pictorial compositions must have had all the trademarks of the revolutionary. What triumphed here was not only a sureness of hand achieved through work; to a certain extent, they constitute documents of primitive atheism (despite all the assurances of our excavators), in the midst of 'creation' humanity began to create, the gods became more dispensable, and don't we all know what can be invented? (The first atheist emerges at the very latest together with the first priest: the atheist being someone who makes himself useful to God.) We've reached the realm of primitives and clerics, but that is essential if we are to pursue the ideas of our artists, the priests of art (of whom quite a few are atheists). The usual objection to being concerned with science, or rather to the demand that artists should present us with images of reality which, in their own way, are just as useful as those of scientists, is this: 'then the world will become so bleak'. In reality, it won't get any bleaker than, in reality, it already is. But it really is bleak. This is where the ugly face of those who ransack the world peeks through most clearly. Humanity must be reshaped so that it can live in a 'bleak' (ransacked) world. Art is supposed to adjust humanity to the world, which is not to be reshaped. The world is over here, humanity is over there, humanity isn't really in the world, the world has already been bought up, you can only rent a room, until further notice. What people need are images of humanity, of worldless humanity indeed, and what people don't need are images of the world that make it possible to get a hold on the world.

The crisis of production of artists who are starting to get involved in changing the world is a side effect of the act of expropriation which is occurring here on a massive scale; the ravages of destruction are unavoidable, and they are worth it. The fearless gaze of a new art also falls on what has been destroyed.

3 *Realism and technique* (continued)

We can only arrive at a free discussion about technique, at a natural attitude to technique, if we are clear in our own minds about the new societal function which the writer fulfils if he wants to write in a realist way, i.e., consciously influenced by reality, and intentionally influencing reality. If we consider the generally accepted technique, especially the pseudo-realist technique, then we can see it as the extraordinarily backward, stunted technique which corresponds to the old function of art. Only very few of our 'realists' have, e.g., taken notice of the development of views on the human psyche in contemporary science and medical treatment. They are still stuck with an introspective type of psychology, a psychology without experiments, a psychology without history, etc. It's not that their descriptions of people are of no interest to psychologists, but in order to get something useful (knowledge of human nature) from them, you must be a psychologist. The statement 'a corner viewed through a temperament' really means 'a temperament viewed through a corner'. These people describe themselves, and nothing but themselves. In order to arrive at their statements about human beings, they subject themselves – each one of them acting as their own guinea pig – to imaginary experiments. As they are prepared to do anything to compel the reader to empathise with their characters – and, as far as they are concerned, the entire artistic value of their work depends on the success of this operation – they narrow down each character who is to be described, and do so in such a way that it must be possible for 'any' reader to empathise. Their human beings resemble one another, both across classes and across the centuries, so that they are not internally stratified, and don't contain real contradictions, and this is much worse than claiming that the *Bellum Gallicum* might have been typed if only typewriters had been available. This technique of representation and human enquiry is utterly primitive, and these writers' knowledge of human nature is recognisably infantile to just about anybody: you certainly couldn't use it to sell a car. The primitive way in which their characters are depicted, their dearth of reactions, their stereotypical nature and lack of development, all this alone would force writers to impose restrictions all over the place. All their processes run their course feebly and schematically. Nuances and abnormalities replace real riches everywhere. You don't discover this as a matter of course when reading these novels, because they appear as self-contained entities and serve up the construct of a world of their own, which of course tends to contain a certain logic: the impression of logic also emerges thanks to this general foreshortening and deformation, and this consistently implemented primitiveness. (By way of example, if you devise a primitive detective for a crime novel, then the criminal has got to be primitive too, etc.) If, however, you extract individual features, parts, characters, actions of characters, and confront them with the real world, you at once see the inadequacy and poverty of these constructs. It's true that undertaking an initiative such as this is condemned as barbaric and philistine by the relevant aesthetic; one has to view the thing as a whole, put oneself in the position of the artist, etc. This reprimand is, of course, only supposed to prevent us from applying our own sound common sense and our own experience of life, which may falter in the case of quite a few problems, but is entirely adequate for these.

Nor should we think that this astonishing primitiveness is not displayed by certain highbrow novels with their depictions of complicated psyches. In the work of these authors we get served up with very complicated psychological constellations, but, wherever you look, no causal relationships can be found; these are psyches cut off from their environment. We also encounter more complicated processes, but these, too, whirr away without causes. What we have here is a highly developed but sterile technique. How, then, should we construct a technique? Certainly not by completely rejecting any technique we come across, just because it is primitive or sterile. Its primitiveness and sterility is a fait accompli. The old technique (which we encounter in stereotypical form) was once capable of fulfilling certain societal functions; it is no longer capable of fulfilling new functions; but the new functions are mixed with the old ones, and we urgently need to study the outdated technique. The more recent, sterile, isolated technique, on the other hand, which has no healthy interaction with the environment, yields significant profit if we study the new functions together with it. We are approaching the problem of the cultural heritage.

4   *Whenever you propose literary models or exemplars*, you must make the effort to be very concrete. You must talk to technicians, and you must do that as a technician. It is very difficult to separate technique (phrasing, 'seeing', composing, etc.) from the respective content: the respective model sees a different world, of course, quite apart from the fact that it sees it in a different way. It is not, of course, enough just to show that a specific historical period is accurately reflected in an exemplary work of art. In literature, you cannot use the same mirror to reflect different periods in the way that you can use one and the same mirror to reflect various heads, and even tables and clouds. It's also not enough to show how the means of representation corresponded to the technological level of the period in question. All that says about a literary technique which we wish to recuperate is that the means of representation must actually correspond to the technological level of our period, which is wishful thinking. It's also wishful thinking to demand that the societal needs of the class we represent should be served 'just as well' by our works as the works of our models served their class. After hints like these, which are of infinite value for literary history, we have at best come to doubt whether we can utilise any of the techniques of our models if they are so closely connected with the contents, techniques and societal aims of other periods. Balzac

wrote in a world that was extraordinarily different from our own, using means of perception and representation that in no way correspond to our technological level (in manufacturing, biology, economics), and writing for a class that was just about to exploit the Code Napoléon. Of course, if we turn our attention to technique and technology, ours has become historical; it is an accumulation of the knowledge and practices of many centuries, i.e., much of the former technology is still alive in ours, it is a continuation, even if it is not a direct descendant or a mere addition. And so, there are technical elements in Balzac, even in Balzac, which we can use. By confronting his world, his class, the technological level of his age, with our world, our class and our technological level, we can gain valuable criteria, but what must be demonstrated at all costs is the *how* of his mode of working, in other words, how he saw and described, which of the methods he applied were different from those of other writers (in characterisation, getting hold of his material, displaying his knowledge, plot composition, etc., etc.). It's also true that the most dangerous thing of all is to speak only of a single model. Apart from the fact that a model such as this, propagated on its own, can never become really three-dimensional, a single model can never be enough under any circumstances. If you assume that technique can be separated from content (which is what you do as soon as you recommend models from different periods), then this act of separation must also succeed with contemporary works. And then it really isn't clear why we cannot study contemporary writing technique, insofar as it is connected to the technological level of our era, with at least the same profit as the technique of previous periods. In their case, too, it is of course essential to apply the above-mentioned criteria. It is to be expected, as a matter of course, that the steam engine, microscope, dynamo, etc., oil conglomerate, Rockefeller Institute, Paramount Films, etc., will have their counterparts in literary technique, counterparts which, like all these new phenomena, cannot simply be buried with the capitalist system. As soon as it's a case of describing the processes in which a human being in late capitalism is located, the forms of the Rousseauesque educational novel are extraordinarily outmoded, as are the techniques with which a Stendhal or a Balzac describe the career of a young bourgeois. The techniques of a Joyce or a Döblin are not merely products of decay; if you get rid of their influence instead of modifying it, then you merely get the influence of epigones, in other words, the Hemingways of this world. The works of Joyce and Döblin display in the grand manner the world-historical contradiction between the forces of production and the relations of production. To a certain extent, productive forces are represented in these works. Socialist writers in particular can become acquainted with valuable, highly developed technical devices[1] in these documents of hopelessness; they see the way out. Many models are needed; what's most instructive is comparison.

5 *What we can learn from a criticism interested in technique* would be, e.g., the difference between representational techniques in Balzac and Dickens. Let us take the representation of legal proceedings in these two authors. At first sight, it seems to be the case that Balzac is the representative of a different class from Dickens, or of the same class in a different situation. (The verdict that one of them speaks for the petty bourgeoisie, and the other for the upper-middle class, would, of course, not be sufficient.) It is a point of considerable interest that it is precisely the moralising mode of writing in Dickens, which sympathises with the object of the judicial process, that gives the impression of digging less deeply into reality than Balzac's mode of writing. Both writers depict the technical side of things, but in Dickens – in his otherwise magnificent representation of legal formalism in, say, *Bleak House* – the real meaning of the bourgeois judicial process, its occasional revolutionary role, is not seen anywhere near as clearly as it is in Balzac. Do understand me correctly, it's not my intention here to denounce advocacy of social reform, that would be absurd. If Balzac has more to offer the social researcher, and I think he does, then it will be because he generalises

---

[1] Interior monologue (*Joyce*), stylistic shifts (*Joyce*), dissectability of elements (*Döblin, Dos Passos*), associative mode of writing (*Joyce, Döblin*), montage of topical events (*Dos Passos*), estrangement (*Kafka*).

at a later stage than Dickens, and only passes judgement after a precise analysis that reveals contradictions; in that respect, what he does is scientific in the best sense of the word. Balzac's moral attitude can never be ours, but Dickens's moral attitude doesn't satisfy us either. Balzac presents us with a deeper knowledge of human nature, he makes it more manipulable. This would need to be shown in detail in a scientific analysis of the historical materialist sort, but with regard to the technical dimension, in other words, the means of representation. (How do Balzac and Dickens depict a judge, the course of a trial, etc.?)

6 On the different societal functions of realism and its variants

It is important, for the practice of realist writers, for literary theory to understand realism in relation to its different societal functions, i.e., as it develops.

The bourgeois revolutionary realist dramatic writing of John Gay, Beaumarchais and Lenz displays the following characteristics: the problems and self-portrayal of the rising bourgeois class are introduced to the stage, which had previously been left to the problems and self-portrayal of the feudal class. Even the takeover of the previously monopolised stage apparatus itself comes across as revolutionary – in John Gay's *Beggar's Opera*, through the fact that the 'underworld' starts up its own opera, and the common people sing. Reality steps on to the stage, i.e., the class that is beginning to control reality steps on to the stage. In this process a peculiar contradiction appears. On the one hand, the high-class stage is desecrated with some relish by the plebs' crude manner of speaking, but at the same time these plebs are consecrated by making use of previously monopolised elevated forms. Deriding the ceremonials of the ruling class, they immediately develop a pathos of their own. Juxtaposed with their *elevated* language, the language of the rulers appears *stilted*. The main thing is that, from now on, the middle class is the focus of attention – in Beaumarchais' *Figaro* and in Lenz's *Court Tutor*, the emancipated minion. That is true realism, because the middle class really had just become the dynamic centre of economic development, and now it was getting ready to become the political centre as well. Figaro the barber, on his own, is still able to sort out to some degree the complicated culinary problems of courtly society; he understands aristocratic relationships better than the aristocracy do. The pimp appears as the really productive person, the consuming stratum are unmasked as parasites who are already incapable of being parasitic. After a performance of *Figaro* you could quite easily say, 'A realist has spoken here.'

Lenz's realism displays different features. They will not disconcert the historical researcher. His court tutor is really a private teacher. The fact that he is still treated as a court tutor, and lets himself be treated as one, while he's actually a private teacher, that is what constitutes his tragedy. Because this German standard work of bourgeois realism is a tragedy at the opposite pole from French realism. You can almost hear the French laughing at the expense of the German private teacher, who, by entering into sexual relations with his female aristocratic pupil, doesn't get on in life, but rather is forced to castrate himself in order to go on performing his duties. The laughter of the French, and the wild protest of the German, both result from a revolutionary realist attitude.

The German realists of the stage, Lenz, the young Schiller, Büchner, the Kleist who wrote *Kohlhaas* (this work can be counted as dramatic literature for various reasons), the young Hauptmann, the Wedekind of *Spring Awakening* – they are also all realists in that their works are tragedies. The tragedy of the middle class gives way to the tragedy of the proletariat (*The Weavers*). The incomplete bourgeois revolution casts its shadow. *The Weavers*, the first great work that presents the emancipation of the proletariat, is a standard work of realism. The proletarian steps on to the stage, and does so as the masses. Everything here has a revolutionary effect. The language, Silesian popular dialect, the milieu in its minute details, the idea that selling the commodity of labour power can be a major subject of art. And yet a monumental weakness can be sensed here, something quite unrealistic in the playwright's attitude. This is the appeal to the pity of the middle class, an entirely futile appeal, i.e., it's futile if it does not simply suggest approving certain reforms of a superficial nature to better exploit the masses.

The Schiller of *The Robbers*, and the Kleist of *Kohlhaas*, had depicted the world in a condition where 'justice' had to shatter all juridical forms in order to win through. In *The Weavers* and in *The Beaver's Pelt*, law and order are not depicted sympathetically either. Realist creative writers give reality its due. They are the advocates of the reality that has developed, and they speak out against traditional and outdated human ideas and modes of behaviour.

Their efforts form one part of the efforts of particular classes, which are themselves realities, driving forces of reality. The societal function of their realism alters, is historical and relative; their realism displays various forms and varying strength.

Even in creative works of one and the same class, and in its rising phase, the practicable benefit of their reality content varies a lot, depending on which tendencies of the respective class the writer represents.

There is no doubt that Goethe's characters are incomparably truer than Schiller's. He was a great realist in his life and in his art. He represented those forces of his class that were dedicated to the natural sciences, strongly revolutionising forces.[2] The historians – Schiller was a historian – had completed their task long before the technicians and those describing nature had completed theirs. And Schiller's characters were all the more one-dimensional, rigid,

---

[2] Cf., however, the passage in *The French Campaign*, which Goethe wrote as a war reporter taking part in the Prussian intervention against the revolutionary Republic: 'They (a squad of riflemen) had hardly left the place when I believed I could pick out a very striking geological phenomenon on the wall where they had been resting; on the little wall built of limestone I saw a ledge of bright green stones all coloured jasper, and was very taken aback as to how such a curious type of stone should have come to be in the middle of these limestone seams in such quantities. However, I was disenchanted in the most unique fashion when, on going up to the spectre, I immediately noticed that it was the middle part of a mouldy loaf of bread which, as they had found it inedible, the riflemen had cut out in good humour and had spread out to decorate the wall.' This passage reveals a good deal about his realism, in the most innocent way.

intellectualised and untrue; the more finished history was, the more the social and revolutionary forces of the middle class were exhausted.

Artists cannot work in a realist manner if they are commissioned by exhausted classes threatened by productive forces, classes which are no longer capable of resolving in a productive way the ensuing difficulties. Hauptmann had worked in a realist way in his early works; in *The Weavers*, as we have said, he produced a standard work of realism, but even this work displays an interesting contradiction if we enquire about who commissioned it, about the class which provoked it. It is entirely possible to discover that the middle class can commission art, to be more exact, certain parts of the middle class, in a provisional alliance at least with parts of the proletarian class; it was commissioned by two parties who were in contradiction with one another. The work was a Naturalist work. Class struggle was depicted, and that was realist, but class struggle was invested with the peculiar character of being natural in the bourgeois sense, i.e., nature was construed metaphysically, the forces fighting against one another had evolved and, to some extent, had a history, but only to some extent, as they were no longer evolving and no longer had any history before them. It was natural that the proletarians were fighting, but it was also natural that they would be defeated. The influence of the environment on human beings was conceded, but not in order to direct the revolutionary spirit towards the environment; the environment appeared as fate, it wasn't depicted as a human construct that could be changed by humans. In his further 'development', Hauptmann turned away from realism. The Weimar Republic no longer saw him as a realist, nor even as a Naturalist, though it reserved the right to give repertory status from now on to his most Fascist work, *Florian Geyer*, which had had no success before the war (and before the nationalist phase of Social Democracy). Then the middle class felt seriously threatened and took serious counter-measures. It no longer saw any chance of securing peace and quiet by raising the living standards of its proletariat; it regarded this as no longer possible under its leadership, it no longer needed to continue educating its workforce for purposes of production, etc., and Hauptmann became a Fascist, but as a private individual; as far as we know, he didn't write any more plays in this capacity. Still, the middle class in Germany is even now setting itself real tasks on a large scale, but in a demarcated area. Contrary to the expectations of many people who surmised that they would represent the war in a completely unnaturalistic way, Fascist creative writers prefer to depict the war naturalistically, i.e., in all its horrors. Naturalistically, not realistically, Naturalism has completely metaphysicised itself, it has turned into sheer mysticism. War is represented as an entirely mechanical, material battle, it has absolutely no societal content, and does not develop.[3] Nevertheless, artistic forms do develop which are supposed to meet the need to subject war to control as a reality, though the ruling class sees war as the only solution.

Realism which is great, all-encompassing, and creative across the whole of society, can only be developed in art in collaboration with rising classes which must intervene in the entirety of societal institutions, in the whole of societal reality, if they themselves are to develop. For realist trends to be possible – partial realism, Naturalism, i.e., mechanistic, mystical, heroic realism – a ruling class must still be able to set sufficient soluble problems of some magnitude. For true realism to be possible, it must be possible to solve all societal problems (to control reality): there must be a new class which can take over the further development of productive forces.

7 Relativity of the characteristics of realism

Some well-known characteristics of realism include realist detail, a certain sensual dimension, the presence of 'unprocessed' raw material, etc. Realist detail provides what is particular, what a particular person has, what, from the point of view of the large-scale action, we more or less don't need to know about, e.g., Caesar's bald

---

[3] Compare these depictions with Grimmelshausen's in *Simplizius Simplicissimus*, where war is shown to be a social phenomenon, to be civil war.

patch, or it provides something which becomes particular in a given situation, perhaps some generally human feature which appears in a large general context in a particular way; we have a realist detail of this sort when Lear is dying, and asks for a button on his coat to be undone. In a learned treatise on the foundations of philosophy by Descartes, we suddenly read, 'Meanwhile, even if our senses occasionally deceive us about small and distant objects, it may well be that, with most other such objects, doubt is quite impossible, even though they are also derived from the senses, as with, e.g., the perception that I am here, sitting by the stove, wearing my winter coat, touching this paper with my hands, etc.' It is fairly certain that we feel this passage to be poetic. Descartes needs the reader to share his thoughts in a particularly realist way here. 'Unprocessed' raw material involves a certain superfluity of material which resists the straight line, a depiction of characters that doesn't just provide what keeps the plot going (human beings with their contradictions), the incorporation of mere facticity which is not to be neutralised in the framework of the action, the recording of what we would not have expected, chance, exceptions, the calculation that doesn't add up, in short, the recording of what constitutes the difference, as people are wont to say, between real life and bureaucratic estimates. There's no doubt that in the organised chaos of our age, calculations are often simple-minded; a calculation which is not simple-minded (it doesn't alert us to additional items) is, in fact, more realistic. This is all to be construed quite practically. If the good soldier Schwejk in Hašek's classic story has 'something' to sort out first in the lower town before he goes somewhere required by the plot, then Hašek displays, in relation to Schwejk, the same realist knowledge of human nature with which he endows Schwejk himself (apart from Hašek's superior position in relation to the real plot, which is, in fact, only a particular in a general context, an everyday adventure). This knowledge involves that clear sight of the oppressed regarding the oppressor with whom he must live, it involves that most sensitive ability to feel out his weaknesses and vices, the profound knowledge of his (the opponent's) real needs and embarrassments, the constant and alert allowance made for the unpredictable and imponderable, etc. (Schwejk's relationship to the military curate). The sensuous dimension of realism, its worldliness, is its best-known characteristic; however, it may mislead. Bodily needs play an enormous role for realists. An absolutely crucial feature is the extent to which realists can free themselves from ideologies and moral horn-blowing, which brand bodily needs as 'base', with a transparent intent. In our era, where human beings exploit human beings, it's true that sensuality appears as a preoccupation with hunger, with poor housing, with socially conditioned illness, with the perversion of sexual relationships. Being preoccupied with these processes is only realist, however, if they are recognised as being societal processes. Sensualism as such is far from being a characteristic of realism. The *capacity for empathy* can be dispensed with to a large degree, at least for the time being. It is entirely possible that writers will be more successful in stimulating the reader's ability to abstract – which is so important for grasping societal processes – if they do not stimulate the reader's sensory capacities. Realism is also not exactly synonymous with the elimination of imagination and invention. Cervantes's *Don Quixote* is a realist work because it shows the obsolescence of chivalry and the chivalrous spirit, yet knights never fought windmills. The largely realist character of Anatole France's *Penguin Island* is in no way spoilt by its imaginative garb. Writers may be permitted to use all the means they need to get control of reality. Even the absence of most of the characteristics we have cited here need not be of any significance. Any realist creative writer might be delighted to have written Lenin's little parable 'On Climbing High Mountains', and this text, a classic minor work of realism, would only be spoilt by, e.g., realist details, superfluity of material, etc.

8   *The realist in art – a realist outside art, too*

Realism in art is treated too often as a purely artistic concern. Art, then, has a realism peculiar to itself, i.e., artists understand realism to be something artistic, and as they have a very fixed view of art, which very often was fixed even before they propagated specifically realist art, the concept of realism also becomes very restricted and fixed. In relation to their own art, too, artists can adopt both an unrealistic, and a realist, attitude. It's a good idea for them to acknowledge how realism is applied in arts different from their own, as well as in non-artistic areas, in politics, in philosophy, in the sciences and in everyday life. Realists can find good mottoes in Francis Bacon's statements '*natura non nisi parendo vincitur*' ('only the person who obeys nature controls nature') and '*ignoratio causae destituit effectum*' ('if the cause is unknown, then the effect cannot be produced'). A realist perspective is one which studies the dynamic forces, a realist mode of action is one which sets the dynamic forces in motion. And Bacon's statements also apply, of course, to human nature. When you write a novel or a play, it's a question of acting realistically. The factor motivating the action of a character in a novel or a play is indicated in a realist way if a different motivating factor would have led to a different action, and no other factor would have led to that same action. It is realist to thrust the causes of processes into the ambit of (being influenced by) society. *The Brothers Karamazov* is not the work of a realist, though it does contain realist details, because Dostoevsky has no interest in thrusting the causes of the processes he depicts into the practical range of society, in fact, he clearly intends to remove them from it. Turgenev's *Diary of a Hunter* is a far more realist work, with its depiction of the oppression of the peasants by the estate owners, although it by no means enables us completely to master the reality in question, as it opens the door to liberal illusions. It's a good idea to define realist works as combative works. In them, reality is given a voice that we don't otherwise get to hear. They report a con-tradiction (and appoint themselves as its spokesman), whereby new dynamic forces come to contradict pre-existing views and modes of action. Realists fight against those who deny the existence of real forces. Realists fight any sort of reductionism, because it does not enable us to control reality. The assertion that German workers work for the sake of their wages may be realistic, compared with the assertion that they work from joy in production as such. Applied to the Spanish munitions workers who are serving the rebellion, this assertion is entirely unrealistic. In the German case, if wages are abolished or excessively reduced, people will stop work unless force is used; in the case of the Spanish workers, they would carry on working in this situation, unless force is used. A depiction which demonstrated to German workers that it was worth their while to make particular efforts for the sake of production would not be realist; workers such as these, who expect to improve their situation (as workers) by making sacrifices for the sake of production, are not realists – something which a realist depiction would establish at once. Realists who write novels or plays will also have a realistic view of their activity as a writer. They won't say that 'a novel takes shape in their head'; they won't rely on their 'intuition' after subjecting it to only minimal scrutiny. They will try to study the laws of nature with all the means that humanity has created in many long years of production. The realist in art is also a realist outside art.

9 All-encompassing nature of realism

The writing realist behaves realistically in every respect: towards his readers, his mode of writing (himself), his material. He takes account of the societal situation of his readers, the class they belong to, their attitude to art, their current goals; he examines his own relationship to the class he belongs to; he obtains his material with circumspection, and criticises it carefully. He does not seduce his readers from their reality into his, he does not appoint himself the measure of all things, he doesn't merely get hold of a few effective backdrops, a bit of local colour and a few obvious themes. He doesn't merely derive his knowledge of reality from sensory impressions; instead, he cajoles nature to display its wiles, with the help of all the expedients of praxis and science, representing nature's regularities in a way that enables them to intervene in life itself, the life of class struggle, of production, of the particular spiritual and bodily needs of our age. In constant struggle with reductionism, ideology and prejudice, he understands reality to be diverse, differentiated, dynamic and contradictory. He understands and manipulates art as a human practice which has specific qualities and a history of its own, but, nonetheless, is one practice amongst others, and is connected with other practices.

['*Notizen über realistische Schreibweise*', BFA 22/620–40.]

Written 1940.

§2 The phrase 'the old picture at Sais' refers to the legend of the veiled picture at Sais in ancient Egypt. Anybody who viewed the picture was said to suffer terrible consequences, in that their joy of life was lost for ever, as recounted in Schiller's 1795 poem *The Veiled Picture at Sais*.

Lévy-Bruhl's 1910 monograph on *The Thought of Primitive Peoples* was published in German in 1926.

§3 Brecht's formulation 'a corner viewed through a temperament' cites Émile Zola's Naturalist slogan 'A work of art is a corner of nature viewed through a temperament' (see Zola's 1866 essays 'My Hates' and 'Naturalism in the Theatre').

§6 John Gay's *The Beggar's Opera* was first performed in 1728, and was adapted in 1928 as *Die Dreigroschenoper* by Brecht and Elisabeth Hauptmann. J. M. R. Lenz's play *The Court Tutor*, written in 1774, was a classic text of the 'Storm and Stress Movement' in late eighteenth-century Germany. Brecht adapted it for the Berliner Ensemble in 1950.

The Weavers (1892) and *The Beaver's Pelt* (1893) were both written by the German Naturalist dramatist Gerhart Hauptmann. Although Brecht refers to Hauptmann's *Florian Geyer* as a Fascist work, it was in fact written in 1896.

Grimmelshausen's seventeenth-century novel *The Adventures of Simplicissimus* (1668), together with its various sequels, was of particular importance to Brecht as it strongly influenced his perceptions of the Thirty Years War. *Mother Courage and her Children* was loosely based on Grimmelshausen's *Biography of the Arch-Swindler and Vagrant Courasche* (1670).

§7 Brecht translated the scene from *King Lear* (act V, scene 3) in *The Messingkauf Dialogues*. The quotation from Descartes is taken from his *Meditations on the Foundations of Philosophy*.

Lenin's parable *On Climbing High Mountains* was published in German in 1924.

§8 Brecht's comment on Spanish munitions workers who are 'serving the rebellion' refers to the Spanish Civil War (1936–9).

59

The Crime Novel

On the Popularity of the Crime Novel

There is no doubt that the crime novel displays all the features of a flourishing branch of literature. It is true that the crime novel hardly ever gets mentioned in periodic surveys of best-sellers, but this need not derive in any way from the fact that it is simply not counted as 'literature'. It is much more likely that the broad mass of the population really does still prefer the psychological novel, and that the crime novel is only championed by a community of connoisseurs which, notwithstanding its numerical strength, is nothing to write home about. For these people, reading crime novels has assumed the character and strength of a habit. It is an intellectual habit.

Reading psychological (or maybe we should say: literary) novels cannot be called an intellectual occupation with the same degree of certainty, because the psychological (literary) novel discloses itself to the reader by means of operations intrinsically different from logical thought. The crime novel is about logical thought, and it requires logical thought from the reader. In that respect it is analogous to crossword puzzles.

Accordingly, it has a pattern, and it shows its strength in variation. No crime novelist will feel the slightest scruples about having his murder take place in the library of a lordly country house, even though that is highly unoriginal. The characters are seldom changed, and there are only a few motives for the murder. The good crime novelist doesn't invest much talent or thought into creating new characters or tracking down new motives for the deadly deed. That's not the point at issue. Anyone who exclaims 'It's always the same', on ascertaining that a tenth of all murders take place in a vicarage, has not understood the crime novel. They might as well exclaim 'It's always the same!' in the theatre as soon as the curtain rises. Originality is to be found elsewhere. The fact that a characteristic feature of the crime novel consists in variations on more or less fixed elements is what confers on the entire genre its aesthetic cachet. It is one of the features of a cultivated branch of literature.

Incidentally, the philistine's 'It's always the same' rests on the same error as the white man's judgement that all black people look alike. There are lots of patterns for the crime novel; all that is important is the fact that there are patterns.

Like the world itself, the crime novel is dominated by the English. The code of the English crime novel is the richest and the most cohesive. It delights in the strictest rules, and these are laid down in fine essayistic writings. The Americans have much weaker patterns and, from an English point of view, they are guilty of fishing for originality. Their murders are delivered on a conveyor belt and have the character of an epidemic. Occasionally, their novels degenerate into thrillers, i.e., the thrill is no longer spiritual, but purely and simply nervous.

Above all, the good English crime novel is fair. It displays moral strength. 'To play the game' is a matter of honour. The reader is not deceived; all the material is laid before him before the detective solves the riddle. The reader is put in a position to set about finding a solution himself.

It is astonishing how much the basic pattern of a good crime novel is reminiscent of our physicists' working methods. First of all, certain facts are noted down. There is a corpse. The clock is broken and is showing two o'clock. The housekeeper has a healthy aunt. Last night the sky was cloudy. Etc., etc. Then, working hypotheses are proposed that are able to fit the facts. The emergence of new facts, or the downgrading of facts that had already been noted, compels us to seek a new working hypothesis. At the end of this process comes the test of the working hypothesis: the experiment. If the thesis is correct, then the murderer must appear at this time and in this place on the basis of a specific measure.

What is crucial is that actions are not developed from characters, but that characters are developed from actions. You see people act, in a fragmented way. Their motives are obscure, and have to be logically inferred. Their actions are assumed to be determined primarily by their interests, almost without exception by their material interests. They are what is looked for.

Note the approximation to the scientific standpoint, and the enormous distance from the introspectively psychological novel.

Accordingly, it is much less important that scientific methods are depicted in crime novels, or that medicine, chemistry or mechanics play a major role; the crime novelist's entire mindset is influenced by science.

We can mention here that in the modern literary novel as well, in the works of Joyce, Döblin and Dos Passos, there is a clearly ascertainable schism between subjective and objective psychology, and such tendencies occur even in the most recent American verism, although this might also be a case of regression. Of course, you must avoid aesthetic evaluations if you are to see the connection between those highly complicated works by Joyce, Döblin and Dos Passos, and the crime novels of Sayers, Freeman and Rhode. If you see the connection, however, then you will acknowledge that, for all its primitiveness (and not just in aesthetic terms), the crime novel suits the needs of people of a scientific age even more than avant-garde works do.

When discussing the popularity of the crime novel, it's true that we must concede the important role played by the reader's hunger for adventurous events, simple suspense, etc., which the crime novel satisfies. It is pleasurable to see people *in action*, and to witness actions with factual consequences that can be established without more ado. People in crime novels leave their traces not only in the minds of their fellow humans, but also in their bodies and even in the soil in front of the library. The literary novel and real life are on one side of the equation, while the crime novel, which is a specific slice of real life, is on the other. People in real life rarely find that they have left their clues behind, at least so long as they don't become criminals and the police hunt down their traces. The life of the atomised mass of the people and the collectivised individual of our age takes its course without trace. This is where the crime novel provides certain substitutes.

An adventure novel could hardly be written in a different way from a crime novel: in our society, adventures are criminal.

However, intellectual pleasure comes about thanks to the *mental task* which the crime novel sets for the detective and the reader.

First of all, our powers of observation are given an arena in which they can play. The event that has taken place is constructed from the deformations of the scenery; the battle is reconstructed from the battlefield. The unexpected plays a role. We have to discover *inconsistencies*. The surgeon has calloused hands; the floor is dry, even though the window is open and it has rained; the butler was awake, but he didn't hear the shot. Then, the witness statements are critically scrutinised: this is a lie, that is a mistake. In the latter case, we observe, as it were, through instruments that record inaccurately, and have to establish the degrees of divergence. This process of making observations, drawing conclusions from them, and thereby coming to decisions, provides us with all sorts of satisfaction, for the simple reason that everyday life seldom permits our thought processes to proceed so effectively, and usually many obstacles intervene between observation and conclusion as well as between conclusion and decision. In most cases, we are simply not in a position to utilise our observations; whether we make observations or not has no influence on the course of our relationships. We are neither masters of our conclusions, nor masters of our decisions.

In the crime novel, we are served up with individually marked-out segments of life, isolated, demarcated, small-scale complexes of events, in which causality functions in a satisfactory way. This produces pleasurable thought. Let's take a simple example, from the history of crime this time, rather than from a novel. The murder was committed by means of town gas. Two people are suspects. One of them has an alibi for midnight, the other for the early hours. The solution is derived from the fact that a few dead flies were found on the windowsill. Hence, the murder took place towards morning: the flies were at the lit window – it's in this sort of way that questions relating to our complicated lives can really be *decided*.

The identification of an unknown murder victim also comes

about by drawing pleasurable conclusions in a restricted area of inquiry. By means of exact observations, his social position is ascertained, together with his geographical location. The small items found on his body are gradually given their biography. His dental bridge was constructed at this or that dentist's. But even before that fact is established, we know that he was in a good financial position when he had the bridge fitted: it's an expensive bridge.

The circle of suspects is also small. Their behaviour can be precisely observed, and be subjected to small tests. The investigator (detective and reader) inhabits an atmosphere remarkably free of conventions. Both the roguish baronet, and the life-long loyal servant, or the seventy-year-old aunt, *may* be the culprit. No Cabinet minister is above suspicion. From a sphere where only motive and opportunity count, the decision will be made as to whether he has killed a fellow human being.

We derive pleasure from the way in which the crime novelist leads us to rational judgements by compelling us to give up our prejudices. In order to do that, he must master the art of seduction. He must provide the people involved in the murder with both unappealing and attractive features. He must be provocative as regards our prejudices. The altruistic old botanist *can't* be the murderer, he has us exclaim. A gardener with two previous con-victions for poaching is capable of anything, he makes us sigh. He leads us astray with his *characterisations*.

Although we've been warned a thousand times (namely by reading a thousand crime novels), we forget once again that only motive and opportunity count. Societal conditions merely make the crime possible or necessary: they violate the character in the way they have shaped him. Of course the murderer is wicked, but, in order to take that view, we have to be able to pin the murder on him. The crime novel does not indicate a more direct way to discover its moral.

It's the same when tracking down the causal nexus.

Pinpointing the causal factors in human actions is the primary intellectual pleasure which the crime novel provides for us.

There's no doubt that we encounter everywhere in our everyday life the difficulties confronting our physicists in the realm of causality, but we do not encounter these difficulties in the crime novel. In everyday life, insofar as societal situations are involved, we are dependent on *statistical* causality, just as the physicists are in particular areas. In all existential questions, with the possible exception only of the most primitive ones, we have to make do with probabilistic calculations. Whether we can obtain this or that position with this or that knowledge is at best a question of probability. We are not even capable of citing straightforward motives for our own decisions, never mind those of other people. The opportunities we encounter are very vague, concealed, blurred. The law of causality works approximately, at best.

In the crime novel, it works perfectly once again. A few tricks remove the sources of disruption. The range of vision is skilfully narrowed down. And conclusions are drawn retrospectively, from the standpoint of the catastrophe. Because of that we arrive at a position which is, of course, very favourable for speculation.

At the same time, we can employ a type of thought here that our life has developed within us.

We are arriving at a crucial point in our little investigation into why it is that the intellectual operations which the crime novel facilitates for us are so exceedingly popular in our age.

We undergo our life experiences in a catastrophic form. We have to infer from catastrophes the way in which our societal coexistence works. We have to think to work out the 'inside story' behind crises, depressions, revolutions and wars. Even when we read newspapers (and also bills, letters of dismissal, call-up letters, etc.), we feel that someone must have done something for this evident catastrophe to have occurred. So who did what? Behind the events that are reported, we suspect other events that are not reported. Those are the *real* events. Only if we knew what they were would we understand.

Only history can instruct us about these real events – to the extent that the protagonists did not manage to keep them completely secret. History is written *after* catastrophes.

This basic situation in which intellectuals find themselves, according to which they are the objects and not the subjects of history, trains the type of thinking that they can pleasurably set to work in crime novels. Existence depends on unknown factors. 'Something must have happened', 'something is coming to a head', 'a situation has emerged' – that's what they feel, and their minds go on patrol. But clarity only comes about after the catastrophe, if at all. The murder has taken place. What came to a head before that? What happened? What sort of situation had emerged? Well, maybe we can work it out.

This point may well not be the crucial one; it may only be one point amongst others. The popularity of the crime novel has many causes. However, this cause seems to me to be one of the most interesting ones.

['*Über die Popularität des Kriminalromans*', BFA 22/504–10.]

Written *c.* 1938. Published in Swedish 1940. Brecht's considerable interest in the crime novel can be dated back to essays he had written on this subject in 1926 (compare no. 7), and he remained an avid reader of crime novels throughout his life.

On the Crime Novel

But the protagonists are sketched very roughly, the motives of their action are solid, the events crude, everything – especially the chain of events – is so improbable, it contains too much chance; a menial spirit is at work. There is no sense in complaining that the protagonists tend to be sketched only superficially. Usually, only as much is said about them as the reader needs to know in order to understand their actions; from the reader's perspective, the construction of the characters generally comes about on the basis of specific traits; there is a constant link with the ways they act. This or that person is vindictive, that is why he is writing the letter, or this or that letter is written by someone vindictive: who is the vindictive party? The reader participates in the construction of the characters as he does in an activity; it is an unmasking that is required. And because the victim, the person whose character sketch is to be produced, usually has to expect disadvantages from it, he only gives away his character traits with great reluctance. He doesn't only express himself, he produces traits, he forges: he disturbs the experiment on purpose. We are reminded again of modern physics: the object being observed is changed by the process of observation. Such peak performances of literary psychology (peak performances, because, from the standpoint of modern scientific psychology, the novel's depiction of human beings is totally outdated) occur in the crime novel precisely because bourgeois life is construed and described as commercial life. Occasionally you may even find creations of a higher order. Poe's chess thinker, Conan Doyle's Sherlock Holmes and Chesterton's Father Brown.

['*Über den Kriminalroman*', BFA 22/510–11.]

Written *c.* 1938.

Part Five

Brecht and German Socialism 1942–1956

(California–Berlin, GDR)

Introduction to Part Five

In the poem 'To those born later' Brecht memorably describes his life's journey through the 'wars of the classes' in the first half of the twentieth century (*Poems*, p. 320). His understanding of the origins of Nazism and the Second World War was classically Marxist, emphasising the primacy of economic power wielded by dominant class interests, which exploited a rhetoric of German racial superiority to justify imperialist expansionism. Brecht's wartime anti-Nazi activity was directed firmly towards a post-Fascist, socialist Germany. His life after the defeat of the Third Reich was dominated by the many conflicts between his engagement with the ideas of socialism and their imperfect realisation. The writings in this part cover these conflicts in the final fourteen years of Brecht's life: during which he returned, in 1947, to German-speaking territory from exile in the United States, initially to Switzerland and Austria, before settling in East Berlin in 1949, where he remained until his death in 1956. Above all, these texts document Brecht's complex relationship with the GDR government, in which political partisanship in the context of the escalating Cold War climate existed alongside an unorthodox aesthetic, and therefore cultural-political, standpoint. In these years Brecht did not produce large-scale reflections on single issues of political aesthetics in the manner of the great essays of the 1930s. Instead, we have an array of smaller and fragmentary pieces, either informal contributions for his own clarification, provoked by particular events and conflicts, or else short declarations, open letters and notes, such as might be published in the journals and newspapers or circulated in the political and arts institutions of the young GDR. His energies were consumed by the awkward negotiations of his situation, as a somewhat dissenting cultural figurehead of the regime. A pivotal event for our understanding of this final phase of Brecht's life and work is the East Berlin workers' uprising on 17 June 1953 and its suppression with Soviet military force. Accordingly, significant room is granted in this section both to Brecht's attempts to exploit the increased breathing space afforded to him in the cultural-political sphere and to his reaffirmation of support for the GDR regime in the wake of the uprising.

His experience of the superficiality of the American Way of Life, described in 'Where I Live' (no. 63) from his home in Santa Monica in 1944, served to reaffirm Brecht's rejection of the Weimar Republic's 'experiment' in capitalist liberal democracy, a view that his appearance before the House Committee on Un-American Activities in 1947 (see no. 64) did nothing to dispel. Throughout his anti-Nazi propaganda activity and perhaps most clearly in 'Report on the Situation of Germans in Exile' (no. 62), he opposed that damning judgement on the German people which came to be known as Vansittartism.[1] Brecht sought always, in line with Communist Party policy, to maintain the distinction between the German people on the one hand and the Nazis and their supporters on the other, amongst whom Brecht counted principally the middle classes. Yet, other texts written before his return to East Berlin already show his difficulties in sustaining that position. They range from the relative optimism of 'On the Declaration of the 26 United Nations' to the more cautious assessment of 'The *Other* Germany: 1943' (nos 60 and 61). In the latter text (published in English) he argued that, not only had working-class organisations been smashed, over a decade the German people's well-being had become increasingly dependent on preparations for military conquest and on its spoils. In those circumstances, 'a world which expects the German people to revolt and turn itself into a peaceful nation is expecting much'. At once a confession of Brecht's acute anxieties about a country ripe for Fascist resurgence, and a withering attack on the alarming intellectual impoverishment of the young generation of Germans, 'Conversations with Young Intellectuals' (no. 65) reveals much about Brecht's attitudes as he considered his future from Feldmeilen in Switzerland in the summer of 1948. The German people did not rise up and overthrow a criminal regime, and Brecht could not conceal his mistrust of that corrupted people, questioning its ability to act as a basis for the development of socialism.[2]

Yet, in Brecht's view, responsibility for Nazism lay always less with the working classes and their representatives than with the educated and moneyed classes. Socialism alone could act as the guarantor of peace. That view rankled with those intellectuals in West Germany who accepted the emerging Western orthodoxy of 'totalitarian theory', which made little distinction between Nazism and Marxism-Leninism. For all his hesitancy about returning to live in Germany, that decision, once taken, could only mean opting for the socialist East. As 'The Arts in Upheaval' (no. 68) demonstrates, only there did Brecht see genuine opportunities for the fruitful new relationship between politics and art that he hoped to realise through the Berliner Ensemble and institutions like the German Academy of Arts in East Berlin.[3] The division of Germany within the deepening ideological antagonism of the Cold War saw some of Brecht's anxieties displaced to the capitalist Federal Republic of Germany (FRG) and the sharpening of an ideological commitment to the German Democratic Republic (GDR). Even though Brecht never joined the ruling Socialist Unity Party for Germany (SED), it followed from his ideological commitment that his overriding loyalty in the Cold War remained to SED rule and to Stalin's rule in Eastern Europe.

The most talented of the many artists and intellectuals who opted for East Berlin, Brecht saw a major role for himself in shaping cultural life in the fledgling socialist state. Nonetheless, from the outset he encountered opposition from an emerging SED orthodoxy that in many ways represented a continuation of disagreements in the 1930s with Lukács over Socialist Realism. The major areas of contention were his dramatic theories and his insufficiently reverential treatment of the cultural heritage, neither of which delivered the uplifting role models from German history and contemporary society that were required of artists by a Party seeking to trumpet the successes of socialist reconstruction. Criticisms of the 'negativity' of the production of *Mother Courage and her Children* in January 1949 set the tone. However, the peculiar dynamics of the immediate post-war political situation added an especially explosive edge to these disagreements. The precarious existence of the GDR and the SED in the context of Stalin's repeated overtures to Western powers concerning a united Germany lent SED cultural policy a desperate, nationalistic dimension. Brecht and his increasingly beleaguered collaborators at the Berliner Ensemble and the Academy of Arts, such as the composers Hanns Eisler and Paul Dessau, could not begin to grasp properly the ramifications of this policy, given the fundamentally open, internationalist attitudes and the belief in the power of the dialectic that informed their understanding of Marxism.[4] In the Attack on Formalism announced in March 1951, the SED modified an instrument imported from Moscow to impose discipline on recalcitrant artists and intellectuals. The Central Committee identified in the aspiration to create something 'completely new' the formalist aim to

achieve a complete break with the classical cultural heritage. That leads to the deracination of the national culture, to the destruction of national consciousness, promotes cosmopolitanism and means, therefore, direct support for the policy of war pursued by American imperialism.[5]

For the SED, the presentation of historical and contemporary socialist role models became a patriotic duty; moreover, a questioning attitude to a tradition that had, after all, spawned Nazism was considered tantamount to treason. Brecht's collaboration with Dessau on the opera *The Trial of Lucullus* was immediately branded as formalist. SED critics complained about the seemingly incomprehensible combination of Dessau's music and Brecht's epic theatre in a piece whose anti-war message, through its mockery of a military leader, was deemed offensive to the Soviet Union and inappropriate during the Cold War (compare the account in *Collected Plays*, vol. 4). Accordingly, Brecht's writings from 1951 reflect a preoccupation with the notion of formalism, in particular as it was applied to the *Lucullus* opera (see nos 69–72). His notes for the defence of the text and music in 'Concerning the Accusation of Formalism' were used in discussions that were designed to give the appearance of open, public debate. Brecht was evidently flattered by the involvement of the GDR President, Wilhelm Pieck. In the interest of clarity for the 'new' audience, Brecht agreed to make substantial changes to his text, which he notes in 'The Discussion about *The Condemnation of Lucullus*', the work's amended title. These exchanges show that, wherever possible, Brecht sought agreement with the Party and did so for ideological, not tactical reasons. At the same time, in private conversations and in a series of short notes throughout 1951, Brecht severely criticised the Formalism Campaign and the employment by SED cultural politicians of precisely the kind of 'medical' vocabulary used by the National Socialists. In his 'Notes on the Discussion about Formalism' and 'What is Formalism?', for instance, he sets down his objections to the vaguely and abstractly articulated arguments in the Party press. In particular in the latter text, he criticises the mis-apprehension that all concerns with form are formalist, pointing out that in composition questions of form and content are inter-dependent and that formal innovation is necessary to convey new material to a new audience: 'it is just as formalistic to impose old forms on material as it is to impose new ones'. Yet, throughout this text Brecht never consciously steps outside the Marxist-Leninist value system and and is happy to see the term formalism deployed against 'depraved, bourgeois culture' where 'formal innovations were used everywhere to make the old appealing again'. Here, as on other occasions during his time in the GDR, his ideological commitment set the limits to his criticisms, so that his relations with the SED are informed by assent shot through by varying degrees of dissent, the latter generally articulated in private.[6]

However, the Party press continued its use of 'medical' language in an attack on the Academy's exhibition of sculptures by the Expressionist Ernst Barlach, an artist vilified by the Nazis in similar terms. In early 1952, this prompted the publication of a key, dissenting statement, 'Notes on the Barlach Exhibition' (no. 74), in the Academy's journal *Sinn und Form*, Brecht's most important publishing platform in the GDR. Lauding Barlach as one of Germany's greatest sculptors, Brecht claimed his best work for the realist tradition, of which Socialist Realism was, of course, the heir. In that way, whilst dissenting from the line of the Party press, Brecht remained within the discourse of Marxist-Leninist aesthetics, a point reaffirmed by his rejection of Barlach's 'mystical' and religious work. These contradictions in Brecht's position in the GDR are exemplified by the composition of his politically partisan 'Open Letter to German Artists and Writers' (no. 73) against the background of his ongoing aesthetic differences with the Party line over *Lucullus*. This statement, strongly supportive of the call by the GDR Minister President Otto Grotewohl for pan-German elections, became famous for its concluding lines, read by Helene Weigel on radio in late 1951: 'Carthage waged three wars. It was still powerful after the first, still inhabitable after the second. It was no longer to be found after the third.' Alluding pointedly to West German publishing practices, Brecht called for freedom of expression with the exception of warmongering works of art. Even a sympathetic writer in the West like Hans Henny Jahnn was at a loss, given his own difficulties with GDR publishers.[7]

The SED's announcement of the Construction of the Foundations of Socialism in 1952 signalled its determination to cut through the contradictions of its position and, in doing so, to discipline internal dissent. In April–June 1953 the Academy was the site for discussions orchestrated by SED cultural hardliner Alexander Abusch, principally the Stanislavsky Conference and the three so-called 'Wednesday Gatherings', at which attacks were launched on Hanns Eisler's *Johann Faustus* that were designed, not as a demonstration of the dialectic in Marxist aesthetics, but to extract from Brecht and his supporters a recantation of their aesthetic positions. Brecht defended Eisler against Abusch's attack in 'Theses on the *Faustus* Discussion' (no. 77), but he and his supporters were saved only by the extraordinary dynamic of events in East Berlin and Moscow around 17 June, which saw Ulbricht nearly toppled and Beria arrested after seeking to jettison the GDR. Brecht led a fight-back by the artistic elite in the Academy against unacceptable restrictions on cultural life through his instrumental involvement in the production of the 'Declaration by the German Academy of Arts' (no. 80), which put forward proposals for the reform of the cultural sphere in the GDR. In a similar vein, the official SED newspaper, *Neues Deutschland*, published Brecht's 'Cultural Policy and Academy of Arts' (*Brecht on Theatre*, pp. 266–70), in which, according to the paper's editor Wilhelm Girnus in a letter to Ulbricht, 'the standpoint was expressed that our entire cultural policy up until now has been wrong'.[8] Yet, Western applause for such publications and for satirical poems like 'Unidentifiable errors of the Arts Commission' and 'The Office for Literature' prompted a clarification in 'Not what was meant', whose final lines offered a sharp rebuke to the West:

> Even the narrowest minds
> In which peace is harboured
> Are more welcome to the arts than the art lover
> Who is also a lover of the art of war
> > (*Poems*, pp. 436–8)

Even now, as 'Concerning 17 June 1953' and 'The Urgent Need for a Major Discussion' (nos 78 and 79) demonstrate – not to mention his letter to Ulbricht (*Letters*, pp. 515–16) – Brecht did not depart from the SED's view of history. In this context, Brecht's efforts to resist the 'opposition' label while the pressure on him was at its fiercest in advance of 17 June (represented in our selection by nos 75 and 76) can be seen to owe as much to ideological commitment as to tactical manoeuvring. Particularly in the essay on Erwin Strittmatter's *Katzgraben*, a play which deals with GDR reality in a manner that eluded Brecht himself, he adopts the language of official cultural policy. Traumatised by the spectre of a resurgent Nazism, which saved him from an even more traumatic questioning of the SED's role, Brecht shifted the principal blame for 17 June from the politicians on to the bureaucrats, who emerge in the 'Preface to *Turandot*' (no. 81, and compare *Collected Plays*, vol. 8) as villains of the piece: 'Unconvinced but cowardly, hostile but cowering, ossified officials began again to govern against the population.' Nor did Brecht permit himself the analogy between Nazism and Stalinism that has often been read into late compositions like the *Buckow Elegies*. Rather, he made suggestions for the improvement of the system like 'The *Volkskammer*', whilst on receipt of the Stalin Prize he reaffirmed his faith in the Soviet Union's leading role in achieving world peace (nos 82 and 83). In 'On the Criticism of Stalin', with which our selection ends (no. 84), Brecht responded to Khrushchev's revelations of Stalin's crimes with a reaffirmation of faith in the dialectic.

Brecht's early death in August 1956 spared him the further severe test for the Left posed by the Soviet invasion of Hungary, but his life choices and statements on art and politics throughout the period leave no doubt as to where his commitment lay, however severely it was tested and however energetic his criticisms of the practice of real existing socialism. In the final analysis, Brecht emerges through his final years in the GDR as the paradigm for that particular intertwining of criticism and loyalty that characterised the artistic elite's relationship to the SED leadership.

---

[1] After the British diplomat Lord Vansittart. See also no. 61 and note.

[2] See journal entry of 9 December 1948, *Journals*, pp. 404–5

[3] For a discussion of Brecht's role within the Academy, see Peter Davies and Stephen Parker, 'Brecht, SED cultural policy and the issue of authority in the arts: The struggle for control of the German Academy of Arts', in Steve Giles and Rodney Livingstone (eds), *Bertolt Brecht: Centenary Essays* (Amsterdam and Atlanta, 1998), pp. 181–95.

[4] For further details, see Peter Davies, *Divided Loyalties: East German Writers and the Politics of German Division 1945–1953* (Leeds, 2000).

[5] Elmar Schubbe (ed.), *Dokumente zur Kunst-, Literatur- und Kulturpolitik der SED* (Stuttgart, 1972), pp. 178ff. For a discussion of the term 'cosmopolitanism', see chapter five, 'Purging "Cosmopolitanism": The Jewish Question in East Germany, 1949–1956', in Jeffrey Herf, *Divided Memory: The Nazi Past in the two Germanys* (London, 1997).

[6] For further discussion, see Matthew Philpotts, *Forms of Literary Assent*

and Dissent in the Twentieth-Century German Dictatorships: Günter Eich and Bertolt Brecht (Ph.D., University of Manchester, 2001).

[7] See Jahnn's letter to Peter Huchel of 1 April 1952 in Bernd Goldmann (ed.), *Hans Henny Jahnn–Peter Huchel. Ein Briefwechsel 1951–1959* (Mainz, 1974), p. 41.

[8] Letter, Wilhelm Girnus to Walter Ulbricht, 27 July 1953, Bertolt Brecht Archive, Z 37/38, published in *Europäische Ideen*, 97 (1996), pp. 22–3.

60

On the Declaration of the 26 United Nations

1 The declaration of the 26 United Nations on 1 January 1942 isolates Nazi Germany and forms the political basis for unifying the military operations of these 26 states. The following suggestions for a unified propaganda campaign aim to isolate the Nazis and militarists inside Germany.

2 The undersigned, all of German extraction, assume that, although opposition to this swashbuckling regime has long been completely paralysed, Germany's military defeats and increasing economic exhaustion must cause it to gain ground amongst large sections of the people. As history teaches us, military and economic defeats make a particularly strong impression on the German middle classes, long since the main supporters of the Nazi regime, so that we may expect a strong and honest propaganda against the regime to have its effect on them too.

3 Such a propaganda campaign would have to be spearheaded by friends and representatives of the German *opposition in exile* and would need centres in Washington, London and Moscow. It would have to be a united campaign by the democratic forces of the entire world. The cause of democracy is indivisible. Without the help of the democrats of the 26 nations, the German people is done for, yet the democratic cause would also suffer seriously in all countries if the peace were not democratic. It is absolutely essential that the representatives of the German opposition in exile find foreign allies who will conduct the propaganda campaign shoulder to shoulder with them.

4 The propaganda must discourage the German classes influenced by the Nazis and militarists while encouraging the opposition. The true relative strength of these groups must be demonstrated incessantly in statistical terms. The regime's military and economic mistakes must be exposed incessantly by experts. The military must be prevented from repeating their First World War tactic of shifting the blame at the appropriate juncture on to the politicians (i.e., this time the Nazis); rather, the Nazis and militarists must be held mutually responsible for the country's defeats, both those which have already occurred and those which will inevitably follow.

5 Above all, propaganda must isolate the Nazis and militarists. The gulf between this system and the actual German people must be shown constantly and enlarged constantly. The leading class must be singled out. A democratic court must be created which, in the name of the entire civilised world, will name each of the regime's atrocities outside and inside Germany, and also expressly name and condemn individual people. Sacrificing German soldiers in wars of conquest must be treated as just as criminal as sacrificing defenceless civilians in the occupied territories.

6 It is to be assumed that express warnings against lending the leading class any especial support are already having an effect in Germany today. Where open rebellion is impossible, skilful sabotage is possible. Radio propaganda could spread technical instructions and call on people to carry out particular acts of sabotage. But even where sabotage is not yet possible, whether for objective or subjective reasons, a popular move away from the Nazis, a concern about associating clearly with doomed groups and individuals, is already of great significance.

7 The idea of an international court was already propagated during the First World War, only far too late, in far too abstract and undemocratic a way, and above all without considering the participation of German democrats in such a court. Ideas or institutions which have not contributed directly to victory cannot be expected to exercise a formative influence on circumstances after the victory.

8 Creating a German government in exile, an idea which has been discussed a great deal recently, would be premature from the point of view of propaganda. Even if any such government were able to win the backing of sufficiently large sections of the exile community, which is highly doubtful, it would certainly not have any

authority whatsoever, neither abroad nor in Germany itself. No German politician, no matter from which party, could achieve anything within Germany from abroad without having secured very precise assurances concerning the future shape of Germany. Such assurances, however, are scarcely to be expected today. On the other hand, involving the German opposition in the propaganda campaign against Hitler is possible and will certainly be fruitful.

['*Zur Erklärung der 26 Vereinigten Nationen'*, BFA 23/7–9.]

Written in 1942. After the entry of the United States into the war in December 1941, the 26 nations allied against Germany and Japan issued a declaration (the United Nations Declaration) in which they gave assurances that they would not make a separate peace with either of the major Axis powers before both were defeated.

61

The *Other* Germany: 1943

In the days when the great powers were not yet fighting Hitler and not a few voices from abroad – some not silent even today – gave him encouragement, the world well knew that he was being fought from within and his enemies were called: the other Germany. Refugees, many of them known throughout the world, and foreign correspondents on furlough, reported that this other Germany really existed. At no time were even half the votes cast for the Hitler regime, and the existence of the most frightful instruments of oppression and the most frightful police force which the world has ever known, proved that the opponents of the regime were not inactive. Hitler ravaged his own country before he ravaged other countries; and the plight of Poland, Greece or Norway is scarcely worse than that of Germany. He made prisoners of war in his own country; he kept whole armies in concentration camps. In 1939 these armies numbered 200,000 – more Germans than the Russians took at Stalingrad. These 200,000 do not comprise the whole of the other Germany. They are only one detachment of its forces.

The other Germany could not stop Hitler, and in the present war which has brought the great powers into conflict with him, the other Germany has almost been forgotten. Many doubted if it really existed or at least denied that it had any significance. One factor was that the fighting democracies had to combat illusions about the striking-power of Hitler's armies. And there were powerful groups that regarded the other Germany with mistrust; they feared it was socialist. But there was also a suspicion that confused the friends of the other Germany, even some who themselves belonged to the other Germany.

The terrible question was: had the war put an end to the civil war which smouldered in Germany all through the first six years of Nazi rule? It is well known, after all, that wars engender fierce nationalism and bind the peoples more securely to their rulers.

The exile's trade is: hoping. It affords no gilt-edged securities. Some forecast that the Nazi regime would not be able to abolish unemployment; and when it was abolished, they forecast that it would go bankrupt. Some placed their hopes upon the Reichswehr, on the pride of caste of the Prussian Junkers, who would not want to go to war under the leadership of a corporal; or upon the Rhineland industrialists who in general must have feared a war. Even when war broke out, some said: 'the regime can keep the war going while it remains a Blitzkrieg fought by boys of twenty and a mechanized army of experts: but no longer.' The workers remain in the factories and at least thirty SS divisions are needed to guard them. The conquest of Poland and Norway, even the subjection of France seemed to be handled by this army of experts. But then came the Russian campaign, and with it an almost universal fear. Especially those who hated the Soviet Union were afraid. For this was no war of experts. The whole people would be drawn in. The higher agegroups who still recalled with a shudder the First World War, hundreds of thousands of workers who regarded Russia as their fatherland were drafted. The workers, precisely that part of the people which the regime itself had always called its most unshakable enemy, entered the war precisely at the moment when it involved the country which they had viewed with special sympathy.

Even those who had hoped most invincibly were silenced. Did no other Germany exist?

A man sticks to his trade, and the exile's trade is: hoping. Very soon therefore all sorts of explanations were available, all more or less technical. The Hitler regime, it was said, had had to keep two countries in the dark about the invasion to the very last minute, the Russians and the Germans. That proves, does it not, that the regime was embarrassed by the whole affair? Investigations of Nazi labor policy during their five years of preparation for war were a more serious matter. Already in the last year of the Weimar Republic the situation of the working class was catastrophic. Rationalisation of industry had created unemployment; the world crisis, which struck Germany with particular force, turned unemployment into a national catastrophe. Competition among the workers themselves became a very war. The German working class was already divided into parties; the parties were now divided against themselves. This legacy was taken over by the great and, as many think, legitimate heir of the Weimar Republic: the Third Reich. Unemployment was done away with in short order. Indeed the speed and scope of the abolition were so extraordinary that it seemed like a revolution. The factories had been taken over by force. The Fourth Estate stormed the Bastille . . . only to remain there in captivity. At the same time the political organisations of the working class were dissolved and decimated by the police. In this manner this class was transformed into an amorphous mob without will or political awareness. From now on the state did not have to deal with organisations, only with individuals. Napoleon had maintained that one need only be stronger at a given point at a given time; Hitler put this strategy to brilliant use. His policies need no longer be approved by these 'private persons'. But that is not all. Peaceful industry, which produces commodities, does not require that the workers take pleasure in their work; modern mechanised war, which is simply the industry of destruction, does not require that the workers take pleasure in war. Destruction is the commodity they deal in. Such is the technical-economic side of a social system which degrades the common man to the status of a tool politically as well as economically.

Such explanations are more illuminating than those of philosophers of history who in foolish and demagogical resortment cry that the German people are by nature bellicose, that their desire to conquer is only equalled by their willingness to obey – and so forth. But these explanations are not the whole truth. They show how the working classes came to be slavishly dependent upon the ruling classes; they do not show how the workers have come to be dependent on the success of their rulers in war. (Emil) Ludwig and Vansittart complain that the German people at least put up with Hitler's war. The truth is that they had to put up with the war because they put up with a system that demands – among other things – wars.

To complain that the German people allows its government to wage a frightful war of aggression is actually to complain that the German people does not make a social revolution. In whose interest is the war being fought? Precisely in the interest of those who can only be removed from their high positions by a social revolution on a gigantic scale. The interests of the industrialists and the Junkers may sometimes diverge, but both need war. They may quarrel about the conduct of the war; but they are alike sure that it should be conducted. Important English journals have described how the Junkers in the Ministry of War whip up competition between the trusts and how effectualy the trusts fight to get influence on the conduct of the war. No group that owns anything is against the war. If the war becomes hopeless the trusts may try to get rid of the Hitler gang or even of the generals for the sake of peace; but they will only make peace in order to make war later with all possible strength and as soon as possible. The important thing for them is naturally to keep what they own, namely, economic power, without which they could never hope to regain the political power which they need to make war. French ministers have described, and General de Gaulle has confirmed their descriptions, how the French industrialists were so afraid of their own people that they could not prostrate themselves before their German conquerors quickly enough. They thought the German bayonets necessary to the preservation of their property. One day the German industrialists will try to find bayonets (and any bayonets will do) in the hope that their loss of political power will only be temporary if their economic power can be salvaged. Is that clear?

But how is it with the rest of the German people, the ninety-nine per cent? Is the war in their interest too? Do they need war? Wellmeaning people are too hasty by half when they confidently answer: No. A comforting reply, but not a true one. The truth is that the war is in their interest so long as they cannot or will not shake off the system under which they live. When Hitler came to power, seven million families, that is more than a third of the population, faced starvation. The system could find no work for them, could not even keep them on relief. When work was found for them it was only in industrial preparations for war. Meanwhile the so-called middle-class was ruined and driven into the munitions' factories. Hundreds of thousands of shops and workshops were closed and closed for good: the cash-registers were melted down. The farmers also were ruined; they are now mere tenants acting under orders. They can cultivate their land only with the cheapest slave-labor, the labor of prisoners of war. Even the smallest factories are ruined for good and their owners have to look for administrative jobs which they can only find if the state is victorious and has occupied territories to dispose of. So they all have a stake in the war. *All*. Is that clear?

Somewhere there must be a terrible miscalculation, that is clear too, and will be clearer still as the war gets worse and worse. In the bombed cities men crouch in the cellars of burning houses shaken by animal fear and begin to learn. Presumably the retreating armies in the south and in the east are also beginning to learn. Where is the miscalculation? Somewhere near Smolensk a Silesian soldier points his gun at a Russian tank which will crush him if it is not stopped. There is hardly time to realize that what he is pointing his gun at is unemployment. And if he does realise, how little has been gained! An engineer is bent over an improvement in the construction of fast fighter-planes. He hardly has time to consider what he is going to do in a poverty-stricken Germany that has lost the war. But surely something in the back of his mind is, however mysteriously, stirred; perhaps he half-suspects there must be a miscalculation somewhere. Hamburg is burning and a crowd of people is trying to get out of the town; a man beats them back home. His parents owned a furniture store in Breslau. It is closed down now. What if the war is lost? What if it is won? He continues to club the crowd. There are many parents in it.

Only the individual can think. Only the group can go to war. It is easier for the individual to follow the group than to think for himself. Every individual in a crowd would perhaps do one thing, but the crowd does another thing. The Russians and the Americans are further away than the sergeant; the RAF is further away than the police. And the war is a fact, whereas thinking is weak and unpractical, a dreamy affair. War demands everything but it provides everything too. It provides food, shelter, work. One can do nothing that is not for the war; to do something good means 'good for the war'. In war all vices and weaknesses are released. But the war also brings out all the virtues: diligence, inventiveness, perseverence, bravery, comradeship and even kindness. And yet there is an enormous miscalculation somewhere.

Where?

When the fate of so much and so many is involved, it is hard to think that only the leaders are responsible for the war. It is easier to assume that the leaders are only responsible for the war's being lost. Now it is very unlikely that the Nazi regime, vicious as it is, would go to war for fun. It has not done so. As far as war and peace are concerned, the regime probably had no choice. Whoever rulers are, they rule not only over bodies but also over minds; they command not only deeds but thoughts. The regime had to choose war because the whole people needed war; *but the people needed war only under this regime and therefore have to look for another way of life.* This is a colossal conclusion. And even when the hand on the reins becomes uncertain, the road to this conclusion is a long one. For it is the road to social revolution.

History shows that peoples do not lightly undertake radical changes in the economic system. The people are not gamblers. They do not speculate. They hate and fear the disorder which accompanies social change. Only when the order under which they have lived turns to an indubitable and intolerable disorder do the people dare, and even then nervously, uncertainly, again and again shrinking back in terror, to change the situation. A world which expects the German people to revolt and turn itself into a peaceful nation is expecting much. It is expecting of the German people courage, determination, and new sacrifice. If our other Germany is to win, it will have to have learned its lesson.

Ending in defeat, the last war freed the German people of their political fetters for a time. In the years after the war the whole people were actively trying to create a government for the people and by the people. Gigantic labor parties and small bourgeois parties, partly under Catholic influence, condemned war and all policies that lead to war. It seemed that war would be discredited for generations. The arts, music, painting, literature, and theatre flourished.

It did not last long. The people had neglected to occupy the key-positions in the national economy. Those who had been used to giving the orders offered their services as specialists of order and their services were accepted. The boasted order which they kept was the order of attacking battalions; the much talked of chaos which they avoided was the occupation by the people of the key-positions in the economy. And after a year or two in which their economic positions had not been even challenged, they took back the political positions, and the preparation of the next war began.

Will all this happen again?

In order to answer this question in the negative one must be able to interpret favorably the very fact which at first seems to make nonsense of the query, namely, the much-reported 'unshakable morale of Hitler Germany'.

The fact that there has been no quick reaction to the privations and defeats of Nazi Germany is admittedly irritating. One must, however, be able to see that precisely this delay indicates how deep and broad the reaction will be. This time the imperialists have no parliaments to turn to when they want someone to end their war for them. Today there are no dynasties which can be sacrificed as scapegoats without in the least endangering the structure of the state. On the other hand if the masses try to fight their way out of the war they will have to confront hundreds of thousands of Hitlerites who can only be defeated in a tremendous civil war, a civil war which must be conducted with the improvised Commandos of a popular government. The people must rise against their torturers – the torturers of the whole world – and defeat them.

One thing is certain. If the German people cannot throw off their rulers, if on the contrary these rulers manage to play a 'Frederickian variation', that is, manage to keep the war going until disagreement among the allies presents an opportunity for a negotiated peace; or, alternatively, if the rulers of Germany are beaten militarily but left in power economically, a pacification of Europe is unthinkable. In the latter case military occupation by the allies would certainly not help. It is hard enough to control India in these days by violent colonization; it would be quite impossible to control Central Europe. Should the allies take up arms not only against the harrassed regime but also against the whole people, they would need immense forces; the Nazis needed more than half a million men, the largest police force in history, and a fanatical block-warden in every block in every town; they also had to hold out a hope of a successful war of conquest without which both the police and the population would starve. The foreign soldier with a gun in one hand and a bottle of milk in the other would only be regarded as a friend worthy of the great democracies that sent him if the milk were for the people and the gun for use against the regime.

The idea of forcibly educating a whole people is absurd. What the German people have not learned when this war is over from bloody defeats, bombings, impoverishment, and from the bestialities of its leaders inside and outside Germany, it will never learn from history books.

Peoples can only educate themselves; and they will establish popular government not when they grasp it with their minds but when they grasp it with their hands.

['The Other Germany', BFA 23/24–30.]

Written in late 1943 or early 1944. The original version of this text has been lost. Brecht sent his text for translation to Eric Bentley, who produced the version reprinted here but was unable to find a publisher for it at the time (see BFA 23/432); (the American and non-standard spellings are retained).

The text is a response to the ideas of the writer Emil Ludwig and the British diplomat Lord Vansittart, who proposed that the causes of National Socialism and the war lay in the innate militarism of the German character, and thus that the Allies should make no distinction between Nazis and Germans. This controversy was one of the most bitter and protracted debates fought out amongst the German exile community. The Communist Party took a consistent line against what it called 'Vansittartism', arguing that the working classes in Germany were also victims of Fascism.

62

Report on the Situation of Germans in Exile

Germans in exile are, it is fair to say, unanimously in favour of Germany's defeat in this war. They regret every victory won by German weapons, they welcome every failure. They know that each failure costs the lives of a thousand German soldiers, but equally that every German victory costs the lives of thousands of German soldiers. The inevitable final defeat of Hitler's Germany will see our country in inconceivable misery. A victory would see the entire inhabited world in such misery, naturally including Germany. This system of bloody oppression, unbridled profiteering and complete lack of freedom would, like a single tidal wave of mud, swallow up everything that the people of different nations had achieved through centuries of sacrifice. The final defeat of Germany, on the other hand, will liberate not only the people of other nations from constant threat, but also the German people. Before Hitler and his backers in the army, diplomatic service and the world of finance subjugated Czechoslovakia, the Scandinavian countries, Holland, Belgium, France, the Balkans and White Russia, they subjugated the German people. That was their first victim. Even if they subjugated the entire world, they would still hold the German people down, under their bloody boot. However weak our voice, the voice of the refugees, may be in the noise of battle which fills ever more continents, it is still not completely inaudible; nothing but this weak sound has survived of the powerful voice of our great and once respected people. We trust that we are saying what the German people itself would say, if it could talk. We say that Hitler and his backers are not Germany, whatever they may claim. Their claim to represent Germany is the first of their barefaced lies. The truth is that they have subjugated the Germans, like they subjugated the Czechs or the French. They have subjugated the German people with the violent authority of the police and with propaganda, just as they have subjugated foreign peoples with the violence of the military and with false promises. They have captured French, English and Czech people with their propaganda, just as they have captured Germans. But these captives will awake. Either they will awake, or they will perish. Either they will allow themselves to be convinced, or they will have to be removed. The German people will have an immense role in the final victory over Hitler and his backers in the military, diplomatic service and the world of finance.

We are not defeatists. We are ready to fight for a German people which is great and free, the master of its own house and the friend of all other peoples.

['*Bericht über die Stellung der Deutschen im Exil*', BFA 23/32–3.]

The text was written in New York some time between November 1943 and March 1944, while Brecht was working on the organisational committee of the Council for a Democratic Germany. The Council, founded officially in May 1944 by the German theologian Paul Tillich, was intended to provide a focus for all anti-Fascist Germans in exile. Brecht's specific role was to recruit new members and to gather material for an 'Information Library of the German Opposition against National Socialism', for the purpose of discrediting the 'Vansittart theory' (compare Introduction).

63

Where I Live

Whenever I say where I live, I always say: in Santa Monica, which is the truth. But everyone repeats: ah, in Hollywood! They are, in fact, different towns, five miles apart, but in some kind of way we do belong to Hollywood. So I hasten to say: we did not choose the place, the ship from Vladivostock set us ashore here, we did not have any money, several other refugees were here, so we stayed. We do have a house here, but only because the mortgage repayments are cheaper than the rent would be anywhere else. The house itself only has one and a half bathrooms, and it is rectangular, a fifty-year-old ranch with another floor added on. The villas all around are built in the Mexican or English style, or they have little towers and curves, the like of which you have never seen. Our house has seven rooms, including two large ones. It is not bad, and the garden is even attractive, rather old, with fig trees, lemon, orange, apricot and pepper trees and grass, there are even paths and corners between wooden sheds, and it looks as if it has been lived in for a long time.

The world is starving and lies in ruins; how can one complain about sitting here? It seemed inconceivable, until the thought struck me that these pretty villas here are built out of the same material as those ruins; as if one and the same ill wind, which tore down those buildings, had swept up all manner of dust and dirt and turned it into villas here. For it is a fact: we live in a town devoid of dignity.

It is difficult to describe, I have often started and given up again. Of course, it might be something to do with the people.

Let us start with the neighbours, simple folk. They are friendly and do not snoop around. They see a woman keeping the house and garden in order, a man sitting at the typewriter; so when the police ask questions about us, they say that we are 'hard-working people' who should be left in peace. They receive figs from our garden and bring us cake. Unlike the German petty bourgeoisie, they are not repressed and neurotic, nor are they obsequious and arrogant. They move more freely, more gracefully, and do not bicker. Of course, there is something vacuous and insignificant about them, just as there is about the characters of superficial novelists eager to please. The schools award marks not only according to how diligent, well-read and intelligent children are, but also according to their popularity. It is hard to object to this: perhaps I only have something against it because I was not popular myself, nor did I want to be. If children are supposed to learn how to conform to society, then what definitely matters too is: to which society? The newspapers, on the other hand, are full of the lower classes' violent rows: men shoot their unfaithful wives, adolescents take an axe to drunken fathers who beat their mothers, etc. This stands in contrast to the better social circles, where these emotional conflicts escalate into financial conflicts, and what is at stake is alimony. Nevertheless, whether in high or low society, these are problems which, one might say, represent equations with only one unknown factor; the seven-line newspaper report already seems exhaustive. The houses around ours have nearly all changed hands several times since we have been living here. People change their jobs and even their professions incessantly and apparently without much reflection, and so they move into districts or towns which are more easily accessible; some move, several times over, across the entire continent. As a result, they hardly get to know their accommodation, have neither a parental home nor a homeland. No friendships grow, nor do any enmities. As far as opinions are concerned, the ideas of the rulers govern almost without restraint. Not agreeing is generally seen as simply not knowing the done thing, as a dangerous inability to conform. Conforming is a school subject in itself; the more intelligent individual will go further, while anyone who resists is a problem for the doctors and psychologists. In order to keep your job (which is always insecure, there are no 'jobs for life' with rights and pensions, not even in government offices), besides having the right qualification (which is not so very important, since everything is geared towards transferability, i.e., towards the minimum) you have to be a 'regular guy', i.e., normal. That leaves little room for individuality. 'The unlimited opportunities' start to sound like a legend, but 'the inevitable crises', they sound like a scientific statement. And the crises rob the population of everything. Bank account, house, freezer and car have to be converted into food, the children's studies are interrupted, marriages end in divorce. Apart from the major universal crises, the minor personal ones are also a threat. The illness of just one member can rob a family of all of its savings and most of its plans for the future. Under these circumstances, the fetid prejudices of large groups of people against the Negroes, Jews and Mexicans, never laid to rest but hardly ever ventilated, take on a sinister significance. The influence of the ill-informed population – the newspapers and the radio are in the hands of a few millionaires – on the country's history is weak. The political machines rule the elections, and they are controlled by large corporate interests. Corruption is on a gigantic scale. Newspapers with dozens of millions of readers hint that the nation's highest civil servant has been 'made' by a group of gangsters. Many people feel that democracy is in such a state that it may disappear from one day to the next. Few dare to imagine what the monstrous brutality fostered here by the economic struggle would then make of the continent.

Vast uncertainty and dependency pervert the intellectuals, making them superficial, timid and cynical. You might say that appearing 'easygoing', 'cheerful' and 'mentally balanced' is part of their job description, and they achieve this by smoking pipes and sticking their hands in their pockets. In the old world, intellectuals still uphold the great fiction that they are working for more than remuneration. Civil servants maintain order, doctors heal, teachers spread knowledge, artists give pleasure, the technical professions produce; they are remunerated 'of course', but that is only because they have to live. Their work has an importance over and above this. Gigantic state institutions, like universities, schools, clinics, administrations, give at least the appearance of being only under public control. But here the universities are openly controlled by the rich, even the ones which are half publicly owned; the same applies to the clinics; and the civil servants in the administration receive weekly cheques and are dependent on the political machines. So the young are a generation of young gods, who are transformed overnight into slaves. Middle-class women over thirty without a bank account are failures. This word 'failure' can barely be translated into a cultured language. It means 'someone who is unsuccessful', and it can be the father, the mother, the teacher, the neighbour, or me. Likewise, the condition of the 'failures' is barely translatable. The word for it is 'frustration', and it means disappointment, despondency, having been thwarted or crossed. This old-maid-like condition affects both sexes and is a social phenomenon, with clinical symptoms.

No wonder that something ignoble, disgraceful, undignified adheres to all human intercourse and has thus affected every object, home, tool, even the countryside itself. The sight of a man reading a volume of Lucretius in his garden early one morning would be in bad taste, while a woman feeding her child would be vulgar. In the half-light, the high-rise flats in Manhattan are breathtaking, but they cannot swell the heart. The slaughter yards in Chicago, the electric power stations in the canyons, the Californian oil fields, all of them have this restrained, frustrated quality; they all come across as failures. Everywhere there is this smell of hopeless rawness, of pent-up violence. In five years I only once saw something approaching art: along the coast of Santa Monica, in front of a thousand bathers, hovering on thin wires like a kite, pulled along by a motor boat, a thin, exquisite form in delicate hues, an advert for a sun lotion company.

['*Wo ich wohne*'*, BFA 23/48–51.]

Written in 1944. Brecht lived in Santa Monica, California, from August 1941 to October 1947, alongside a number of other prominent Germans in exile. During this time he came under observation by the FBI.

64

Statement to the House Committee on Un-American Activities in Washington, 1947

I was born in Augsburg (Germany), as the son of a factory director, and studied science and philosophy at the Universities of Munich and Berlin. At the age of twenty, as a medical orderly in the First World War, I wrote a ballad which Hitler's regime cited fifteen years later as the reason for depriving me of my citizenship. The poem attacked the war and those who wished to prolong it.

I became a playwright. For a while, Germany seemed on the road to democracy. There was freedom of speech and artistic expression.

In the second half of the 1920s, however, the old militaristic forces of reaction gained ground once more. At that time, I was at the height of my career as a playwright; my play *The Threepenny Opera* was being staged throughout all of Europe. But in Germany there were already calls for an end to freedom of artistic expression and speech. Humanist, socialist, even Christian ideas were called 'un-German', a word which I can now hardly imagine without Hitler's wolf-like intonation. At the same time, the people's cultural and political institutions were being attacked furiously.

Despite all its flaws, the Weimar Republic had a powerful slogan, recognised by the best writers and artists of every kind: *art to the people*. The German workers, who were indeed greatly interested in art and literature, formed a particularly important section of the general reading and theatregoing public. Their sufferings in the catastrophic economic crisis, which was posing an increasing threat to their cultural standards, and the growing power of the old militaristic feudal, imperialist riff-raff alarmed us. I began to write poems, songs and plays, which described the people's feelings and attacked their enemies, who were now marching openly under Adolf Hitler's swastika.

Persecution in the cultural sphere gradually increased. Well-known painters, publishers and editors of periodicals were persecuted by the courts. Political witch-hunts were staged, both at the universities and against films like *All Quiet on the Western Front*. Of course, these only prepared the way for more drastic measures. When Hitler seized power, painters were forbidden to paint, writers to write, and the Nazi Party snapped up the publishing houses and film studios for itself. But even these attacks on the cultural life of the German people were only the beginning. They were devised and carried out as the intellectual preparation for total war, which is the total enemy of culture. The war which followed put an end to all that. The German people now lives without a roof over its head, without sufficient food, without soap, without the bare rudiments of culture.

At the beginning only very few people were in a position to see for themselves the connection between the reactionary restrictions in the cultural sphere and the ultimate attack on the physical life of the people. The efforts of the democratic, anti-militarist forces proved far too weak.

I had to leave Germany in February 1933, on the day after the Reichstag Fire. An exodus of writers and artists began, the like of which the world had not seen before. I settled in Denmark and from then on devoted my entire literary work to the fight against Nazism, writing plays and poems.

Several poems were smuggled into the Third Reich, and the Danish Nazis, supported by Hitler's embassy, soon began to demand my deportation. The Danish government refused. But in 1939, when war seemed imminent, I moved to Sweden with my family. I was only able to stay there one year. Hitler invaded Denmark and Norway.

We continued our flight north and reached Finland. Hitler's troops followed. Finland was already filled with Nazi divisions when we emigrated to America in 1941. We crossed the USSR in the Trans-Siberian Express, which was carrying German, Austrian and Czech refugees. Ten days after we had left Vladivostock on a Swedish ship, Hitler invaded the USSR. The ship loaded copra in Manila. Several months later, Hitler's allies invaded this island.

I assume that several of my plays and poems, written during the struggle against Hitler, have prompted the House Committee to summon me here.

My activities, even those against Hitler, were always purely literary, and they were dependent on no one. As a guest of the United States I engaged in no activities regarding this country, not even literary ones. Let me mention incidentally that I do not write screenplays. I am not aware of any influence, political or artistic, which I might have exercised on the film industry.

However, now that I have been summoned before the House Committee on Un-American Activities, I feel tempted for the first time to say a few words concerning American affairs. Looking back on my experiences as a playwright and poet in Europe during the last two decades, I would like to say that the great American people would lose a great deal and risk a great deal, if it were to allow anyone to restrict free competition of ideas in the cultural sphere or to intervene against art, which must be free, if it is to be art.

We live in a dangerous world. The state of our civilisation is such that mankind already possesses all the means to be thoroughly rich, but as a whole is still afflicted by poverty. We have borne suffering in great wars; as we hear, we face greater ones. One of them may very well devour mankind in its entirety. We may be the last generation of the human species on this earth. The ideas about how we might use the new possibilities of production have not been developed much further since the days when horses had to do the work which men could not. Do you not think that in such a critical situation every new idea ought to be examined carefully and freely? Art can make such ideas clearer and even nobler.

['*Anrede an den Kongressausschuss für unamerikanische Betätigungen in Washington, 1947*', BFA 23/59–61.]

Written in October 1947. Brecht became caught up in the anti-Communist witch-hunts along with other left-wing Germans in exile who were working in and around the film industry. He was summoned before the House Committee on Un-American Activities, which was investigating supposed 'Communist influences' in Hollywood. Brecht's hearing took place on 30 October 1947. Translations of some of his works had been submitted to the committee as evidence against him. Brecht was not permitted to read out his text, which he had prepared for the hearing, on the grounds that it was, in the words of the Committee Chairman, Karl E. Mundt, not relevant to the investigation. The hearing ended without a formal indictment; in his journal entry of 30 October 1947 Brecht puts this down to the fact that he had generally kept his distance from the Hollywood studio system, that he had never intervened publicly in US politics, and that other witnesses refused to incriminate him (see *Journals*, p. 372).

65

Conversations with Young Intellectuals

[. . .]

No, I do not understand you young people, you can talk freely to me.

No, I cannot raise your hopes. Even if I could – why should I? The question is whether one can look at you without fear.

It is as if you were searching for someone who could use you again. You wish that he would not abuse you this time. But why do you wish that someone would use you?

For a great goal? But you do not have one? Fair enough, those who do have one will use you. Perhaps it really is better, considering your present mood, if you have nothing against dictatorship and instead content yourselves with searching for a great goal. Only that is not easy either. Really, you are dangerous brethren.

In a periodical, which shouldn't be called *Dionysos*, a man who claims to be young complains: 'He shattered illusions . . . and today we feel only frost engulfing us. Distance has a cooling effect. It impedes empathy, understanding . . .' A frosty encounter.

*

I feel tempted to say: even I do not want to expose you to the feelings which would come if you understood.

But isn't there something for us to hold on to? No.

But won't it all turn out well? No.

No, I am not a nihilist, thank you. But where nothingness is, there is nothing.

Mustn't one be afraid? Certainly. Of you.

Nothing but abuse, that is more than nothing.

Should we allow ourselves to be ordered how to write, paint and make music? – What would you give if I told you?

I do not expect the sight of the ruined cities to shock me excessively. The sight of the ruined human beings has already done so.

The houses seem rather like snails' houses to me. You do not think of them separately, as accommodation for any particular snails. What I see is not cities no longer able to shelter any human beings, but rather human beings without cities. Throughout my fifteen years in exile, I felt no sense of regret at no longer being able to be in my home city or in Berlin. The places I remembered from childhood, the yards where the boys built tree houses, the cement slope of a river dam, good for sunbathers; in the hands of the Nazis these had for me become places like the crime scenes pictured in smutty newspaper photographs. Furthermore, in my imagination these cities had increasingly come to carry the stigma of destructibility, as if people had planned to create the impending gigantic heaps of rubble by bombing cities erected specially for this purpose – a roundabout and obviously rather expensive method. In my eyes the large cities still standing today are branded with the same mark of Cain.

*

I agree, these lyricisms are in dubious taste. The argument is simply this: these cities, or at least the modern parts of them, had been erected for the purpose of speculation, or to consume profits of some kind or other; so they were warlike enterprises which could spread at any time. They were built, a sword in one hand, a trowel in the other, and these were not the hands of the owners. Unfortunately I cannot find a word meaning the opposite of *collapse*, i.e., something which comes into existence through violence.

Incidentally, whenever I speak of myself, I do not do so out of a desire to force my own individual perspective on to you, or to turn my thoughts or impressions or impulses into yours. I simply present myself to you, as it were, so that by seeing a particular person before you, a playwright who had to flee his country, you can work out where you stand.

I think nothing of sympathy which produces only helpfulness and not anger too.

I know the statistics about resistance fighters murdered in the Third Reich. The numbers are enormous. More people fell there than in France and Norway; more people fought there than in the English and American armies. I cite the statistics at every possible opportunity. But I also know that the surviving fighters do not dare to speak of their deeds today, out of fear of being declared traitors now. Talking about this shames me, I do not know why.

A country which rewards its traitors for fighting against its shameful deeds is one which people might like to have as a fatherland.

I think I could talk about that: I did not live through it all.

'It is certainly the greatest defeat which a people has ever experienced, the deepest misery, the bitterest suffering.' And the most accursed vanity.

*

For a while, let us speak of the *people* no longer. Let us speak of the population.

'Who recommended trading straight away, scarcely returned from the concentration camps? Who organised the black market?' Fine, one good suggestion: you suppress your bourgeoisie, and I won't say anything if you suppress the Jewish bourgeoisie too.

The events in Auschwitz, in the Warsaw ghetto, in Buchenwald would doubtless not bear any literary description. Literature was not prepared for such events, nor has it developed any means of describing them.

'The motives which kept millions of individuals in the Nazi armies can surely not only have been opportunism or fear. There must have been idealistic motives.' I agree that ideals must be regarded with gloom.

In view of the danger that there is someone in your midst who might understand after all, whom I might fail to reach if I remained too hostile: without having recourse to bourgeois ideals, the Nazis could never have carried out their monstrous acts of destruction. The war had to be seen as one of the conceivable, indeed natural means by which conflicts are fought out; the subjects' blind obedience had to have prior sanction, etc., etc. Take Kaiser Wilhelm's sentence, 'I no longer recognise any parties, I recognise only Germans' and replace the word 'recognise' with 'tolerate'; then take Bismarck's sentence, 'We Germans fear God and none other on earth' and replace the word 'God' with 'Hitler', and the Nazis are revealed as epigones. They did not bring anything earth-shatteringly new; I knew this huge bestiality and this huge narrow-mindedness when they were still small – from the bourgeoisie.

Of all Goebbels's claims, none is more absurd than the claim that they carried out a revolution. What they carried out was a counter-revolution. And it was as bestial as counter-revolutions generally are. The bourgeoisie took its revenge for the humiliations of 1918. It hired the avengers and equipped them with the necessary financial and legal means, before starting the great blood-letting which robbed the proletariat of many of its leaders and all of its organisations. This blood-letting was so thorough that the humiliations were not repeated after the second war, which was more criminal by far. The delay of the second front permitted the last and decisive blow.

The bourgeoisie, and not only in Germany, now speaks of these special measures as the *Nazis' excesses*. What ungrateful cheek! Making this growth out to be a tumour! They ordered a fillet, and the inhuman butcher murdered a calf!

As if the concentration camps were not necessary, when a war like this was needed! After all, one could not entice the workers and their representatives into this kind of war just by asking them nicely! After all, it wasn't out of pure sadism that all these SS units, these high-bred master warriors were taken out of military service!

But the 14th of July! The generals' planned strike as a substitute for a general strike. The only chance of continuing the war with some hope of success, by rupturing the enemy alliance and offering to ally with one enemy against the other. The repetition of the Nazi trick at the start of the war. An act of plagiarism!

Aha, now my true colours are coming to light.

The Church does not seem to be preparing for a beautiful death but rather for a prosperous one. A high-ranking spiritual dignitary – what a word! – recently hinted that sinister plans were afoot to nail people like him to the cross, just like Jesus of Nazareth. Of course, on the cross *he* would still have a wallet in his hand.

Do you really mean to claim that more people have worked for their money than inherited it? Or that it is not harder for the sons of the destitute to buy education on the market?

The papal privy purse helped to finance the butcher Franco, so I hear. It might be true, but how dull! It might be dull, but what if it were true?

Religion offers a stay. But the horse doesn't take much notice of the stay which the saddle gives the rider.

I realise that the example is lame. It is not the riders who are generally religious, but rather the horses.

Correct, our country struggles against jazz. And against cocaine.

['*Gespräche mit jungen Intellektuellen*', BFA 23/97–103.]

This text, thought to have been written in the summer of 1948, is believed to have been prompted by discussions held with young intellectuals under the auspices of the *Kulturbund*, an umbrella organisation for the arts across the whole of Germany, set up in the Soviet Occupied Zone in August 1945 and then banned in the West. Brecht may have been informed of these discussions by the theatre critic Herbert Ihering who had taken part in them.

In October 1947 an article had appeared in the Berlin cultural journal *Dionysos* accusing Brecht of trying 'to destroy the old forms of drama. He destroyed our illusions. He distanced the stage from the audience.'

Brecht's reference to Kaiser Wilhelm stems from the Kaiser's address to the Reichstag at the outbreak of World War I. On 14 July 1944 Klaus von Stauffenberg aborted a second assassination attempt on Hitler's life. His unsuccessful attempt was carried out on 20 July. On 1 April 1939 Pope Pious XII sent a congratulatory telegram to Franco on the foundation of the Fascist dictatorship in Spain. No evidence exists of the financial support alluded to by Brecht.

66

Bringing the World Peace at Last

1 Mother Courage and her Children shows that ordinary people cannot hope to gain anything from war (in contrast to the powerful). Ordinary people pay for the defeats and the victories.

2 Creative literary activity is greatly obstructed in America by the economic dictatorship of the bourgeoisie, which threatens its enemies with economic ruin. Now, after the war, progressive writers are suffering from direct political persecution to boot.

3 It gave me great pleasure, only one day after my return to Berlin, the city which launched one of the most terrible wars, to be able to attend a demonstration of intellectuals for peace. The sight of the horrific devastation filled me with one wish alone: to contribute in my way to bringing the world peace at last. It is becoming uninhabitable without peace.

['*Dass die Welt endlich Frieden bekommt*'*, BFA 23/103–4.]

Written 25 October 1948. The text was written following a peace rally, organised by the *Kulturbund* in Berlin, which Brecht attended on 24 October 1948. Brecht had returned to Berlin in October 1948 for the production of *Mother Courage*, which premiered on 11 January 1949.

67

The Emblem of the Berliner Ensemble

The Berliner Ensemble has taken Picasso's valiant dove of peace as its emblem: the site of knowledge of human nature, of social impulses and of entertainment.

['*Wahrzeichen des Berliner Ensembles*'*, BFA 23/117.]

Thought to have been written in the autumn of 1949. The Berliner Ensemble did not move into its own permanent theatre until 19 March 1954.

68

The Arts in Upheaval

At the moment of their self-liberation, the exploited and oppressed proletarian masses have an extraordinary hunger for art. It is the hunger to enjoy life, part of this immense, suppressed hunger. More often than not, at the terrible but wonderful time of the final battle, the 'last fight', and during the great struggles of the initial effort of construction, naked bodily hunger still rules. It is the intellectual hunger which can be more quickly satisfied. The masses also see the arts as a weapon in their struggle.

Art is generally the first thing the bourgeoisie throws overboard when its ship begins to sink, and not only because the best artists have already begun to contribute to the sinking of that ship. The proletariat recalls these artists when it takes power.

How staggering the care with which the new Soviet government, attacked from within and without, in the midst of war, in the midst of hunger, treated the theatre! It helped with coal, with special rations, and with immediate commissions. Two and a half decades later this is repeated in the conquered Berlin, when, in the very first few days, the Soviet commander decrees that the theatres closed by Hitler should be reopened. The enemy, beaten down with such effort, was invited into the theatres. The first measures taken by the victors are to provide bread, supply water and open the theatres! After the revolution, before it built up its heavy industry, the Russian proletariat built up its film industry. Two and a half decades later, its victorious soldiers are helping the German people, who destroyed a considerable part of its heavy industry, towards a new film industry!

What is certain: with the great upheaval, a great period for the arts is beginning. How great will they be?

['*Die Künste in der Umwälzung*', BFA 23/129.]

Written around 1950. The 'last fight' makes reference to the chorus of the 'Internationale'. The DEFA (German Film Company) was founded by the Soviet military administration on 17 May 1946.

69

Concerning the Accusation of Formalism

1 In the opera *The Trial of Lucullus* the action – posterity's condemnation of wars of conquest – is located in the underworld. This is an artistic device which the classics often use (the prelude in heaven in *Faust* / the classical Walpurgis night in *Faust* / *Orpheus and Eurydice* by Gluck, etc., etc.). This artistic device serves by no means simply to conceal an idea (i.e., like a slaves' language); instead, art expects to gain by it, for spectators who are allowed to discover the topical relevance for themselves will experience this more intensely and profoundly. Indeed, the enjoyment of art in general (and the enjoyment which art produces in acts of recognition and new stimuli) is increased if the audience is made to produce, discover and experience intellectually.

2 Artists here often suspect that when people attack formalism they mean form in general. That is to say that any sign that content has been given form, any sign of an individual and even beautiful shape, already leads people to suspect frivolity. If accepted, this would simply paralyse artistic production, instead of encouraging and endorsing it.

3 The Berliner Ensemble has staged a new production of my play *The Mother* (incidentally, although this was very loosely based on motifs from Gorky's novel and so doesn't constitute an adaptation of the classic, Gorky authorised it nonetheless) because we wanted to endear the Soviet Union to our workers, and also to our petty bourgeoisie and our intellectuals. As many statements testify, very few people are able to resist this effect. This work has very little to do with Agitprop and Proletkult, for it is the poetic description of an already classical epoch. Formally, the work is based – incidentally, along with only very few recent works – on the structure and expressive manner of the national German theatre (from Goethe's *Götz* to Büchner's *Woyzeck*). The fact that, again in order to maximise the impact of the ideas, we strove to make the production visually attractive, does not in my opinion diminish the work's realism in any way; on the contrary.

4 GDR artists have a particularly complicated war to wage. On the one hand, they have to overcome the old capitalist isolation of the working masses; on the other they cannot afford to isolate themselves completely from the rest of Germany, as far as the language of their art is concerned. In my opinion they do well to focus as much as possible on content and ideas. The *Lucullus* affair will make many people think that in the GDR we prioritise questions of taste and form over content and ideas.

5 I find it extremely difficult to understand and agree with the condemnation of the music. 'The music is thin and fragmented' (ND). In my eyes (or ears) that means that the musical structure is beautifully transparent, a feature which I value in the classics, and that the music is divided into individual pieces (in contrast to the 'unceasing melody' of Wagner and his pupils), something which we likewise find in the classics.

[*Appendix*]

Our artists' optimism and determination to engage in reconstruction do not only find expression in their choice of optimism and reconstruction as themes, but also when they themselves create powerful works which fight the old and advocate the new, and when they educate the young and fill them with enthusiasm for socialism. Through these means they are participating in the Herculean task of the GDR's working populace, and it is not necessary to check constantly that Hercules's face also looks as if he is optimistic and enjoying the work.

['*Zum Vorwurf des Formalismus*'*, BFA 23/135–7.]

Written in 1951. Brecht's libretto for the opera *The Trial of Lucullus* (music by Paul Dessau) was based on his radio play, *Lucullus on Trial*, which was first broadcast in 1940. The play uses a chorus of Roman plebeians to expose the general's claims that the Roman people have benefited from war. The opera was premiered in Berlin on 17 March 1951 before an invited public, having already become the target of concerted attacks by SED hardliners. After a meeting with Pieck and other officials, Brecht agreed to make substantial changes to his text, renaming it *The Condemnation of Lucullus* and, after a further meeting with Pieck on 5 May 1951, the opera was declared fit for public performance, and was produced in both East and West Germany.

Brecht's adaptation of Maxim Gorky's novel *The Mother*, which was first performed in 1932, and which was designed to demonstrate the didactic principles of epic theatre, had always been a bone of contention with proponents of Socialist Realist aesthetics. The revival of the play, which premiered at the Berliner Ensemble on 12 January 1951, came under attack almost immediately for 'formalism', marking the beginning of the public campaign to undermine Brecht's aesthetic stance. For the production history of these plays, compare *Plays* 3 and 4.

70

Notes on the Discussion about Formalism

The discussion about formalism is not helped by the fact that the wrong people are supporting the right side, and the wrong arguments are being presented for the right position. The progress of certain critics of formalism has diminished to a snail's pace; people moan on about eternal artistic laws in the interest of completely transforming our cultural life. Medical vocabulary is replacing political vocabulary: instead of demonstrating that this or that work of art involves something useless for, or detrimental to, society, they assert that it's a case of sickness. If the doctor isn't called out to produce healthy works of art, then the police are called out to punish a crime against the people. This sort of thing hampers efforts and struggles to develop art which is of value to society.

One thing which artists find particularly unhelpful, and indeed annoying, is the attitude of certain critics of formalism who draw a clear, or even unclear, distinction between themselves and the people. They never talk about a work of art's impact on themselves, and always about its impact on the people; they themselves don't seem to be part of the people. By the same token, they know exactly what the people want and recognise the people by virtue of the fact that the people want what they want. 'The people can't understand that,' they say. 'Did *you* understand it?' asks the artist. 'If not, at least have the decency to say that you didn't understand it, and I can cite you as a witness.' In fact, people like this underestimate quite outrageously the people they value so much.

The disillusioned complain, of course, that the people want first and foremost to see trash, full stop. What this leads to is that some of the 'disillusioned' party simply do not produce art for the people, or else just produce trash for the people. What you have to do is define what the people is. And see the people as a highly contradictory entity, in a process of development, as an entity of which you yourself are a part. When the people are brought face to face with the artist as the audience, the people aren't only the customer or the consumer, but also the supplier; they supply ideas, they supply dynamism, they supply the material, and they supply the form. Inconsistent, and constantly changing, the way they are.

['*Notizen über die Formalismusdiskussion*', BFA 23/141–2.]

Written in 1951. This text appears to have been written as part of Brecht's preparations for the debates over the *Lucullus* opera. He refers to the attitudes of proponents of Socialist Realism, such as the critic Heinz Lüdecke, whose articles in the Party newspaper *Neues Deutschland* set the tone of the debate. Lüdecke wrote not about his personal response to the music, but instead made assumptions about the (negative) response of the public.

71

What is Formalism?

As far as proletarians are concerned, bourgeois freedom is a kind of formalism, something that exists only 'on paper', an empty phrase, eyewash; because proletarians are only free 'in formal terms'. The extravagant statement in the Weimar Constitution, 'Anybody can acquire a plot of land', is merely formal progress as compared to eras when only particular classes could acquire plots of land; because proletarians still can't acquire a plot of land – it's just that the less extravagant statement, 'who has the necessary cash', has been omitted. The possibility of acquiring an allotment some day does not turn the proletarian into a landowner either. The worst kind of formalism was the socialism of the Nazis, a type of socialism that virtually screamed out for quotation marks; it duped many people. There was the 'people's community' of the entrepreneurs and the entrepreneured, of the earners and the well-earned; there was the 'economic upturn', the 'economic miracle' thanks to rearmament. And, on paper, the people had a Volkswagen, though in the cold light of day it became a tank.

You see, you can do lots of things with form, carry out all sorts of swindles and fake improvements which then simply exist in 'external form'.

Form plays a major role in art. Form isn't everything, but it's so substantial that neglecting it will destroy a work. It isn't something external, something that the artist confers on content, it's so much a part of content that it often comes across to the artist as content itself; because, in the process of making a work of art, certain formal elements usually occur to the artist at the same time as the material, and sometimes even in advance of it. The artist may feel like making something 'light', a poem with 14 lines, something 'dark' with heavy rhythms, something extensive, colourful, etc. He blends words which are unusually tasty, deceitfully marries them off, plays with them. In the process of construction, he plays around, tries this or that, directs the action first this way and then another. He seeks out variety and contrasts. He cleans his words, they gather dust easily; he freshens situations up, they get stale easily. He is not always aware, not every moment when he's 'creating', that he's constantly in the process of forming an image of reality or an 'expression' of what reality outside him is doing to him inside. He occasionally dries up, to the detriment of his work, but the dangers of the procedure don't make it wrong or avoidable. The 'great formal artists' are often in danger, and they occasionally perish. Excessive 'smoothing out' ruins a fair amount of creative writing, and it's also true that 'volcanic eruptions' do the same. At any rate, we should note that creative writers don't 'mince their words', unless we're counting on them having rather strangely shaped gobs. They form and they formulate. But that does not turn them into formalists.

It would be utter nonsense to say that we should lay no emphasis on form and the development of form in art. We must. If it does not introduce formal innovations, creative writing cannot introduce new strata in the audience to new materials and new perspectives. We construct our buildings differently from the Elizabethans, and we construct our plays differently too. If we wanted to retain Shakespeare's construction methods, we would probably have to explain the origins of the First World War, say, in terms of one individual's need for self-assertion (Kaiser Wilhelm, caused in his case by his stunted arm). But that would be absurd. That really would be formalism: it would mean that we were renouncing a new perspective on a changed world simply in order to retain a particular construction method. Because it is just as formalistic to impose old forms on material as it is to impose new ones.

In our case, however, the trenchant critique of formalism emerged in the face of *new* artistic forms which presented nothing new other than formal innovation. By way of example, psychological factors continued to be seen as the engine of world events, and in that sense everything stayed as it was, but psychology was changed by the introduction of psychoanalysis or behaviourism, and that was what was new. What underlay this process was the unease which had entered depraved, bourgeois culture – the worn-out mare of psychology was thrashed into performing new tricks and running new races. In painting, the apple became a problem of form and colour. What underlay this was a new impatience with nature which elsewhere, in biology, led to the creation of new kinds of fruit. An American Presbyterian used certain innovations in acting techniques, which had been developed for the revolutionary representation of social problems, to bring about the contemplative apotheosis of a New England congregation. At the same time, his brothers in the pulpit introduced film and jazz into church services that were losing their popular appeal. The so-called Existentialists discovered that the existence of bourgeois human beings had become rather dubious, but because a decisive battle has to be fought (which Churchill also thinks), and in order to draw the sting from this new and interesting thought, they spoke only of the existence of 'human beings', without troubling the adjective 'bourgeois', and so we were left with the old ploy in a new guise, and pessimism was recommended as a new pick-me-up. In short, formal innovations were used everywhere to make the old appealing again, the threadbare old pair of trousers was turned inside out, which didn't make it any warmer, but it did look nicer (and warmer).

It's no wonder that, in the end, formal innovations fell into disrepute. People saw too clearly that something existed which might be called the autonomous dynamic of form, and is very dangerous. A few new principles are found, they make a name for themselves, a new short cut seems to have been discovered. In the beginning the new form promises this and that, but it soon begins to demand this and that independently of materials and function. If this happens, you can be sure that it was a dead end, and that now people are just making themselves at home in it. The new trend in art did not correspond to a new trend in politics or in public affairs. The new form was a new order, of the sort that was experienced in National Socialism, a new, striking, agreeable arrangement of the old scheme of things, a formalism.

It's clear that we must fight illusory innovations such as this, at a time when everything depends on humanity rubbing out the dust that's been thrown into its eyes. It is equally clear that we can't return to the old, but must march on towards true innovations. Just consider the immense innovations that are currently happening all around us. In territories as populous as France and England combined, new classes have conquered the land and the means of production; ancient China, as large as the English Empire at the time of its 'heyday', is entering world history with new social principles, etc., etc. – how are artists supposed to produce images of all that with the old artistic methods?

['*Was ist Formalismus?*', BFA 23/143–7.]

Written in 1951. This is another text belonging to the complex of responses to the debate about the *Lucullus* opera. The People's Republic of China had been founded two years earlier, on 1 October 1949.

72

The Discussion about *The Condemnation of Lucullus*

The opera had already been accepted when the campaign against formalism was launched. In the Ministry for Public Education doubts were raised. The authors were advised to withdraw the opera. They, however, were prepared only to cancel the contract and not to withdraw the opera, since they did not consider the opera formalist. The arguments put forward did not convince them, those put forward by musicians actually seemed to them to be formalist. They emphasised the importance of the content, namely the condemnation of wars of plunder. And they suggested continuing rehearsals for the opera, which had already begun, until a closed performance could be staged to allow a responsible audience and the artists to reach an understanding. The suggestion was accepted, and very great resources were mobilised to facilitate this understanding. At the performance, the content made a very strong impression on the audience, precisely because it corresponded to the GDR's policy of peace, of condemning wars of plunder. However, there were also strong reservations and, in a three-hour discussion between prominent members of the government, led by the GDR President, and the authors, it transpired that in its present form the work might introduce a certain confusion into the new campaign, which is of the utmost importance since its role is to close the undeniable gulf between the arts and their new audience. The text's parabolic character made it harder to understand. The music, diverging from the classical line, did not take the majority of the audience's current level of musical education sufficiently into account. Moreover, the music was dominated by those parts which described the aggressors and which were consequently gloomy and vehement. Brecht and Dessau declared themselves willing to make additions in the spirit of the discussion and to resubmit the work. When, in a second discussion organised on the same basis, the new texts were submitted and the composer also proposed certain changes, it was decided to allow the work to proceed to performance and to present it to public criticism.

['*Die Diskussion über* Die Verurteilung des Lukullus', BFA 24/276–7.]

Written in 1951. In this text, Brecht attempts to summarise the controversy over *Lucullus*. See note on no. 69, above.

73

Open Letter to German Artists and Writers

It is with horror that I, like many others, have learned from Otto Grotewohl's speech, in which he calls for pan-German consultations in preparation for free elections, how serious the government of the German Democratic Republic considers the situation in Germany.

Will there be war? The answer: if we arm for war, we will have war. Will Germans shoot at Germans? The answer: if they do not talk to each other, they will shoot at each other.

In a country, which has for a long time taken a unified approach to its affairs and which has been suddenly and violently torn apart, there are many conflicts which need arbitration, everywhere and at every moment. This can happen in many ways. If there are armies, it will happen in a warlike way. At the very latest, when there is a danger that such armies are being created, new efforts must be made to find a peaceful path to reunification. Notwithstanding the huge advantages of such unity, this would remove the source of conflicts. People from all professions, all equally threatened, must contribute towards removing the tensions which have arisen. As a writer, I turn to German writers and artists to call on their representative institutions, that they might discuss the following suggestions at an early stage in the negotiations we hope for.

1   Complete freedom for the written word with one proviso.
2   Complete freedom for the theatre   with one proviso.
3   Complete freedom for the visual arts   with one proviso.
4   Complete freedom for music   with one proviso.
5   Complete freedom for film   with one proviso.

The proviso: no freedom for writings or works of art which glorify war or present it as inevitable, nor for those which promote hatred between peoples.

Great Carthage waged three wars. It was still powerful after the first, still inhabitable after the second. It was no longer to be found after the third.

['*Offener Brief an die deutschen Künstler und Schriftsteller*', BFA 23/155–6.]

Written and published in September–October 1951. The text is a declaration of support for the appeal by the *Volkskammer* (the GDR parliament) to the West German *Bundestag* on 15 September 1951, which expressed the regime's disquiet at the proposed remilitarisation of the Federal Republic (which began in earnest in 1952 and ended with the FRG's entry into NATO in October 1954, further entrenching the Cold War division between East and West Germany). The GDR Minister President Otto Grotewohl proposed talks with the West German government on setting up a freely elected national assembly for the whole of Germany. The

West German Chancellor, Konrad Adenauer, rejected the proposals.

Brecht's text, with its pointed reference to the three Punic Wars between Carthage and Rome (264–146 BC), was greeted euphorically in places, particularly in the East, but provoked controversy in the West.

74

Notes on the Barlach Exhibition

The Barlach exhibition and the discussions concerning it must be seen as a sign of the significance attached to art in the GDR. The discussion may not yet have the thorough and all-encompassing quality for which we should strive, nor do I like the impatient and zealous tone of some pronouncements, but Barlach's work has never before been discussed in so important a forum.

I consider Barlach one of the greatest sculptors we Germans have ever known. The accomplishment, the significance of the message, the craftsman's genius, beauty without embellishment, unforced greatness, harmony without superficiality, vitality without brutality make Barlach's sculptures masterpieces. At the same time, I do not like all his creations, and even if we can learn a lot from him, we are still entitled to ask: what? when? by whom?

Barlach's religious sculptures do not mean a great deal to me, nor do all those which have something mystical about them. And I cannot quite decide whether he has not also occasionally delivered up his beggars and apathetic mothers to religious feeling alone, which, after all, accepts economic *and* spiritual poverty piously and humbly. But in the sculptures which I consider his most beautiful, he allows human substance, social potential, to triumph splendidly over injustice and humiliation, and this shows his greatness.

There is the *Woman beggar with bowl*, in bronze, from 1906. A powerful person with hard self-assurance, from whom no thanks for alms are to be expected. She seems immune to a corrupt society's hypocritical attempts to persuade her that she can achieve something by being diligent and making herself useful. She blames it coldly for the fact that her strength is paralysed. Around 1906 there were already women who declared war on this society; she is not one of them. There were also artists who were already fashioning such female fighters (Gorky was just creating his Vlassova); Barlach is not one of these artists. That may be a pity, but I am willing to stand by his contribution and thank him for it.

Then there is the *Melon cutter*, a bronze from 1907. In the German plastic art of recent centuries we will scarcely find another work which depicts a common man eating with such sensual power. (Am I wrong? I'd be grateful for correction.) He has sat down in the exact position which is best for precisely this activity, and he is not lost in his work. It would be perfectly possible to discuss working conditions with him and other things besides. He may not yet know enough, but his class need not be ashamed at least to have him as a precursor, I think.

Three singing women, a wood carving from 1911, stout women, leaning against each other and singing raucously in all directions, and I like them because I find the connection between strength and singing agreeable.

The singing man, a bronze from 1928, is singing differently from the three women of 1911, boldly, freely, clearly working at his song. He is singing alone but seems to have listeners. Barlach's humour intends him to be a little vain, but no more than is compatible with practising art.

The fact that the angel of the Güstrow Monument (bronze 1927) overpowers me is not surprising. It has the face of the unforgettable Käthe Kollwitz. I like angels like this. And although we have never seen either an angel or a man fly, it is still a glorious depiction of flying.

The blind man and the cripple, a stucco relief from 1919, a blind man who is dragging a cripple. The picture is not executed in the usual parabolic manner, with a degree of abstraction, with unindividualised figures. It is executed with realism, and the real, individual event attains the status of a parable. (It makes a difference, whether, on hearing the words 'a rich man had a vineyard',

I imagine the landed class, or on seeing a blind man dragging a cripple, uphill at that, I think of the trade unions who in 1919 were dragging the Social Democratic Party. I am by no means certain that Barlach was thinking anything of the sort.) The group has a wonderful inner dynamic due to the realistic drawing of limbs walking with a heavy burden.

Old woman dancing, coloured plaster, from 1920. An image whose humour is extremely rare in German sculpture. What grandeur the old woman has, lifting her skirts and daring another little dance! Her gaze is raised upwards: she is digging in her memory for the right steps!

The *Kissing groups I* and *II*, bronzes from 1921, are of great interest, because here the sculptor developed his subject matter and, by roughening and thus actually coarsening the material, achieved a greater depth. The work is a welcome change from the cute sexless Amor-and-Psyche groups in the front parlours of the petty bourgeoisie.

From now on, with the sculptures from the years after '33, you have to look at the date of their genesis. There is the *Man reading a book*, the bronze from 1936. A man sitting down, leaning forward, holding a book in his heavy hands. He is reading with curiosity, confidently, critically. He is clearly searching for solutions to urgent problems in the book. Goebbels would probably have called him 'a beast of an intellectual'. I prefer the man reading a book to Rodin's famous thinker, who only shows the difficulty of thinking. Barlach's sculpture is more realistic, more concrete, unsymbolic.

In the *Old woman freezing* (teak, 1937), a cowering maid or peasant woman, so patently abandoned both physically and mentally by society, her large, work-worn hands leap to our attention: she has been unable to protect them from the cold. She sees to the freezing as if it were a task, and she shows no anger. But the sculptor shows anger, far more anger than pity; let us thank him for that.

Old woman seated, a bronze sculpture from 1933. Again our gaze is directed towards the face and hands, but this woman possesses spirit; her face and hands show what we might call nobility, were this word not associated with the Hindenburgs and Hohenzollerns. (Again, incidentally, the clothing is depicted masterfully. It does not only hint at the body, but allows us to survey it in one, just as a successful rhyme allows us to do with a thought. One minute detail makes it utterly realistic: the woollen scarf.) The body is very beautiful; it shows tenderness and strength in noble proportions. The old woman holds herself erect, she is thinking. Her smile hints at experiences, which she has gleaned like ears of wheat by the grassy roadside, one after the other. Faced with this sculpture, created in the fateful year 1933, memories and comparisons resurface. One year earlier in Berlin, Weigel played Vlassova on stage. Instead of passivity, activity; instead of inhumanity's victim, humanity. I can imagine a worker nudging Barlach's old woman with his elbow: seize power! You have everything it takes.

Symbolism is pretty much lost on me, but I would like to let Barlach's *The terrible year 1937* (in plaster) stand. It is an upright, emaciated young woman, wrapped in a shawl. It could be the *Old woman seated* in her youth. She is looking into the future, worried, but her worry is proof of the sculptor's optimism. The image signifies a vehement rejection of the Nazi regime, of Goebbels's optimism. I can well imagine this young woman as an activist in 1951.

From the same terrible year 1937 comes the *Old woman laughing* (in wood). Her cheerfulness is irresistible. Her laughter is like singing, it has released her entire body, which looks almost young. Goebbels and Rosenberg would not particularly have liked seeing her laugh either, I think. Barlach is said to have made his *Old woman laughing* on hearing that many of his sculptures, removed from museums on the grounds of 'degeneracy', were being sold in Switzerland to pull in foreign currency to produce guns. It is interesting how historical perspective deepens our enjoyment of works like this.

All of these sculptures seem to me to have the mark of realism: there is much depth and nothing superfluous about them. Ideas, real models and material determine the pleasurable form. Barlach's love of man, his humanism, are also undeniable. Of course, he gives man little hope; even some of his most beautiful works awaken the sad thought of the *deutsche Misere* which has so damaged our arts. The 'idiocy of country life', which has cruelly branded Barlach's figures, is not the target of his attack; at times he even takes on the appearance of being 'hefted to the soil', 'eternal', 'divinely ordained'. If a tractor driver from today can nevertheless benefit from looking at these splendid depictions of poor people, then this is because the artist endowed his class, so long oppressed, the very monopoly on humanity in a bestial world. – Barlach writes: 'It is probably the case that the artist knows more than he is able to say.' But perhaps it is actually the case that Barlach is able to say more than he knows.

I am not making notes here about the works which I like less (like *The avenger, The doubter, The abandoned,* etc.), since in those cases the form given to them seems to me a deformation of reality. I too am of the opinion that our young artists should not be called on to learn from such works. However, it is not acceptable to lump these works together with the others, particularly if neither group is dealt with concretely. Abstract criticism does not lead to realistic art.

['*Notizen zur Barlach-Ausstellung*', BFA 23/198–202.]

Written in January 1952 and published in the January–February 1952 edition of *Sinn und Form.* The Academy of Arts opened an exhibition of Ernst Barlach's sculptures in December 1951, which immediately drew attacks in the Party press. On 13 January 1952, the sculptor Gustav Seitz shared with Brecht his concerns about those press attacks and encouraged Brecht to visit the exhibition. This text consists of Brecht's thoughts dictated to Käthe Rülicke as he went around the exhibition.

The writer and sculptor Ernst Barlach (1870–1938) was one of the most significant artists connected with German Expressionism, though he always kept his distance from the movement's major groupings and controversies. Some of his most important public works were destroyed by the Nazis.

Deutsche Misere was a term used to describe the idea that there was a fundamental flaw at the heart of the historical development of Germany, which had ultimately led it off the 'normal' path followed by other nations; in the Marxist interpretation of this idea, the root cause lay in the backwardness and division which resulted from the Thirty Years War

(1618–48). Brecht's ongoing concern with this idea is further illustrated in his contributions to the discussion about Hanns Eisler's *Johann Faustus*, see no. 77.

75

On the Death of Stalin

The oppressed people of five continents, those who have already liberated themselves, and all those who are fighting for world peace, must have felt their hearts miss a beat when they heard that Stalin was dead. He was the embodiment of their hopes. But the intellectual and material weapons which he produced remain, and with them the method to produce new ones.

['*Zum Tod Stalins*'*, BFA 23/225.]

Written between 6 and 7 March 1953. On 8 March 1953 the official SED newspaper, *Neues Deutschland*, published the reactions of numerous prominent figures to Stalin's death on 5 March 1953. Brecht's somewhat restrained contribution appeared under the heading 'National Prize Winner, Bertolt Brecht' and was reproduced alongside the responses of other members of the East Berlin Academy of Arts in the March–April edition of *Sinn und Form*.

76

Erwin Strittmatter's *Katzgraben*

Erwin Strittmatter is one of the new writers who did not rise from the proletariat, but with the proletariat. He is the son of a farm worker from Niederlausitz, tried his hand at many jobs, as a farm-worker, baker, furrier and so on, and after 1945 he became a village mayor, people's correspondent, writer. Without the German

Democratic Republic he would not only not have become the writer he is, he would probably not have become a writer at all. His novel *Ox-driver* immediately placed him in the none too long line of significant German writers, due to his strength in structuring the material, his originality, conviction, knowledge and linguistic power. His peasant comedy *Katzgraben* shows him in a process of rapid development. He is proceeding along new paths, but not without knowledge of the old ones.

The German peasants have appeared on stage in plays by Anzengruber, Ruederer and Thoma, and in dialect plays which are only known locally. *Katzgraben* is to my knowledge the first play to put the modern class struggle in the village on the German stage. It shows peasants with large, medium and small holdings, and a party secretary, after the Junkers had been driven out of the German Democratic Republic. The characters in the play are full of individuality, with delightful idiosyncrasies, likeable or hateable, full of contradictions and at the same time unambiguous, characters who are worthy companions of the more familiar characters of dramatic literature. The language of the play is extraordinarily plastic, rich in imagery and strong, full of new elements.

[. . .]

I consider it a significant achievement that we hear our workers and peasants speaking on stage like the heroes of Shakespeare and Schiller.

The plot of the play is also shaped magnificently. We see the village of Katzgraben in two successive years and then a further six months later. These chronological leaps, however, by no means break up the action. One and the same theme runs through and develops logically, and the class struggle proceeds to ever higher stages. In 1947, the new peasant has to give in to the powerful peasant in the matter of a road intended to link Katzgraben more closely to the town, because he still needs his horses to meet the cultivation plan: in order to double his harvest, he has to plough deeply. In 1948, his double harvest has brought him an ox, and he is in a position to force the road through against the will of the powerful peasant. But the ox is very lean and there is no fodder. In

1949, the lack of ground water becomes urgent, and unless this problem is solved, all the previous work is at risk. Again, the problem is political, and in the epilogue, a solution is sought on the broadest possible basis: a tractor replaces the ox. All this is depicted poetically. Such 'prosaic' things as potatoes, roads, tractors, become poetic!

The new people in his play are, of course, the most important thing for Strittmatter. *Katzgraben* is a hymn of praise to their new virtues. To their unrelenting patience, their inventive courage, their practical goodwill towards one another, their critical sense of humour. By leaps and bounds, in the course of the play, social being changes their consciousness. The peasants who attended the first preview performance recognised themselves in the play and discussed the author's views with him in an open, friendly way.

The play does not only show things. It draws the spectator powerfully into the great process of productively transforming the village, a process driven by the dynamo of the Socialist Party of the German Democratic Republic. It fills him with the spirit of bold progress.

Learn and change, learn from this anew.

And change again!

['*Erwin Strittmatters* Katzgraben', BFA 24/437–41.]

Written 3 June 1953. The text relates to the Berliner Ensemble's production of *Katzgraben*, written by the GDR playwright Erwin Strittmatter, which premiered on 23 May 1953 (and the text of which Brecht had revised with Strittmatter the previous year). The production of Strittmatter's highly orthodox agricultural comedy is often viewed as a tactical sop to SED cultural politicians, in response to the increasing pressure the Berliner Ensemble faced in early 1953 as a result of its perceived failure to follow the prescribed dramatic method of the Soviet theoretician Constantin Stanislavsky (see also 'Some of the Things that can be Learnt from Stanislavsky' and 'Notes on Erwin Strittmatter's Play *Katzgraben*', *Brecht on Theatre*, nos 45 and 47). That this piece, couched starkly in the orthodox language of SED ideology, was published in *Sinn und Form* after 17 June 1953, when that pressure had been lifted, is a strong indication of Brecht's genuine commitment to the social and economic project of East German socialism. Brecht was also seeking to promote new GDR literary talent and to develop a German comic tradition with the Ensemble.

77

Theses on the *Faustus* Discussion

1 Although the work requires music in order to achieve its full effect, it is a significant literary work

due to its great national theme,
due to the linkage of the character of Faust and the Peasants' War,
due to its magnificent conception,
due to its language,
due to the richness of its ideas.

2 Even with all these qualities, the work might still be rejected if it were asocial or unpatriotic. However, because of these qualities our investigation must proceed carefully.

3 A careful investigation will show that the work can be called neither asocial nor unpatriotic.

4 The treatment of a great literary character in a new manner and another spirit should not be rejected. Such an undertaking by no means signifies an attempt to destroy the character. Some poetic undertakings of this kind can be found in ancient Greek drama.

5 Eisler's Faustus is by no means a distorted character. Like Goethe's Faust, he is a divided, restless individual with brilliant talents and lofty goals. Of course, his development occurs during his downfall, like that of the Shakespearian heroes; in contrast to Goethe's play, this is a tragedy.

6 I read the content as follows: Faust, the son of a peasant, has crossed over to the ruling classes in the Peasants' War. Faust's attempt to develop his personality fails as a result. He finds it impossible to carry his betrayal through completely. His guilty conscience forces him at the last moment to continue to execute his ambitious plans so rebelliously that he fails to win the favour of the ruling classes. To his own disadvantage, he has recognised the truth. From being a life-giving potion, it becomes poison for him. When the peasants' slave drivers finally recognise him, he breaks down and achieves the insight which he proclaims in a confession.

7 The moral message of the work is hard to discern because the betrayed peasants are in my opinion insufficiently represented by Karl, a veteran of the Peasants' War, who although well-drawn makes only a fleeting appearance. They dominate Faustus's every thought and deed, but are thus only psychologically present. If they were – or were to be – depicted as great antagonists, it would hardly be *possible* to continue to misinterpret the work as negative.

8 We must assume unconditionally the truth of the sentence: 'A conception which only sees *Misere* in German history and where the people as a creative potential are absent, is not true' (ND). However, the creative powers of the people are not absent from Eisler's *Faustus*, they are the peasants of the great Peasants' War led on by Münzer. Faustus's creativity is broken because he deserts them. And anyone who, like Eisler, talks of *deutsche Misere* in order to combat it, himself belongs to the creative forces, to those who make it impermissible to talk of German history as nothing but *Misere*.

9 Can we also assume that this sentence is true: 'that it would be not only a grave artistic, but also an ideological shortcoming, were Faust to appear from the outset as a traitor, as a condemned man, as someone doomed to failure, so that there could no longer be any question of an inner development, either positive or negative' (ND)? The sentence as a whole is not acceptable, for every person in a tragedy from Oedipus to Wallenstein is doomed to failure from the outset. But if in Faustus we simply had a traitor before us who did not develop at all, then I too would consider the work a failure. That, however, is not the case. In fact, the play begins with a Faustus who wavers for a long time. Then he seals the pact with the devil, and there follows one attempt after another to develop his personality by exploiting the pact. They all fail, since Faustus's guilty conscience prevents him from staging the attempts *without inhibitions*. However, it is precisely Faustus's conscience which these attempts develop powerfully, and what ensues is the great confession, the horrifying recognition that there can be no true

development for a traitor to the people. As in every genuine tragedy, recognition provides no rescue from damnation: the traitor is fetched by the devil.

10 I do not agree with Ernst Fischer's interpretation of the work. Fischer calls the basic idea of Eisler's creation: the German humanist as renegade (ND). Perhaps Fischer is basing his remarks on the volume of the Soviet Encyclopaedia devoted to Germany, which states: 'Out of fear of the Peasants' Revolution, the humanists crossed over to the side of the reaction and persecuted materialism and science with no less hatred than the Catholic clerics.' That is a very severe judgement, in my opinion too severe. In Eisler's work the assessment of the humanists is by no means negative. Faustus is not 'only a renegade', just as Oedipus is not 'only a father killer and mother violator', or Othello 'only a wife murderer'. In Faustus the truth, hard won in the Peasants' Revolution, lives on until his demise; he cannot eradicate it himself, and it brings him finally to book. His self-condemnation does not, of course, make him an exemplary figure – let him go to the devil! – but it is worth depicting.

11 At an historic moment, when the German bourgeoisie is once again calling on the intelligentsia to betray the people, Eisler holds up a mirror to them: may each person recognise or not recognise himself in it! Writing a play like this is the opposite of unpatriotic.

12 Has Eisler tried to destroy our classical image of Faust completely (ND)? Is he removing the soul from a wonderful figure in the German heritage, falsifying, destroying it (Abusch)? Is he revoking Faust (Abusch)? I think not. Eisler rereads the old folk legend and discovers a different story from Goethe, and a different figure, which strikes him as significant. Of course, significant in a different way from Goethe's creation. In this way I feel that Faust's dark twin comes into being, a sinister, great character which neither can nor should replace or overshadow his lighter brother. On the contrary, the light brother is brought more sharply into relief by the darker brother and becomes even lighter. Creating something like this is not vandalism.

I shall summarise my points once more. I agree with Eisler's critics that German history should not be depicted as negative, and that German literature, one of whose most beautiful works is Goethe's *Faust*, should not be abandoned, but that serious attempts must instead be made now to turn it into the property of the people. I do not agree with Eisler's critics that Eisler disagrees with them. He has in my opinion taken sides with the forces of light which in Germany fought, and are still fighting, with the forces of darkness, and he has supplied a positive contribution to the great Faust question, of which German literature need not be ashamed.

['*Thesen zur* Faustus-*Diskussion*', BFA 23/246–9.]

Written in May 1953, first published in *Sinn und Form* in the late summer of 1953. The theses are a discussion piece presented by Brecht to the second of three special 'Wednesday Gatherings', held at the East Berlin Academy of Arts in May and June 1953 to discuss Hanns Eisler's *Johann Faustus*. Towards the end of 1952, Eisler, arguably the most prominent GDR composer of the time, had published the libretto for an opera based on the Faust legend. Publication of the libretto in the GDR and an enthusiastic review by the Austrian Marxist Ernst Fischer provoked a storm of controversy – entirely disproportionate to Eisler's little-read text – which extended through the first half of 1953. Eisler's *Faustus* was heavily criticised in public by SED hardliners, above all because of its perceived negative depiction of the Faust figure, located by Eisler in the immediate context of the German Peasants' War (1525), and its apparent depiction of *deutsche Misere* (see no. 74). Brecht makes reference in his text to two such attacks: an editorial piece, 'The Faust-Problem and German History', which appeared in *Neues Deutschland* on 14 May 1953 (abbreviated as 'ND'); and Alexander Abusch's essay 'Faust: Hero or Renegade in German National Literature?' which appeared in the GDR weekly *Sonntag* on 17 May 1953 (abbreviated as 'Abusch').

Brecht, who had looked through Eisler's text with him in August 1952 (see *Journals*, p. 445) and whose own production of Goethe's early play on the same theme, known as *Urfaust*, had been forced to close by SED cultural officials, became drawn into the controversy which was played out to its climax at the 'Wednesday Gatherings'. At these meetings, the aesthetic debate concerning the appropriate attitude to the German literary tradition and the representation of German history was subsumed by an internal political struggle between SED cultural hardliners and the increasingly marginalised faction around Brecht and Eisler. Eisler's treatment of the Faust legend seems to have struck a nerve concerning the historical legitimacy of the SED regime itself. The defensive tone of Brecht's theses betrays the severe pressure which Brecht and Eisler felt themselves to be under. Only a combination of the new political course emerging from Moscow in early June and the subsequent workers' uprising of 17 June allowed Brecht to counter-attack and effectively secure his position within GDR culture until his death in 1956.

78

Concerning 17 June 1953

The demonstrations of 17 June showed that a considerable section of Berlin's workers were dissatisfied with a series of misguided economic measures.

Organised Fascist elements attempted to abuse this dissatisfaction for their bloody ends.

For several hours, Berlin stood on the brink of a third world war.

It is only thanks to the speedy and assured intervention of Soviet troops that these attempts were frustrated.

It was obvious that the Soviet military intervention was by no means directed against the workers' demonstrations. It was quite patently directed exclusively against the attempts to kindle another global conflagration.

It is now up to every individual to help the government eradicate the errors which triggered dissatisfaction and which are endangering our indubitably great social achievements.

['*Zum 17. Juni 1953*'*, BFA 23/249–50.]

Written after 17 June 1953. This text represents one of Brecht's several responses to the events of that day. Provoked by the government's decision of 28 May to raise by ten per cent the output required of industrial workers, the popular uprising could only be put down with the help of Soviet tanks. This text, together with his letter of 1 July 1953 to his West German publisher Peter Suhrkamp (see *Letters*, pp. 516–18), demonstrates that Brecht largely subscribed to the official SED interpretation of the unrest, namely that it was orchestrated by Fascist insurgents from the West. Brecht's belief in the social achievements of the GDR is also apparent.

Compare also the more coded comments in poems from the same time, the *Buckow Elegies*.

79

The Urgent Need for a Major Discussion

On the morning of 17 June, when it became clear that the workers' demonstrations were being abused for the purposes of war-mongering, I expressed my commitment to the German Socialist Unity Party. I hope now that the provocateurs are being isolated and their lines of communication cut. At the same time, however, I hope that the workers who demonstrated out of justified dissatisfaction will not be equated with the provocateurs, so that the major discussion concerning the mistakes made on all sides, which is so urgently needed, will not be rendered impossible from the outset.

['*Dringlichkeit einer grossen Aussprache*'*, BFA 23/250.]

Written 21 June 1953, first published in *Neues Deutschland*, 23 June 1953. This text represents Brecht's attempt to clarify in public his attitude to the events of 17 June, following the decision by *Neues Deutschland* to publish only the final unequivocally supportive sentence of the letter he had written to SED First Secretary Walter Ulbricht on the morning of 17 June, expressing his solidarity with the regime (see *Letters*, pp. 515–16). However, Brecht's bitter complaints over the treatment of that letter remained private. This text constitutes the full extent of Brecht's public questioning of the regime's culpability in the workers' unrest and its aftermath, and was published alongside other contributions under the heading 'No Mercy for Fascists'.

80

Declaration by the German Academy of Arts

Suggestions submitted to the government

In the endeavour to support the government of the German Democratic Republic in its task of establishing German national unity and securing peace, the German Academy of Arts declares:

1 The artist's responsibility to the public must be restored. The responsibility for repertoire must lie with the theatre manager, for concerts with the impresario or artistic director, for literary works with the author and publisher, for exhibitions with a jury composed of artists. State bodies should promote art in every conceivable way but refrain from all administrative measures in questions of artistic production and style. Criticism must be left to the public.

2 It is necessary to develop and promote a variety of themes and forms in all areas of art which will appeal to the different sections of the population.

3 The German Academy of Arts suggests that the government of the German Democratic Republic should consult it as an assessor and adviser on all decrees and laws concerning art. It considers its participation necessary in the selection of leading individuals responsible for artistic matters, in order to guarantee that they are professionally qualified.

When public commissions are awarded, monuments conceived, or art exhibitions, prize ceremonies, competitions etc. organised, the advice and judgement of the German Academy of Arts should be listened to on principle. The same applies to the development of curricula and examination regulations as well as all other matters concerning our talented young artists. At the same time, the Academy suggests that the government should listen to the appropriate professional associations where artistic matters are concerned.

4 The language of our daily newspapers must correspond to the

manifold needs and receptive capacity of the population. Bureaucratic, mechanical language paralyses the population's interest in public affairs. At the same time, such language impedes communication between both parts of Germany.

5 Radio has failed as a decisive means of forming public opinion. It has left the task of informing and influencing the population to the misleading broadcasters on the opposing sides. Only a fundamental reorganisation – including the artistic sphere – can place radio in a position to recapture the interest and trust of listeners and to force a decline in the influence of rival broadcasters.

6 In contrast to the years immediately after 1945, when the films we produced appealed to broad sections of the population, in recent years the subject matter has been narrowed more and more, so that they only interest a small circle of people. The Academy suggests that, in order to increase production and thematic variety, artistically independent production groups should be formed in the DEFA's feature film studio. It suggests furthermore that the DEFA should produce more films with pan-German appeal. Where the weekly newsreel is concerned, the same statements apply as to the daily press and radio.

7 The German Academy of Arts suggests that the government should also award National Prizes to artists who do not live in the German Democratic Republic, irrespective of whether or not they are currently able to accept them.

8 The responsibility for editing art and culture periodicals should lie with the appropriate associations and organisations or with individual persons or groups of artists.

9 The Academy suggests examining whether it was appropriate to dissolve the Union of German Theatre Workers. It sees the dissolution of the *Volksbühne*, the broadest organisation of theatregoers, as overhasty and inappropriate.

10 The events of 17 June have proved that the arts must also redouble their efforts in the fight against Fascism in all its manifestations.

['*Erklärung der Deutschen Akademie der Künste*', BFA 23/253–5.]

Written in June 1953, first published in *Neues Deutschland*, 12 July 1953. Following 17 June 1953, Brecht was appointed on 18 June to a special commission of the East Berlin Academy of Arts, charged with putting forward proposals for the reform of cultural policy in the GDR. At a plenary meeting of the Academy on 26 June Brecht read out a preliminary list of eight proposals, which was extended to ten and approved by the Academy at a meeting on 30 June. The SED tried strenuously to block the publication of the Academy's proposals and objections were raised above all to point five. This public statement criticising the workings of cultural policy in the GDR constitutes a significant act of dissent against the SED regime. Nonetheless, the introduction to the text and point ten demonstrate ongoing support. The BFA (23/549) erroneously dates the first presentation of the Academy proposals to 16 June 1953, thereby connecting the establishment of the commission to the new political course originating from Moscow rather than to the uprising of 17 June.

81

Preface to *Turandot*

At the beginning of the summer in which I wrote the play in question, a terrible event had shocked every intelligent person in the Republic. Since the end of Hitler's war, which had led to the Soviet occupation of this part of Germany, socialist measures like the expulsion of the warmongering Junkers, the nationalisation of many factories and the admission of workers' and peasants' children to higher education had effected a powerful change in the way people live. They had not succeeded, of course, in effecting an equally great change in the way people think. There were many reasons for this. First of all, the economic system had to be transformed at a time when the economy had been weakened by the war. Hitler's regime had exhausted the last reserves of national prosperity, and the economic restoration, tackled conscientiously and ingeniously by workers and peasants, also suffered initially from the necessity of making amends for at least some of the monstrous devastation which the German people had perpetrated during their invasion of the Soviet Union under Hitler's regime: this country too had reached the limit of its resources.

Furthermore, the socialist measures were new; those who were putting them into practice had little or no experience in such matters, every step was an experiment on virgin territory, even with Russian support. Everywhere, mistakes were made, people were harmed or had their feelings hurt, expensive detours or expensive short cuts were taken, again and again decrees took the place of persuasion.

A revolution had not taken place; not even in the last days of battle had the population risen against a regime which had plunged them into misery and crime. The German proletariat, disunited, weakened by unemployment, terrorised by a militarised petty bourgeoisie, formed underground fighting troops which achieved the superhuman but did not go beyond passive resistance. Many of its best leaders were murdered. Towards the end of Hitler's war, the bombing raids on the cities also annihilated new organisations which might have been able to seize power during the collapse. Whatever measures for reconstruction were instigated, they were undertaken for the majority of the population but not by them.

It is, particularly in the chaos of military defeat in a highly civilised system with a high degree of division of labour, impossible to do without a state apparatus, but difficult to establish an entirely new one. So, under the new commanders, the Nazi apparatus once more set itself in motion. Such an apparatus cannot be imbued with a new spirit through control from above; it needs control from below. Unconvinced but cowardly, hostile but cowering, ossified officials began again to govern against the population.

['*Vorwort zu* Turandot', BFA 24/409–10.]

Written in late summer 1953. Although ostensibly one of Brecht's theatrical writings, this foreword to his play *Turandot or the Whitewashers' Congress* (see also *Plays 8*), written at Brecht's summer retreat in Buckow at the same time as his *Buckow Elegies*, represents arguably the most significant of Brecht's statements on the events of 17 June 1953. Through this text, Brecht again reveals his genuine belief in the achievements of the SED regime in the GDR, but he also highlights the errors which have been made during the process of post-Hitler reconstruction in East Germany. Most strikingly, Brecht's paranoia concerning the re-emergence of Fascism within East Germany reveals itself, a theme which also runs through the *Buckow Elegies* and his letter to Suhrkamp (*Letters*, pp. 516–18). In particular, Brecht identifies bureaucrats and civil servants as a reactionary force within the GDR undermining the project of East German socialism. This, above all else, seems to have been the source of his 'alienation' expressed in his diary entry of 20 August 1953 (*Journals*, pp. 454–5) and the principal lesson which Brecht drew from the events of 17 June 1953.

82

The *Volkskammer*

Perhaps we make too little of our *Volkskammer*. It works, as I hear, in its committees, but this goes on 'behind closed doors', and the population finds out little about it. We could, however, set the People's Chamber up as a great instrument through which the government could contact the population and the population could contact the government, as a great instrument for speaking and listening. The newspaper reports on public matters still meet with little interest, partly because they are clumsily written, partly because they tackle the population's real concerns only rarely and, all too evidently, just 'dispatch' voices of dissent. The radio is, despite some endeavours, as dead as ever. The deputies of the People's Chamber might, if they sought genuine contact with the population in large-scale assemblies, be able to use questions and answers to awaken the initiative of the active sections of the population in public matters, which we so greatly miss. Of course, they too would not only have to talk, but also to ask questions. The thousands of major and minor complaints should be directed to them, so that we can transform them into suggestions. The people would have to be able to write letters to their deputies, anonymous ones too, and the deputies would have to answer the letters, in assemblies, in sessions of the *Volkskammer*, and in letters. This would give the government a valuable overview of the mood, the concerns, the ideas of the population, and it would give the population a mouthpiece.

['*Die* Volkskammer', BFA 23/283.]

Written in 1954. Brecht sent this text to the GDR Minister President Otto Grotewohl in July 1954, with an accompanying letter complaining that the work of the GDR parliament, the *Volkskammer*, was seen to be secretive and distant from the people, and criticising the superficiality of the GDR radio's reporting of politics. He also enclosed a newspaper cutting with the radio listings for 22 July 1954, consisting largely of what he considered trivial light entertainment, with the handwritten comment: 'This programme is typical!' Grotewohl did not forward the text to the *Volkskammer*.

83

Peace is the Be-all and End-all

Speech at the presentation of the International Stalin Peace Prize in Moscow

It is one of the astonishing customs of the Soviet Union, this most astonishing state, to award an annual prize to several people for their efforts on behalf of world peace. Such a prize seems to me the most valuable which can be awarded today, the one for which it is most worth striving. Whatever anyone seeks to persuade them, the people of all nations know: peace is the be-all and end-all of every humanitarian activity, of all production, of all the arts, including the art of life.

I was nineteen years old when I heard of your great Revolution, twenty when I glimpsed the reflection of the great fire in my home country; I was a medical orderly in an Augsburg field hospital. The barracks and even the field hospitals emptied, the old town filled suddenly with new people, coming in great droves from the suburbs, with a vitality unknown to the streets of the rich, of the offices and merchants. Several days long, working women spoke in the hastily improvised councils, taking the young workers in soldiers' dress to task, and the factories heard the commands of the workers.

Several days, but what days they were! Everywhere fighters, but at the same time peaceful people, constructive people!

These struggles did not, as you know, lead to victory, and you know why. In the following years of the Weimar Republic, it was the writings of the socialist classics, which had been newly invigorated by the great October, and the reports of your bold construction of a new society, which committed me to these ideals and furnished me with knowledge. The most important lesson was that a future for mankind was becoming visible only 'from below', from the standpoint of the oppressed and exploited. Only by fighting with them does one fight for mankind.

A gigantic war had taken place, an even more gigantic war was being planned. From this perspective, from below, the hidden causes of these wars could be discerned; this class had to pay for them, the defeats and the victories. Here, far down below, peace also had a warlike aspect.

Deep within and all around the sphere of production, violence reigned, whether the open violence of the river tearing down the dams, or the secret violence of the dams holding down the river. It is not a matter of whether guns were being produced or ploughs – in the wars over the price of bread, the ploughs are the guns. In the continual and inexorable class struggles over the means of production, the periods of relative peace are only the periods of exhaustion. It is not the case that a destructive warlike element interrupts peaceful production time and again, but rather that production itself is founded on the destructive warlike principle.

Throughout their whole lives, people under capitalism fight for their bare existence – against each other. Parents fight for their children, children for their inheritance, the small retailer fights for his shop with the other small retailers, and all of them fight with the large retailer. The peasant fights with the townsman, the pupils fight with the teacher, the ordinary people fight with the authorities, the factories fight with the banks, the companies fight with companies. How, given all this, are nations to end up not fighting nations?

The nations whose people have fought successfully for a socialist economy have adopted a wonderful position with regard to peace. People's instincts are becoming peaceful. The struggle of everyone *against* everyone is being transformed into the struggle of everyone *for* everyone. Anyone who benefits society benefits himself. Anyone who benefits himself benefits society. The people who have it good are those who are useful, no longer those who are harmful. Progress ceases to mean stealing a march on the competition, and discoveries are no longer kept secret from anyone, but are instead made accessible to all. The new inventions can be received with joy and hope, instead of with horror and fear.

I myself have experienced two world wars. Now, approaching old age, I know that a monstrous war is being prepared anew. But a quarter of the world has now adopted peace, and in other parts socialist ideas are advancing. Ordinary people everywhere have a deep desire for peace. In the intellectual professions many people with different levels of awareness are fighting for peace. That includes the capitalist states. But our best hope for peace lies with the workers and peasants, in their own states and in the capitalist states. Long live peace! Long live your great peaceful state, the state of the workers and peasants.

['*Der Friede ist das A und O*', BFA 23/345–7.]

Written and published in 1955. Brecht gave this speech in Moscow on 25 May 1955 on the occasion of his acceptance of the Stalin Peace Prize. The Russian translation was made on Brecht's insistence by the writer Boris Pasternak, at that time living in enforced isolation from public life in the Soviet Union. Brecht's acceptance of the Stalin Prize led to outrage in the Federal Republic and to a boycott of his plays in certain West German theatres.

84

On the Criticism of Stalin

Perhaps you could inform Sch. of several of my opinions concerning the criticism of Stalin.

1 The escape from the barbarism of capitalism may itself still have barbaric features. The first period of proletarian rule may have inhuman features due to the fact that the proletariat, as Marx describes it, is held in bestial subjugation by the bourgeoisie. The revolution unleashes wonderful virtues and anachronistic vices simultaneously. The liberation from these vices needs more time than the revolution. The second time around (in China) it will already be somewhat easier, and the same applies to less backward countries, where the original accumulation of capital is already more advanced.

2 One of the severe consequences of Stalinism is the atrophy of the dialectic. Without knowledge of the dialectic, such transitions as that from Stalin as motor, to Stalin as brake are not comprehensible. Nor is the negation of the party through the state apparatus. Nor the transformation of struggles over different viewpoints into struggles for power. Nor the transformation of the technique of idealising and mythologising a leader in order to win over the vast, backward masses into a reason for the distance and paralysis of the masses.

3 Historians must work on the historical appraisal of Stalin. The liquidation of Stalinism can only succeed if the Party mobilises the wisdom of the masses on a gigantic scale. That lies on the direct path to Communism.

4 The (painful) transition from the worship of Stalin into a renunciation of prayer.

['*Über die Kritik an Stalin*'*, BFA 23/417.]

Written in 1956. At the 20th Conference of the Soviet Communist Party in February 1956, Nikita Khrushchev, in his famous 'secret speech', had attacked the crimes of the Stalin era, laying the blame on Stalin's style of rule and the 'personality cult'. The text of this speech began to circulate widely, causing consternation in the Communist world and panic in the ranks of the GDR regime, who were only just beginning to stabilise their authority after the uprisings of June 1953. Brecht had always had private reservations about Stalin, which he had never expressed in public for fear of weakening the struggle against Fascism (see his cool response to Stalin's death, no. 75); as was the case with many Communists, he dealt with the shock of Khrushchev's revelations by interpreting Stalinism as an undialectical perversion of Marxism. This attitude is consistent with his position on questions of aesthetics in his conflicts with the SED cultural line.

The abbreviation 'Sch.' may refer to the Marxist historian and Professor of History at the University of Leipzig, Albert Schreiner, whom Brecht had known since his work for the Council for a Democratic Germany in New York (see note to no. 62).

Select Bibliography

The standard German edition of Brecht's writings is the *Große kommentierte Berliner und Frankfurter Ausgabe* (Berlin and Frankfurt: Aufbau/Suhrkamp, 1988–2000), on which our selection of texts is based.

In English, the major publications of Brecht's non-literary writings are:

Brecht on Theatre, edited and translated by John Willett (London: Methuen, 1964)

Brecht on Film and Radio, edited and translated by Marc Silberman (London: Methuen, 2000)

Journals 1934–1955, translated by Hugh Rorrison and edited by John Willett (London: Methuen, 1993)

Letters 1913–1956, translated by Ralph Manheim and edited by John Willett (London: Methuen, 1990)

The Messingkauf Dialogues, edited and translated by John Willett (London: Methuen, 1965)

In addition, a wide range of important material, above all as it pertains to individual plays, is contained in the volumes of *Collected Plays 1–8*, edited by John Willett, Ralph Manheim and Tom Kuhn.

Useful further literature in English includes:

L. Althusser, *For Marx* (London: Verso, 1982)

R. Barthes, *Critical Essays* (Evanston: Northwestern UP, 1972)

—— *Image–Music–Text* (London: Fontana, 1979)

W. Benjamin, *Understanding Brecht* (London: New Left Books, 1973)

P. Brooker, *Bertolt Brecht: Dialectics, Poetry, Politics* (London: Croom Helm, 1988)

S. Giles, *Bertolt Brecht and Critical Theory: Marxism, Modernity, and the 'Threepenny Lawsuit'* (Bern: Peter Lang, 1998)

S. Giles, R. Livingstone (eds), *Bertolt Brecht: Centenary Essays* (Amsterdam: Rodopi, 1998)

F. Jameson, *Brecht and Method* (London: Verso, 1998)

E. Lunn, *Marxism and Modernism. An Historical Study of Lukács, Brecht, Benjamin and Adorno* (London: Verso, 1985)

Screen (special issue, 15, 2, Summer 1974: *Brecht and a Revolutionary Cinema*)

D. Suvin, *To Brecht and Beyond: Soundings in Modern Dramaturgy* (Sussex: Harvester, 1984)

R. Taylor (ed.), *Aesthetics and Politics. Debates between Bloch, Lukács, Brecht, Benjamin and Adorno* (London: Verso, 1977)

P. Thomson, G. Sacks (eds), *The Cambridge Companion to Brecht* (Cambridge: CUP, 1994)

B. N. Weber, H. Heinen (eds), *Bertolt Brecht. Political Theory and Literary Practice* (Manchester: MUP, 1980)

J. Willett, *The Theatre of Bertolt Brecht. A Study from Eight Aspects* (London: Methuen, 1977)

The annual publication of the International Brecht Society, *The Brecht Yearbook*, provides a further resource of current scholarly articles.

Index

Index

Index